Virtue:
Way To Happiness

St. Thomas Aquinas

Translated with an Introduction

Virtue:
Way To Happiness

St. Thomas Aquinas

Translated with an Introduction

by

Richard J. Regan

SCRANTON: UNIVERSITY OF SCRANTON PRESS

Library of Congress Cataloging-in-Publication Data

Thomas, Aquinas, Saint, 1225? - 1274.
    [Summa theologica. Prima secundae. English. Selections]
                                 / St. Thomas
Aquinas ; translated with an introduction by Richard J. Regan.
    p. cm.
    Includes bibliographical references and index.
    ISBN 0-940866-77-3 (hardcover). – ISBN 0-940866-78-1 (pbk.)
    1. Act (Philosophy) 2. Virtue.   I. Regan, Richard J. II. Title.
B765.T53S816 1999
171' .2–dc21   99-11402
                                                       CIP

Distribution:

**University of Scranton Press
Chicago Distribution Center
11030 S. Langley
Chicago IL 60628**

PRINTED IN THE UNITED STATES OF AMERICA

CONTENTS

ST I-II

PREFACE

The writings of St. Thomas deserve wide circulation for several reasons. First, they have had so much influence on other thinkers. Second, no serious student of Western thought can be considered well-educated without acquaintance with St. Thomas's grand synthesis of faith and reason. Third, St. Thomas's thought, in my opinion, has intrinsic merit and perduring relevance. Even those who do not share St. Thomas's philosophical and theological perspectives should find his writings intellectually stimulating.

This volume is an anthology of St. Thomas's thought about the moral dimensions of human action, as expressed in the first part of the second volume of the *Summa theologiae*: the ultimate human goal, human acts, emotions, and virtues. As the selections make clear, St. Thomas generally approaches these topics from the perspective of human reason. Reading these selections in isolation from the theological purpose of the *Summa*, however, risks misinterpreting his thought. The *Summa* is professedly a summary of theology, not philosophy, and St. Thomas's overarching perspective is that of a believer seeking to understand his faith. Nonetheless, St. Thomas proposes certain propositions and analyses on the basis of reason, and it is important for believers and unbelievers to weigh the merits of those propositions and analyses on that basis. Within such a context, this anthology is selective, and informed readers can judge for themselves whether the texts selected are sufficiently representative and comprehensive.

Although I believe this anthology to be relatively comprehensive regarding St. Thomas's treatment of the subjective ingredients of human action, the anthology does not include his treatment of the objective norm of morality governing human action (ST I-II, QQ. 90–108). Robert J. Henle has recently provided an excellent translation of, and commentary on, most of the latter (QQ. 90–97): St. Thomas Aquinas, *The Treatise on Law* (Notre Dame, Ind.: U. of Notre Dame Press, 1993).

xiii

To assist the reader, I have provided a glossary of key terms. Hackett Publishing Company has graciously allowed me to incorporate and adapt definitions from the glossary that Professor William P. Baumgarth and I provided in our anthology of St. Thomas's writings on law, morality, and politics: St. Thomas Aquinas, *On Law, Morality, and Politics* (Indianapolis: Hackett, 1988).

I wish to thank Professor Baumgarth, my colleague in the Department of Political Science of Fordham University, for his help in selecting the texts in this volume. I also wish to thank the Reverend Brian Davies, O.P., Professor of Philosophy of Fordham University, for his helpful suggestions for the Bibliography.

NOTE ON THE TEXT AND TRANSLATION

This translation is from the 1952 recension of the Leonine text of the *Summa*. In citing books of the Bible and numbering the Psalms, I have followed the Revised Standard Version. I have translated St. Thomas's biblical quotations as he phrases them, not as they appear in the Vulgate. I have cited Plato according to the Stephanus divisions, and Aristotle according to the Bekker divisions. For patristic citations or quotations, I have referred the reader to the Migne edition. Unless otherwise indicated, note references to the *Summa* are to the first part of the second volume (I–II).

Translators should be faithful to the text and express the meaning of the text in felicitous English. The two objectives are often difficult to reconcile. Fidelity to the text has been my highest priority, although I am confident that the reader will find the translation clear and idiomatic. The translation of certain key words inevitably involves interpretation. I have, for example, generally translated participial use of the Latin infinitive "*esse*" as "existing" or "existence." Since I interpret St. Thomas to understand "being" in the absolute participial sense to mean "existing," I have chosen to make that interpretation explicit. The translation of other key words varies with the context. I have, for example, translated "*ratio*," the generic Latin word for reason, as "argument," "aspect," "consideration," "nature," "reason," "reasoning," or "respect" as appropriate for different contexts.

Richard J. Regan

INTRODUCTION

The *Summa theologiae* represents a major attempt to introduce the method of Aristotle, and many of his principles, into the study of Christian theology. Although many contemporaries in the Augustinian tradition found St. Thomas's basically Aristotelian treatment of the human soul unacceptable, even heretical, they and St. Thomas were in solid agreement about the heavenly destiny and earthly responsibilities of human beings.

The central purpose of the *Summa* is to show whence human beings come, whither they are destined to go, and how and why they can get there. St. Thomas is not simply concerned about God, creation, and the human constitution as things in themselves worthy of study; he is also and primarily concerned about the ultimate goal of cognitive and affective union with God, and the behavior required of human beings in order to attain the heavenly goal. One quantitative indication of the dominance of this theme is the fact that St. Thomas in the second part of the *Summa* devotes more than twice as much space to fundamental and applied moral questions than he in the first part devotes to the combined treatment of God, creation, and the human constitution.

THE HUMAN END

St. Thomas begins his treatment of moral questions with consideration of the human end. He approaches this consideration from an Aristotelian perspective, and he basically follows Aristotelian methodology.

Every kind of thing has a nature that aims to achieve its specific perfection, which is its end. Seedlings grow into mature plants and trees capable of fully exercising vegetative functions, colts grow into mature horses capable of fully exercising animal functions, and babies grow into mature adults capable of fully exercising rational functions. Accordingly, human beings differ from other kinds of

xvii

living material things (and, of course, from all nonliving material things) in that human beings have the power to understand and reason. And because the power of reason is the specific perfection of human beings, they attain their ultimate perfection, the state of happiness, by activities of reason and activities according to reason. St. Thomas rejects any contention that human happiness consists in one or another kind of material good, and he in this respect echoes Aristotle, St. Augustine, and the Christian tradition. Rather, St. Thomas holds that human happiness involves activities of the soul, namely, theoretical and, in this life, practical intellectual activities.

Up to this point, St. Thomas is in basic agreement with Aristotle. But when St. Thomas comes to specify the object of human happiness, he decisively parts company with Aristotle; the object of human happiness, says St. Thomas, is the intellectual vision of God's essence, albeit not a comprehensive vision. St. Thomas argues that human beings will not be perfectly happy as long as there remains something more for them to know, that they are constituted by nature to seek to know God, and that they in this life cannot know what God is in himself. (As presently constituted, the human intellect depends on sense images and so knows God only through his perceptible effects, that is, only as the cause of perceptible things and the possessor of the perfections of perceptible things in an infinitely superior way.)

Aristotle was satisfied with the limited, albeit daunting, goal of theoretical wisdom as the most important ingredient of human happiness. Human beings intuitively understand that the coming-to-be of things is due to causes, and that human beings by the use of their reason can discern the ultimate causes (efficient, final, formal, and material) of all changeable things. In so doing, human beings become theoretically wise and attain the perfection of their specifically rational nature.

St. Thomas does not deny that theoretical wisdom is a major ingredient of human happiness in this life. Moreover, he agrees with Aristotle that human beings, to be happy in this life, need a body (indeed, a suitable body), external goods, and the company of friends. But St. Thomas insists that the happiness attainable in this life is incomplete and imperfect, a pale reflection of the perfect happiness of beholding God's essence, and that nothing material or created, including human friendship, is essential to such perfect happiness.

Both Aristotle and St. Thomas recognize that human happiness in this life also requires right reason to govern external actions and internal emotions, and a rightly ordered will regarding the requisite ends of human actions and emotions. St. Thomas, however, goes beyond Aristotle to maintain that rectitude of will is necessary for happiness not only because happiness results from the due ordination of the will toward the goal of acting according to right reason, but also because willing that end necessarily entails loving as good whatever God loves. For St. Thomas, there is no complete rectitude of will without conformity to God's will and his commands, whether these are communicated by reason or revelation.

Thus, despite the large measure of agreement that Aristotle and St. Thomas share regarding the human end, they differ sharply about the sufficiency of theoretical and practical wisdom for the happiness of human beings. This is quite understandable. On the one hand, the pagan Aristotle does not—and is not culturally disposed to—conceive God in personal, providential terms, and so he does not look to the beatific vision as the final goal of human beings. On the other hand, St. Thomas conceives God in salvific terms, and so he cannot look to the theoretical and practical wisdom accessible to human beings in this life, or even a more complete theoretical wisdom without the beatific vision in the next life, as the ultimate human end. One might be tempted to argue that St. Thomas's position about the human end is derived from faith, but St. Thomas argues that the beatific vision is the ultimate human end because the intellect *naturally* desires it.

Philosophers will need to weigh the merit of St. Thomas's argument that only the vision of God's essence can make human beings perfectly happy. But his position, if accepted, raises serious philosophical and theological problems.

On the one hand, the fact that human beings have a desire from nature for the complete happiness of the beatific vision seems to suggest that God, who created human beings with such a desire, should fulfill the desire if human beings act according to right reason. On the other hand, to suppose that God could have not bestowed the beatific vision on those who follow the dictates of right reason seems to imply that God could have left unfulfilled the natural desire of human beings for complete happiness in the vision of himself.

St. Thomas's position in this regard is that human beings can attain an incomplete and imperfect happiness in this life by their natural power to acquire intellectual and moral virtue, but that they cannot by their natural power attain the complete and perfect happiness of the beatific vision. In other words, the beatific vision is a gift that God freely deigns to bestow on those who do his will. God endows human beings with the requisite freedom and grace to carry out his will and thereby provides the requisite means for human beings to qualify for the complete and perfect happiness of the beatific vision. But however much human beings may cooperate in the disposition of themselves for the beatific vision, the vision itself remains beyond their natural power to attain.

As a Christian, St. Thomas firmly believes that God has destined worthy human beings for eternal union with himself. As a Christian theologian, St. Thomas explains that union in terms of the beatific vision and seeks to demonstrate that the vision befits the rational nature of human beings. On the one hand, the beatific vision is a free gift from God. On the other, the beatific vision complements the natural desire of human beings to know God in himself. Beyond that, St. Thomas is apparently not prepared to speculate about the hypothetical possibility of a suitable and worthy human nature on which God would not deign to bestow the beatific vision.

But is such a state possible? The position of St. Thomas and Christian tradition on the gratuity of participation in God's life would seem to suggest that a state of pure nature, one in which human beings would not be destined to share in God's life, is possible. And if such were to be the case, the maximum happiness that human beings could attain would be theoretical and practical wisdom for the human composite in this life, and the highest theoretical wisdom for the immortal soul in the life hereafter. This happiness, of course, would be incomplete and imperfect in comparison with the beatific vision, but it would be as complete and perfect as human beings could by their natural power attain. And the latter conception of "perfect" virtue seems to be the position of Aristotle, at least regarding this life.

Some Christian theologians, especially St. Bonaventure, a contemporary of St. Thomas, while agreeing that perfect human happiness is only possible in the heavenly union with God, argued that it is the love of God in such a union, not the knowledge of his essence, that makes human beings perfectly happy. The significance of this dispute may be exaggerated. On the one hand, St. Thomas holds that love of God necessarily accompanies the cognitive vision of God's essence, since the will necessarily seeks goodness, and God's essence is goodness itself. And on the other, St. Bonaventure holds that the cognitive vision of God's essence necessarily accompanies perfect love of God, since the will is the faculty of intellectual desire and so can find perfect satisfaction in God's goodness only insofar as the intellect knows his essence. Nonetheless, there is a difference of emphasis reflecting the larger question of the relative rank of cognition and affection in the rational life of human beings.

HUMAN ACTS AND VIRTUE

St. Thomas considerably expands on Aristotle's treatment of the will and human acts. St. Thomas clearly identifies the will as a faculty. He distinguishes voluntary activity or inactivity from involuntary activity or inactivity. He considers whether (or when) force, fear, concupiscence or ignorance could cause activity or inactivity to be involuntary. He examines circumstances and how they affect external acts. The object of the will is the good, even an apparent good. The intellect moves the will by presenting an object to the will, emotions may dispose the will regarding objects, and God is the primary cause of the will and its acts as such. But neither the intellect nor lower appetites nor God (unless by a special grace) determine the will to will or not to will particular means to attain happiness. Reason ordains, that is, structures, what the will wills, and the will freely chooses anything less than perfect goodness known as such. Deliberation by reason precedes choice, but choice involves consent of the will. And reason can command sense powers and external bodily members to carry out the will's choice.

Human acts derive their moral goodness from the suitability of the acts' objects for the ultimate human end, observance of requisite circumstances, and the ends to which the acts themselves are put. Conversely, human acts derive their malice from the lack of any of these things. The goodness of the will itself depends exclusively on the will's object, and so on reason, which presents the object to the will as in accord or discord with right reason. Since the light of human reason participates in the eternal law, the goodness or malice of the will depends even more on that law. Every will acting contrary to reason, even erroneous reason, is evil, but some acts of the will in accord with erroneous reason may be evil, since human beings may be directly or indirectly (through vincible ignorance) responsible for their reason judging erroneously.

The most striking contrast between St. Thomas's treatment of human acts and Aristotle's is the attention St. Thomas pays to the moral goodness and malice of individual human acts. Aristotle was largely concerned about the moral character of human acts in connection with the development of moral virtue, that is, with the consequence of morally good and bad acts for acquiring morally good habits. St. Thomas, while similarly concerned about that result of human acts, is also and primarily concerned about the consequence of the moral character of individual human acts for gaining heavenly bliss or meriting eternal damnation. St. Thomas is concerned about the moral character of human acts not only in relation to dictates of right reason and the acquisition of virtue in this life, but also and primarily in relation to dictates of God's law and the acquisition of the beatific vision in the next life.

For Aristotle, as a virtuous life constitutes its own reward, so a vicious life constitutes its own punishment. For St. Thomas, as a virtuous life in this world does not confer complete happiness on human beings, so a vicious life in this world does not sufficiently punish human beings with unhappiness. Moreover, morally bad acts are not only bad for their perpetrators, in St. Thomas's view, but they are also and primarily offenses against God and so deserve retribution from him. Accordingly, the morality of every human act involving serious matter is of supreme importance for human beings. For example, murder is not only contrary to the humanity of the murderer and an offense against the victim, but it is also a serious offense against God that deserves the punishment of hell. Conversely, just acts are not only just to others and virtuous, but they are also acts that by God's grace merit the reward of heaven.

St. Thomas holds that some external acts are intrinsically evil, since the acts frustrate the intrinsic ends of the acts. For example, he argues that lying is always wrong because it frustrates the intrinsic purpose of communicative speech (ST II–II, Q. 110, A. 1). Similarly, he argues that some sexual behavior is always wrong because it is contrary to the intrinsic purpose of sex (ST I–II, Q. 154, especially A. 11). The bottom line of this position is that no larger purpose, however good, can render such acts morally good, and the position differs from the emphasis and most of the substance of Aristotle's position.

Aristotle (*Nichomachean Ethics* II, 6. 1107a9–27) held that certain emotions (e.g., spite, envy) are always morally wrong, since such emotions are by definition disordered, that is, contrary to right reason, and so unvirtuous. With regard to actions, he cited adultery, murder, and theft as among those that are intrinsically wrong, presumably because they involve injustice, but he did not specify any other. St. Thomas does, especially but not exclusively in regard to sexual matters. For example, St. Thomas condemns all acts of lying, fornication, homosexuality, and contraception. He invokes the intrinsic finality of specific acts (e.g., speech, sex) to justify his definitive conclusions about the acts' moral character, and he thereby goes beyond not only Aristotle's conclusions in such regard but also beyond Aristotle's concerns and mode of analysis.

St. Thomas in his treatment of moral virtues follows Aristotle very closely. As with Aristotle, the key virtue in moral matters is intellectual. Practical wisdom, that is, practical reason, directs moral virtues by prescribing their ends (e.g., justice, moderation, courage) and by choosing the means to achieve those ends. And in the cultivation of justice and mastery of emotions, St. Thomas echoes Aristotle on the necessity of habituation. But St. Thomas is not content to rest there. To live a consistently virtuous life, human beings after the fall of Adam need added help, and so God infuses supernatural moral dispositions in the just to strengthen the natural power of human beings to acquire moral virtue. Moreover, God infuses in the just the theological virtue of charity, which informs every moral virtue, whether the moral virtue is naturally acquired or supernaturally infused.

Neither Aristotle nor St. Thomas is optimistic about the likelihood of the mass of humanity, left to itself, living a virtuous life. Natural aptitude, of course, will decidedly limit the possibility of most people acquiring intellectual virtues, and the dominance of inordinate desires will limit the possibility of most people, left to themselves, acquiring moral virtues. (For Aristotle, the dominance of passions in most people is simply a fact; for St. Thomas, it is the result of original sin.) But both Aristotle and St. Thomas think that rightly organized community could considerably rectify the situation, even if moral evil and its social consequences can never be eliminated. Both Aristotle and St. Thomas look to enlightened political leaders, that is, those with highly developed practical wisdom, to guide the community by framing laws that encourage virtue and discourage vice. Unlike Aristotle, St. Thomas also and primarily looks to the church to inculcate moral virtue, that is, to promise the virtuous the reward of heavenly bliss and to threaten the vicious with the punishment of hell.

St. Thomas, like Aristotle, devotes considerable attention to the nature of emotions and their influence on human behavior. St. Thomas, like Aristotle, distinguishes between ordinate and inordinate movements of sense appetites, that is, between emotions in accord with right reason, and emotions contrary to right reason. For example, emotions of desire for sexual intercourse with one's spouse in proper ways, times, and places are in accord with right reason and so, if willed, morally good, while emotions of desire for sexual intercourse with someone else's spouse, or with one's own spouse in improper ways, at an inappropriate time, or in an inappropriate place, are contrary to right reason and so, if willed, morally bad.

St. Thomas also follows Aristotle in classifying emotions as movements of sense appetites regarding the pleasurable (concupiscible emotions) and movements of sense appetites regarding the useful that involves difficulty and overcoming opposition (irascible emotions). Neither St. Thomas nor Aristotle investigates noncognitive or unconscious mechanisms that may trigger emotional responses. In this respect, their analysis is radically incomplete. Although St. Thomas and Aristotle are well aware that individuals respond emotionally to cognitive stimuli in different ways, they rest content with attributing the different responses to the different dispositions of individuals without any attempt at further explanation or empirical research.

THE STRUCTURE AND METHOD OF THE *SUMMA*

As St. Thomas makes clear at the beginning of the *Summa*, the work is designed for "beginners," "novices," in the study of theology, although the *Summa* evidently presupposes substantial academic preparation on their part. The *Summa* is thus expressly theological, and its audience Christian believers, presumably clerics and aspiring clerics, interested in understanding their faith more deeply. Nonetheless, the *Summa* proposes many theses and arguments about God, human beings, and the world that do not rely on Scripture or the church's teaching. Such theses and arguments merit study by believers and nonbelievers alike, by students of philosophy as well as by those of theology.

The *Summa* is divided into three parts. In the first part, St. Thomas considers God and his attributes, creation, angels, human beings, and Adam's condition before the fall. The second part, itself divided into two parts, deals with the ultimate end of human beings, the nature of specifically human acts, sin, law, and the virtues. The third part deals with the role of Christ and the sacraments in the redemption and salvation of the human race. The *Summa* thus progresses cyclically: human beings proceed from God and, despite Adam's fall, are destined to return to God if they freely cooperate with the graces won by Christ and communicated by the sacraments.

This volume of translations is from the first part of the second part of the *Summa* and deals with St. Thomas's views on the moral dimensions of human decision making. St. Thomas poses a series of questions related to these topics, and the questions are divided into articles raising specific points of inquiry. Each article poses a problem in the form of a question (e.g., Q. 2, A. 1: "Does the Happiness

of Human Beings Consist in Riches?"). The article begins with
objections to the position that St. Thomas will adopt. Each objection
cites at least one Scriptural, patristic, theological, philosophical, or
popular statement. St. Thomas then declares his contrary position,
typically citing a Scriptural, patristic, or philosophical text in sup-
port. Next, St. Thomas elaborates one or more arguments in favor of
his position. Lastly, St. Thomas answers each objection in turn.
While many of the objections are superficial or plays on words,
others provide the opportunity for him to make clarifications or
distinctions that he deems important.

Why do the articles have this formal structure? The short answer
lies in the academic conventions of the University of Paris and other
medieval universities. Faculty masters or student degree-candidates
would at appointed times defend theses against all comers, and the
format resembled that of a modern debate. The first step in the
process was to recapitulate an opponent's position in such a way that
the opponent could agree that his position was correctly stated and
interpreted. Only then would the master or student explain and
defend his own position.

The longer explanation of the formal structure of the articles in
the *Summa* is that the medieval thesis-defense format invited
audience participation in a way similar to that of a Platonic dialogue.
As Plato implicitly invites readers of the dialogues to become
intellectually involved in the exchange of ideas between Socrates and
his interlocutors, so St. Thomas and other medieval masters
explicitly invited their audience, and implicitly continue to invite
readers, to become intellectually involved in resolving the questions
posed. The objections in the medieval format thus take on the role of
Socrates's interlocutors in the Platonic dialogues. Unlike the
Socrates represented in the dialogues, however, St. Thomas and other
medieval masters clearly enunciated their own positions and directly
distinguished the terms involved in the discussions. Where Plato
progressively raised a series of questions to indicate the presup-
positions of Socrates's interlocutors, and the need to go beyond
conventional understanding of the world and human experience, St.
Thomas gives explicit answers to clearly framed questions. In this
respect, St. Thomas has more in common with modern academic

conventions than Plato does, however much both seek to involve their respective audiences.

St. Thomas's treatment of the ultimate end of human beings, happiness, may serve to illustrate the logic of his method of inquiry. St. Thomas argues in Q. 1 that human beings use their reason to attain ends, that there is an ultimate end of human life (happiness), and that human beings will every willed good in order to attain happiness. In Q. 2, he considers in what human happiness consists. In AA. 1–6, he rejects various material goods (riches, honor, glory, power, health, pleasure). In A. 7, he rejects as constitutive of happiness even the soul and the things belonging to the soul. And in A. 8, he argues that nothing created can satisfy the desire of the human will for unlimited good, and that only God can. In Q. 3, A. 8, St. Thomas is still more specific: complete human happiness consists in beholding God's very essence. In the next two questions, he takes up the requirements for happiness (Q. 4) and the attainment of happiness (Q. 5).

CONCLUSION

The issues that concerned St. Thomas in the topics included in this volume of translations—the ultimate human end, human acts, emotions, and virtues—reflect the concerns of the Christian theologian he was. It is accordingly necessary to study St. Thomas in the context of the Christian faith. But the import of much of his thought transcends the bounds of Christian theology. St. Thomas proposes most of his views about the moral dimensions of human activity in terms of reason, and he would expect his readers to examine his arguments in those terms. The questions St. Thomas raised about the moral dimensions of human activity may need to be reformulated or nuanced, the answers he gave to the questions may need to be modified or rejected, and new questions may be pertinent, but the topics and his many insights merit careful consideration.

BIBLICAL ABBREVIATIONS

Cor.	Corinthians
Eph.	Ephesians
Gal.	Galatians
Gen.	Genesis
Heb.	Hebrews
Hos.	Hosea
Is.	Isaiah
Jas.	James
Jn.	John
Lk.	Luke
Mt.	Matthew
Pet.	Peter
Phil.	Philippians
Prov.	Proverbs
Ps.	Psalms
Rev.	Revelation
Rom.	Romans
Sir.	Sirach
Tim.	Timothy
Wis.	Wisdom

OTHER ABBREVIATIONS

A	Article
Chap.	Chapter
Comm.	Comment
Dist.	Distinction
Lect.	Reading
PG	J. P. Migne, *Patrologia Graeca*
PL	J. P. Migne, *Patrologia Latina*
Obj.	Objection

Q   Question
ST   St. Thomas Aquinas, *Summa theologiae*
Supp.   Supplement
Tract.   Treatise

WORKS CITED BY ST. THOMAS

Most titles are in Latin, according to common usage.

Alexander of Hales
    Summa theologiae
Ambrose
    Super Lucam
Aristotle
    De anima
    De animalium motione
    Categories
    De coelo
    Ethics (Nicomachean)
    Historia animalium
    De memoria et reminiscentia
    Metaphysics
    De partibus animalium
    Physics
    Politics
    Posterior Analytics
    Rhetoric
    Topics
Athanasius
    Vita sancti Antonii
Augustine
    De bono conjugali
    The City of God
    Confessions
    De doctrina Christiana
    Enarrationes in Psalmos
    Enchiridion
    Epistolae
    Contra Faustum
    Super Genesim ad litteram

Contra Iulianum
De libero arbitrio
Contra mendacium
De moribus Ecclesiae Catholicae et Manichaeorum
De natura boni
Octoginta trium quaestionum
Retractationum
De sermone Domini in monte
Sermones ad populum
De Trinitate
De vera religione

Averroes
In De anima
In De coelo

Avicenna
De anima
Metaphysics
Sufficientia

Benedict
Regulae ad monachos

Boethius
On the Consolation of Philosophy
De differentia topicorum
De duabus naturis
In librum Aristotelis De interpretatione

Bonaventure
In librum Sententiarum

Cicero
De inventione
De oratore
Tusculanae disputationes

Damascene
De fide orthodoxa

Denis
Coelestia hierarchia
De divinis nominibus
De mystica theologia

Glossa
Glossa ordinaria
Gregory the Great
    Homiliarum in Evangelia
    Moralia
Hilary
    De Trinitate
Liber de causis
Lombard
    Sententiae
Nemesius
    De natura hominis (erroneously attributed by St. Thomas to Gregory of Nyssa)
Plato
    Meno
    Phaedo
    Timaeus
Prosper
    Librum sententiarum
Sallust
    Bellum Catilinae
Simplicius
    Super librum Praedicamentorum
Thomas Aquinas
    Commentary on the Ethics

AUTHORS CITED BY ST. THOMAS

Alexander of Aphrodisias (late second century A.D.)
Alexander of Hales (A.D. 1170/85–1245)
Ambrose, St. (340?–397)
Anaxagoras (500?–428? B.C.)
Aristotle, "the Philosopher" (384–327 B.C.)
Athanasius, St. (A.D. 293?–373)
Augustine, St. (A.D. 354–430)
Averroes, "the Commentator" (A.D. 1126–1198)
Avicenna (A.D. 980–1037)
Benedict, St. (A.D. 480?–547?)
Boethius (A.D. 470/75–524?)
Bonaventure, St. (A.D. 1217?–1274)
Cicero (106–43 B.C.)
Damascene, St. John (A.D. 700?–754?)
Denis, the Pseudo-Areopagite (early sixth century A.D.)
Gellius, Aulus (second century A.D.)
Gregory the Great, Pope St. (A.D. 540?–604)
Hilary, St. (A.D. 315?–367?)
Lombard, Peter (A.D. 1100?–1160)
Nemesius (late fourth century A.D.)
Plato (428?–348/47 B.C.)
Prosper of Aquitaine, St. (A.D. 390?–463?)
Sallust (86?–35/34 B.C.)
Simplicius of Cilicia (early sixth century A.D.)

Question 1

On the Ultimate End of Human Beings

[This question is divided into eight articles, one of which is included here.]

Fourth Article

Is There an Ultimate End of Human Life?

I proceed in this way to the fourth article: it seems that human life has an unlimited succession of ends rather than an ultimate end.

Obj. 1. Good by its nature pours itself out, as Denis makes clear in his *De divinis nominibus.*[1] Therefore, what results from good, if it also is good, needs to pour out another good, and so there is an unlimited succession of goods. But good had the nature of end. Therefore, there is an unlimited succession of ends.

Obj. 2. We can endlessly add to the number of conceptual things, and so also do we endlessly add to mathematical quantities. The species of numbers are for this reason likewise unlimited, since, given any number, reason can conceive another number that is greater. But the desire of an end results from a conception of reason. Therefore, it seems that there is also an unlimited succession of ends.

Obj. 3. Goods and ends are the object of the will. But the will can be directed on its very self an endless number of times, for I can will something, and will that I will it, and so on endlessly. Therefore, the human will has an unlimited succession of ends rather than an ultimate end.

On the contrary, the Philosopher says in the *Metaphysics* that "those who suppose something infinite, take away the nature of good."[2] But good has the nature of end. Therefore, it is contrary to the nature of end that there be an unlimited succession of ends. Therefore, we need to posit an ultimate end.

I answer that, absolutely speaking, there cannot be a succession of ends that is in every respect limitless. For in every case where things are intrinsically related to one another, the things subordinate to the first thing are necessarily taken away when the latter is taken away. And so the Philosopher proves in the *Physics* that there cannot be an endless succession of causes of motion, since there would then be no first cause of motion, and that the other causes cannot cause motion when the first is taken away, since the other causes only cause motion because the first cause moves them.[3]

And we find two orders of ends, namely, the order of striving and the order of accomplishing, and there needs to be something first in both orders. For what is first in the order of striving is, as it were, the source that moves an appetite, and so nothing would move the appetite if that source were taken away. And the source in accomplishing is the source from which activity originates, and so no one would begin to do anything if that source were taken away. And the source of striving is the ultimate end, while the source of accomplishing is the first means to that end. Therefore, in neither respect can there be an unlimited succession of ends. For nothing would be sought if there were no ultimate end, nor would any activity cease, nor also would the striving of efficient causes come to a state of rest. And no one would begin to do anything if there were no first source of means to the end, and the process of deliberation would not cease but go on endlessly.

On the other hand, nothing prevents things not intrinsically related but joined to one another by chance from being unlimited in number, since there is no fixed number of chance causes. And so there may by chance be an unlimited number of ends and means.

Reply to Obj. 1. It belongs to the nature of good that something flow from itself, but not that it itself come from something else. And so, since good has the nature of end, and since the first good is the ultimate end, the cited argument establishes that there is an unlimited succession of goods from the first presupposed good regarding means, but not that there is no ultimate end. And this would indeed be proper if we were only to consider the power of the first good, which power is unlimited. But since the first good pours out good by means of its intellect, and it belongs to such an outpouring to flow into effects by fixed forms, a fixed means is employed for the flowing of goods from the first good, from which all other goods share the power to pour out good. And so the outpouring of goods is not an unlimited succession, as the Book of Wisdom says: God arranged everything "in number, weight, and measure."[4]

Reply to Obj. 2. In intrinsic matters, reason starts with naturally known principles and reaches conclusions. And so the Philosopher proves in the *Posterior Analytics* that the process in demonstrations is not endless, since we in demonstrations attend to an order of certain things that are intrinsically and not by chance linked to one another.[5] But nothing prevents reason from proceeding endlessly in the case of things linked by chance. And it is by chance that a quantity or unit is added to a quantity or preexisting number as such. And so nothing prevents reason proceeding endlessly in such cases.

Reply to Obj. 3. The multiplication of acts of the will directed on its very self is by chance related to an order of ends. And this is evidenced by the fact that the will is indifferently directed once or often on its very self with respect to one and the same end.

Notes

1. *De divinis nominibus* 4. PG 3:693.
2. *Metaphysics* Ia, 2. 994b12–13.
3. *Physics* VIII, 5. 256a13–b2.
4. Wis. 11:21.
5. *Posterior Analytics* I, 3. 72b7–15.

Question 2

In What the Happiness[1] of Human Beings Consists

[This question is divided into eight articles, one of which is included here.]

Eighth Article

Does the Happiness of Human Beings Consist in a Created Good?

I proceed in this way to the eighth article: it seems that the happiness of human beings consists in a created good.

Obj. 1. Denis says in his *De divinis nominibus* that God's wisdom "links the limitations of higher things to the foremost parts of lower things,"[2] and we can thereby understand that the highest perfection of a lower nature is to attain the lowest perfection of a higher nature. But the highest good of human beings is happiness. Therefore, since nature ordained the superiority of angels to human beings, as I maintained in the First Part,[3] it seems that the happiness of human beings consists in human beings attaining the condition of angels.

Obj. 2. The ultimate end of anything consists in its being made complete, and so the parts of anything exist for the whole as their end. But we relate the entire created universe, which we call the "greater world," to human beings, whom the *Physics* calls the "lesser world,"[4] as the complete to the incomplete. Therefore, the happiness of human beings consists in the entire created universe.

Obj. 3. Human beings are made happy by the satisfaction of what they by nature desire. But the desire of human beings from nature does not extend to a greater good than one that they are capable of receiving. Therefore, since human beings do not have the capacity to receive a good that surpasses the limitations of all created things, it seems that some created good can make human beings happy. And so the happiness of human beings consists in a created good.

On the contrary, Augustine says in *The City of God*: "As the soul is the life of the flesh, so God is the happy life of human beings, and the Psalm (144:15) says about them, 'Happy are the people whose Lord is their God.' "[5]

I answer that the happiness of human beings cannot consist in a created good. For happiness is a complete good, one that completely satisfies the appetite; otherwise, there would be no ultimate end if there still remained something to be sought. But the object of the will, that is, the human appetite, is universal good, just as the object of the intellect is universal truth. And so it is evident that nothing other than universal good can satisfy the will of human beings. And we find such good only in God and not in any created good, since every creature has shared goodness. And so only God can satisfy the will of human beings, and the Psalm accordingly says that he is the one "who satisfies your desire with good things."[6] Therefore, the happiness of human beings consists in God alone.

Reply to Obj. 1. The higher perfection of human beings analogously attains the lowest perfection of the angelic nature, but human beings do not rest in that perfection as their ultimate end. Rather, they progress ultimately to the universal source of good, which source is the universal object of the happiness of all the blessed and exists as infinitely and completely good.

Reply to Obj. 2. If a whole is not an ultimate end but ordered to a further end, the ultimate end of parts is not the whole itself but something else. But the universe of created things, to which we relate human beings as parts to the whole, is not an ultimate end but ordered to God as the ultimate end. And so God himself and not the good of the universe is the ultimate end of human beings.

Reply to Obj. 3. Created goods are goods that human beings have a capacity to receive as things internal to, and inhering in, them, but created goods are inferior to the unlimited good that human beings have capacity for as an object. And the good in which angels and the entire universe share, is a limited and restricted good.

Notes

1. See Glossary, s.v. "Happiness."
2. *De divinis nominibus* 7. PG 3:872.
3. Q. 96, A. 1, *ad* 1. Q. 108, A. 2, *ad* 3, and A. 8, *ad* 2. Q.111, A. 1.
4. Aristotle, *Physics* VIII, 2. 252b26–27.
5. *The City of God* XIX, 26. PL 41:656.
6. Ps. 103:5.

Question 3

What Happiness Is

[This question is divided into eight articles, one of which is
included here.]

Eighth Article

*Does the Happiness of Human Beings Consist in Beholding
God's Essence?*

I proceed in this way to the eighth article: it seems that the happiness
of human beings does not consist in beholding God's very essence.
Obj. 1. Denis says in his *De mystica theologia* that the highest
perfection of the intellect unites human beings to God as something
completely unknown.[1] But what we behold essentially is not completely unknown. Therefore, the ultimate perfection of the intellect,
that is, happiness, does not consist in our beholding God essentially.
Obj. 2. A higher perfection belongs to a higher nature. But to behold
God's essence is a perfection that belongs to his intellect. Therefore,
the ultimate perfection of the human intellect does not reach so far
and falls short of beholding God's essence.

On the contrary, the First Letter of John says: "When he has
appeared, we shall be like him and see him as he is."[2]

I answer that our ultimate and complete happiness consists only
in beholding God's essence. To prove this, we need to consider two
points. First, indeed, that human beings are not completely happy as
long as something remains for them to desire and seek. The second
point is that we take note of the perfection of any power by the
nature of the power's object. But the object of the intellect is "what
something is," that is, the thing's essence, as the *De anima* says.[3]
And so the more the intellect knows a thing's essence, the more
perfect the intellect becomes. Therefore, if an intellect should know

the nature of an effect and not be able to know the nature of the effect's cause, that is, not to know "what the cause is," we do not say that the intellect attains the cause absolutely, although the intellect can by the effect know "that the cause exists." And so, when human beings know an effect and know that the effect has a cause, they also retain a natural desire to know "what the cause is." And this desire belongs to wonderment and causes inquiry, as the beginning of the *Metaphysics* says.[4] For instance, a person aware of an eclipse of the sun considers that the event comes about by some cause, and wonders about the cause, since the person does not know what it is, and in the course of wondering investigates it. Nor is that inquiry satisfied until the person comes to know the nature of the cause.

Therefore, if the human intellect, knowing the nature of a created effect, should know nothing about God except "that he exists," the intellect's perfection does not yet attain the first cause absolutely and still retains a natural desire to seek the cause. And so the human intellect is not yet completely happy. For complete happiness, therefore, the intellect needs to attain the very essence of the first cause. And then the intellect will possess its perfection by union with God as its object. And human happiness consists only in this object, as I have said before.[5]

Reply to Obj. 1. Denis is speaking about the knowledge of those who are proceeding to their end, those who are striving for happiness.

Reply to Obj. 2. We can comprehend an end in two ways, as I have said before.[6] In one way, with respect to the very thing desired, and then the ends of higher and lower natures, indeed of all things, are the same, as I have said before.[7] In the second way, with respect to attaining the thing desired, and then the ends of higher and lower natures differ regarding the natures' different dispositions toward the thing desired. Therefore, the happiness of God, whose intellect comprehends his essence, is superior to the happiness of human beings and angels, who behold but do not comprehend his essence.

Notes

1. *De mystica theologia* 1. PG 3:1001.
2. 1 Jn. 3:2.
3. Aristotle, *De anima* III, 6. 430b27–28.

4. Aristotle, *Metaphysics* I, 2. 982b11–21.
5. Q. 2, A. 8. Q. 3, AA. 1, 7.
6. Q. 1, A. 8.
7. Ibid.

Question 4

On the Prerequisites of Happiness

[This question is divided into eight articles, seven of which are included here.]

First Article

Is Pleasure Necessary for Happiness?

I proceed in this way to the first article: it seems that pleasure is not necessary for happiness.

Obj. 1. Augustine says in his *De Trinitate* that "seeing God is the total reward of faith."[1] But the prize or reward of virtue is happiness, as the Philosopher makes clear in the *Ethics*.[2] Therefore, only the vision of God is necessary for happiness.

Obj. 2. Happiness is "the most self-sufficient good," as the Philosopher says in the *Ethics*.[3] But what needs something else, is not self-sufficient. Therefore, since the essence of happiness consists in the vision of God, as I have shown,[4] it seems that pleasure is not necessary for happiness.

Obj. 3. "The activity of felicity" or happiness ought to be "unimpeded," as the *Ethics* says.[5] But pleasure impedes intellectual activity, since "pleasure weakens the judgment of practical wisdom," as the *Ethics* says.[6] Therefore, pleasure is not necessary for happiness.

On the contrary, Augustine says in his *Confessions* that happiness is "joy about truth."[7]

I answer that something is necessary for something else in four ways. In one way, as prefatory and preparatory for the very other thing; for example, learning is necessary for theoretical knowledge. In the second way, as perfecting something else; for example, the soul is necessary for the life of the body. In the third way, as an external help; for example, friends are necessary in order to do something. In the fourth way, as something attendant; for example, if we should say that heat is necessary for fire. And pleasure is necessary for happiness in the latter way. For pleasure results from the fact that an appetite is satisfied in the good that it has attained. And so there cannot be happiness without attendant pleasure, since happiness consists in nothing other than the possession of the highest good.

Reply to Obj. 1. The will of a person deserving a reward is satisfied, that is, takes pleasure in the fact that the reward is rendered to the person. And so pleasure is included in the very consideration of the reward rendered.

Reply to Obj. 2. The very vision of God produces pleasure. And so the person who beholds God cannot lack pleasure.

Reply to Obj. 3. The pleasure accompanying intellectual pleasure does not impede that very activity but rather strengthens it, as the *Ethics* says,[8] for we do with greater care and perseverance what we do with pleasure. But extraneous pleasure impedes intellectual activity. Extraneous pleasure indeed sometimes impedes our attention, since we are more intent on things that delight us, as I said, and our attention is necessarily drawn away from one thing when we are more intent on another. And extraneous pleasure also sometimes impedes intellectual activity by reason of opposition; for example, sensual pleasure contrary to reason impedes judgment by the practical intellect rather than judgment by the theoretical intellect.

Third Article

Is Comprehension Necessary for Happiness?

I proceed in this way to the third article: it seems that comprehension is not necessary for happiness.

Obj. 1. Augustine says to Paulina: "To attain with one's mind is great happiness, but to comprehend him is impossible."[9] Therefore, there is happiness apart from comprehension.

Obj. 2. Happiness is the perfection of human beings regarding their intellectual component, in which there are only the powers of intellect and will, as I have said in the First Part.[10] But the vision of

God adequately perfects the intellect, and pleasure in his very self adequately perfects the will. Therefore, comprehension is not necessary as a third element.

Obj. 3. Happiness consists in activity. But the objects of activities determine activities. And there are two universal objects of activities, the true and the good; the true corresponds to the vision of God, and the good corresponds to the pleasure in that vision. Therefore, comprehension is not necessary as a third element.

On the contrary, the Apostle says in the First Letter to the Corinthians: "So run that you may comprehend."[11] But the finish line of the spiritual race is happiness, and so the Apostle says in the Second Letter to Timothy: "I have fought the good fight, I have finished the race, I have kept the faith; for the rest, there is laid up for me a crown of righteousness."[12] Therefore, comprehension is necessary for happiness.

I answer that, since happiness consists in attaining our ultimate end, we need to consider the prerequisites for happiness from the very ordination of human beings to their end. And human beings are ordered to their intelligible end partially by their intellect and partially by their will. By the intellect, indeed, inasmuch as some imperfect knowledge of the end preexists in the intellect. And by the will, indeed first by love, which is the first movement of the will, and second by the concrete disposition of the lover to the beloved object, which disposition can exist in three ways. For example, sometimes the beloved object is present to the lover, and the beloved object is then no longer sought. And sometimes the beloved object is absent and cannot be attained, and then it is likewise not sought. But sometimes the beloved object can be attained but is so superior to a person's capacity to attain it that the person cannot immediately possess it. And the latter is the disposition of those who hope for the thing they hope for, the only disposition that causes them to seek the end.

And certain components of happiness itself correspond to these three things. For example, perfect knowledge of the end corresponds to imperfect knowledge, and the presence of the very end corresponds to the disposition of hoping for it, and love results in pleasure in the end now present, as I have said before.[13] And so, for happiness, three things need to coalesce, namely, the vision of God, which is perfect knowledge of our intelligible end; comprehension, which implies the presence of our end; pleasure or enjoyment, which implies the satisfaction of the lover in the beloved object.

Reply to Obj. 1. We speak about comprehension in two ways. In one way, comprehension denotes the inclusion of the comprehended object in the comprehending subject, and then everything finite things comprehend, is finite. And so, in this way, no created intellect can comprehend God. In the second way, comprehension denotes only the possession of something already actually possessed; for example, we say that a person has another in his or her grasp when the person lays hold of the other. And it is in the latter way that comprehension is necessary for happiness.

Reply to Obj. 2. As hope and love belong to the will, since it belongs to the same power to love something and to strive for it when it is not possessed, so also both comprehension and pleasure belong to the will, since it belongs to the same power to possess something and to be satisfied by it.

Reply to Obj. 3. Comprehension is not an activity added to vision; rather, comprehension is a disposition regarding an end already possessed. And so the very vision, or the thing beholden as actually present to the beholder, is the object of comprehension.

Fourth Article

Is a Rightly Directed Will Necessary for Happiness?

I proceed in this way to the fourth article: it seems that a rightly directed will is not necessary for happiness.

Obj. 1. Happiness consists essentially in intellectual activity, as I have said.[14] But a rightly directed will, by reason of which we call human beings pure, is not necessary for perfect intellectual activity, for Augustine says in his *Retractationum*: "I do not approve what I said in the prayer, 'O God, you who willed only the pure to know the truth.' For there can be the rejoinder that even many impure persons know many truths."[15] Therefore, a rightly directed will is not necessary for happiness.

Obj. 2. Things prior do not depend on things subsequent. But activity of the intellect precedes activity of the will. Therefore, happiness, which is the perfect activity of the intellect, does not depend on a rightly directed will.

Obj. 3. A means ordained for something as an end is not necessary after the end has been attained; for example, a ship needs no means of navigation after the ship reaches port. But a rightly directed will, which exists by reason of virtue, is ordained for happiness as our end. Therefore, a rightly directed will is not necessary after happiness has been attained.

On the contrary, the Gospel of Matthew says: "Happy are those of pure heart, since they will see God."[16] And the Letter to the Hebrews says: "Let us pursue peace with everyone, and holiness, without which no one will see God."[17]

I answer that a rightly directed will is necessary for happiness both as an antecedent and as a concomitant. As an antecedent, indeed, because the will is rightly directed by being duly ordered to our ultimate end. And we relate ends to means as we relate form to matter. And so, as matter can attain form only if the matter be duly disposed to receive the very form, so nothing attains its end unless it be duly ordered to the very end. And so no one can attain happiness unless the person should have a rightly directed will.

And a rightly directed will is necessary for happiness as a concomitant, since, as I have said,[18] our ultimate happiness consists in the vision of God's essence, which is the very essence of goodness. And so the will of those beholding God's essence necessarily loves in subordination to God everything that the will loves, just as the will of those not beholding God's essence necessarily, under the general aspect of good that the will knows, loves everything that the will loves. And this very fact is what causes the will to be rightly directed. And so there evidently cannot be happiness without a rightly directed will.

Reply to Obj. 1. Augustine is speaking about the knowledge of the truth that is not the very essence of goodness.

Reply to Obj. 2. An act of the intellect precedes every act of the will; nonetheless, some acts of the will precede some acts of the intellect. For example, the will tends toward the ultimate act of the intellect, that is, happiness. And so the rightly directed inclination of the will is a prerequisite for happiness, just as an arrow's rightly directed motion is a prerequisite for the arrow to hit the target.

Reply to Obj. 3. When an end is attained, not every means to the end ceases to be necessary, but only a means, like motion, that is essentially imperfect. And so means of travel are not necessary after one arrives at one's destination, although the due order of the means to the end is necessary.

Fifth Article

Is the Body Necessary for the Happiness of Human Beings?

I proceed in this way to the fifth article: it seems that the body is necessary for happiness.

Obj. 1. The perfection of virtue and grace presupposes the perfection of nature. But happiness is the perfection of virtue and grace. And the soul cannot have the perfection of nature apart from the body, since the soul is by nature part of human nature, and every part is incomplete when separated from the whole of which it is a part. Therefore, the soul cannot be happy apart from the body.

Obj. 2. Happiness is a perfect activity, as I have said before.[19] But perfect activity results from being perfect, since only something that is an actual being, acts. Therefore, since the soul does not have perfect existing when separated from the body, as neither does a part when separated from the whole of which it is a part, it seems that the soul cannot be happy apart from the body.

Obj. 3. Happiness is the perfection of human beings. But the soul apart from the body is not a human being. Therefore, the soul cannot have happiness apart from the body.

Obj. 4. "The activity of happiness," in which the state of happiness consists, is "unimpeded," as the Philosopher says in the *Ethics*.[20] But the activity of the separate soul is impeded, since, as Augustine says in his *Super Genesim*, "there is present in the soul a desire from nature to govern the body, and the soul is somehow impeded by this desire from progressing with all its striving toward the highest heavens," that is, to the vision of God's essence.[21] Therefore, the soul cannot be happy apart from the body.

Obj. 5. Happiness is a sufficient good and satisfies desire. But such does not belong to the separated soul, since the separated soul still desires to be united to the body, as Augustine says.[22] Therefore, the soul cannot be happy when separated from the body.

Obj. 6. Human beings in the state of happiness rank with angels. But souls without bodies do not rank with angels, as Augustine says.[23] Therefore, the soul is not happy apart from the body.

On the contrary, the Book of Revelation says: "Happy are the dead who die in the Lord."[24]

I answer that happiness is of two kinds: one imperfect, which we have in this life, and the other perfect, which consists in the vision of God. And we evidently need a body for the happiness of this life. For the happiness of this life consists of intellectual activity, whether activity of the theoretical or the practical intellect. And there cannot be intellectual activity in this life apart from sense images, which are present only in bodily organs, as I have maintained in the First Part.[25] And so the happiness capable of being possessed in this life depends in some way on the body.

But with respect to perfect happiness, which consists in the vision of God, some have held that no such happiness can come to the soul apart from an existing body, and they say that the saints' souls separated from bodies do not attain perfect happiness until the Day of Judgment, when they regain their bodies.

And both authority and reason indeed show that the foregoing opinion is false. Authority indeed evidences this, since the Apostle says in the Second Letter to the Corinthians: "As long as we are in the body, we are exiles from the Lord,"[26] adding: "For we walk by faith and not by sight."[27] And this shows that persons are not yet in the presence of God as long as they, lacking the vision of God's essence, walk by faith and not by sight. But the saints' souls separated from bodies are in the presence of God, and so the Apostle adds: "But we are courageous and prefer to be exiled from the body and to be in the presence of the Lord."[28] And so the saints' souls separated from bodies evidently walk by sight, beholding God's essence, in which true happiness consists.

Reason likewise shows that there can be perfect happiness for the soul apart from an existing body. For intellectual activities need a body only for sense images, in which the intellect regards intelligible truth, as I have said in the First Part.[29] But we evidently cannot behold God's essence by means of sense images, as I have demonstrated in the First Part.[30] And so the perfect happiness of human beings, since it consists in the vision of God's essence, does not depend on the body. And so the soul can be happy apart from the body.

But we should note that something belongs to a thing's perfection in two ways. In one way, to constitute the thing's essence; for example, the soul is necessary for the perfection of human beings. In the second way, what belongs to the thing's well-being is necessary for the thing's perfection; for example, bodily comeliness and mental agility belong to the perfection of human beings. Therefore, the body, although it does not belong to the perfection of human happiness in the first way, nonetheless belongs to such perfection in the second way. For, since activity depends on the nature of the thing acting, the more perfect the soul will be regarding its nature, the more perfectly will the soul have capacity for its characteristic activity, in which happiness consists. And so Augustine in his *Super Genesim*, in the course of having hypothetically posed the question, "Can we allow that perfect happiness to the souls of the dead lacking bodies?" answers: "They cannot see the unchangeable substance as the holy angels see it, either due to some other, more hidden reason, or because they have from nature a desire to govern the body."[31]

Reply to Obj. 1. Happiness is perfection of the soul regarding the intellect, by which perfection the soul transcends bodily organs, but not perfection of the soul as the natural form of the body. And so the perfection of nature by which happiness is necessary for the soul abides, but the perfection of nature by which the soul is the form of the body does not abide.

Reply to Obj. 2. The soul is otherwise disposed toward existing than other parts of human beings are. For the existence of a whole does not belong to any of the whole's parts. And so either parts completely cease to exist when the whole is destroyed, as the parts of an animal cease to exist when the animal is destroyed, or parts, if they remain, have a different actual existence, as parts of a line have a different existence than the whole line. But for the human soul, the composite's existing abides after the demise of the body, and this is so because there is one and the same existing of the form and the matter, which existing is the composite's existing. And the soul subsists in its existing, as I have demonstrated in the First Part.[32] And so we conclude that the soul has perfect existing after separation from the body and so can also have perfect activity, although the soul does not have the complete nature of the species.

Reply to Obj. 3. Happiness belongs to human beings by reason of their intellect, and so they can have the capacity for happiness by reason of their intellect abiding. Similarly, an Ethiopian's teeth, by reason of which we call the Ethiopian white, can remain white even after the teeth have been extracted.

Reply to Obj. 4. Something else impedes something in two ways. In one way, by way of opposition; for example, cold impedes the causal activity of heat. And such an impediment to activity is incompatible with happiness. In the second way, by way of some deficiency, namely, in that the impeded thing does not possess everything necessary for it to be perfect in every way. And such an impediment is not incompatible with happiness but incompatible with happiness itself being perfect in every way. The body impedes the soul from tending toward the vision of God's essence with all its striving. For the soul desires to enjoy God in such a way that the very enjoyment overflows into the body as much as possible. And so, as long as the soul itself enjoys God apart from the body, the soul's desire is satisfied with what the soul possesses, but in such a way that the soul would still wish its body to attain a share in the enjoyment.

Reply to Obj. 5. The separated soul's desire is completely satisfied regarding the object of its desire, namely, in that the soul possesses what suffices to satisfy its appetite. But the separated soul's desire is not completely satisfied regarding the subject that desires, in that the one desiring does not possess the desired good in every way that one would wish to possess it. And so, when persons regain their bodies, their happiness increases in scope but not in intensity.

Reply to Obj. 6. We should not understand the statement in the cited text, "The souls of the dead do not behold God as the angels do," regarding an inequality of magnitude. We should not so understand the statement, since some souls of the blessed are even now raised to the higher ranks of angels and behold God more clearly than lower angels do. Rather, we understand the statement regarding an inequality of proportion, since angels, even the lowest, possess all the perfection of happiness that they will possess, while the separated souls of the saints do not.

Sixth Article

Is Any Bodily Perfection Necessary for Happiness?

I proceed in this way to the sixth article: it seems that bodily perfection is not necessary for the perfect happiness of human beings.
Obj. 1. Bodily perfection is a material good. But I have shown that happiness does not consist in material goods.[33] Therefore, a perfect disposition of the body is not necessary for the happiness of human beings.
Obj. 2. The happiness of human beings consists in the vision of God's essence, as I have shown.[34] But the body produces nothing for such activity, as I have said.[35] Therefore, no disposition of the body is necessary for happiness.
Obj 3. The more the intellect is drawn away from the body, the more perfectly the intellect understands. But happiness consists in the most perfect intellectual activity. Therefore, the soul needs to be drawn away from the body in every way. Therefore, no disposition of the body is any way necessary for happiness.

On the contrary, happiness is the reward of virtue, and so the Gospel of John says: "You will be happy if you have done these things."[36] But God promises to reward saints not only with the vision of himself, and with pleasure, but also with a good disposition of the body. For the prophet Isaiah says: "You will see, and your heart will rejoice, and your bones will flourish like the grass."[37] Therefore, a good disposition of the body is necessary for happiness.

I answer that, if we should speak about the happiness of human beings as they can possess it in this life, it is obvious that a good disposition of the body is necessarily required for happiness. For such happiness consists "in completely virtuous activity," as the Philosopher says.[38] And indisposition of the body can evidently hinder human beings in every kind of virtuous activity.

But if we should speak about perfect happiness, then some have held that no disposition of the body is necessary for happiness; on the contrary, the soul, for happiness, needs to be completely separate from the body. And thus does Augustine in *The City of God* cite the words of Porphyry, who said that "we need to shun every material substance in order that the soul be happy."[39] But this opinion is inappropriate. For it cannot be the case that the soul's perfection should exclude its natural perfection, since it is natural to the soul to be united to the body.

And so we need to say that, for happiness in every way, perfect disposition of the body is necessary both as a condition and as a consequence. As a condition, indeed, because, as Augustine says in his *Super Genesim*, "If the body be such that its governance be difficult and burdensome, as flesh that passes away and burdens the soul, the mind is turned away from that vision of the highest heavens."[40] And so he concludes that "when this body will no longer be animal but spiritual, then it will be ranked with the angels, and what was burdensome, will be for its glory."

And perfect disposition of the body is necessary as a consequence of perfect happiness, since the happiness of the soul overflows into the body, that the body may also obtain its perfection. And so Augustine says in his letter to Dioscorus: "God made the soul to be of so powerful a nature that the strength of its indestructibility overflows from its most abundant happiness to the lower nature."[41]

Reply to Obj. 1. Happiness does not consist in material good as an object of happiness, but material good can contribute to the adornment or perfection of happiness.

Reply to Obj. 2. The body, although it contributes nothing to the intellectual activity whereby we behold God's essence, could nonetheless be an obstacle to that activity. And so perfection of the body is necessary lest the body impede the mind's ascent.

Reply to Obj. 3. Being drawn away from the present destructible body, which is a burden to the soul, is indeed necessary for perfect intellectual activity, but not being drawn away from the spiritual body, which will be completely subject to the spirit. And I shall discuss this matter in the Third Part of this work.[42]

Seventh Article

Are Any External Goods Necessary for Happiness?

I proceed in this way to the seventh article: it seems that external goods are also necessary for happiness.

Obj. 1. Things that God promises to reward to the saints belong to happiness. But God promises external goods, such as food and drink, riches, and royal power, to the saints, since the Gospel of Luke says: "[I shall appoint] that you eat and drink at my table in my kingdom."[43] And the Gospel of Matthew says: "Lay up treasures for yourselves in heaven,"[44] and "Come, blessed of my Father, take possession of the kingdom."[45] Therefore, external things are necessary for happiness.

Obj. 2. Happiness is "the condition made perfect by the aggregation of every good," as Boethius says in his *On the Consolation of Philosophy*.[46] But external things are some goods belonging to human beings, although the least, as Augustine says.[47] Therefore, such very goods are also necessary for happiness.

Obj. 3. The Lord says in the Gospel of Matthew: "Your reward is great in heaven."[48] But to be in heaven is to be in a place. Therefore, at least an external place is necessary for happiness.

On the contrary, the Psalm says: "For what is there for me in the heavens? And what on earth do I wish from you?"[49] This as if to say that I desire only what follows: "It is good for me to cling to God."[50] Therefore, no other external thing is necessary for happiness.

I answer that external goods are necessary for such imperfect happiness as we can possess in this life, not as if such goods are realities that belong to the essence of happiness, but as if such goods are means that contribute to happiness, which consists in virtuous activity, as the *Ethics* says.[51] For example, human beings in this life need bodily necessities both for contemplatively virtuous activity and for practically virtuous activity, and they need for the latter even more other things, as means to perform deeds of practical virtue.

But such goods are in no way necessary for perfect happiness, which consists in the vision of God. And this is because all such external goods are necessary either to sustain our animal bodies or for activities that we perform by means of our animal bodies, activities that befit human life. And the perfect happiness that consists in the vision of God will be either in the soul apart from the body or in the soul united to a body that is no longer animal but spiritual. And so such external goods are in no way necessary for perfect happiness, since they are ordained for animal life.

And the happiness of contemplation in this life, since it, as even more God-like, as is evident from what I have said,[52] comes closer to resembling that perfect happiness than the happiness of action does, accordingly has less need of such bodily goods, as the *Ethics* says.[53]

Reply to Obj. 1. We need to understand metaphorically all the material promises contained in sacred Scripture, since Scripture is accustomed to indicate spiritual things by material things, "so that we may rise from things we know, to desire unknown things," as Gregory says in a homily.[54] For example, food and drink signify the pleasure of happiness, riches signify the sufficiency of God for human beings, royal power signifies the raising of human beings up to union with God.

Reply to Obj. 2. The goods that contribute to animal life do not belong to the spiritual life in which perfect happiness consists. And yet there will be in such happiness an aggregation of every good, since we shall possess in the supreme fount of goodness the totality of everything good that we find in goods that contribute to animal life.

Reply to Obj. 3. Scripture does not say that the reward of the saints exists in a material heaven; rather, Scripture understands by heaven the sublimity of spiritual goods, as Augustine says in his *De sermone Domini in monte*.[55]

But nonetheless, a material place, namely, the highest heavenly sphere, will attend the blessed, albeit by reason of a certain suitability and adornment.

Eighth Article

Is the Company of Friends Necessary for Happiness?

I proceed in this way to the eighth article: it seems that friends are necessary for happiness.

Obj. 1. Scripture often designates future happiness by the term "glory." But glory consists in the fact that many persons come to know a human being's goodness. Therefore, the company of friends is necessary for happiness.

Obj. 2. Boethius says that "the possession of no good is pleasing without fellowship."[56] But pleasure is necessary for happiness. Therefore, the company of friends is also necessary.

Obj. 3. Love is perfected in happiness. But love includes love of God and neighbor. Therefore, it seems that the company of friends is necessary for happiness.

On the contrary, the Book of Wisdom says: "Everything good came to me along with her,"[57] namely, divine wisdom, which consists in contemplating God. And so nothing else is necessary for happiness.

I answer that, if we should be speaking about the happiness of our present life, a happy person indeed does not need friends for their usefulness, since a happy person is self-sufficient, or for pleasure, since a happy person as such takes complete pleasure in the person's virtuous activity. Rather, a happy person needs friends for good acts, namely, that the happy person may do good for them, and take pleasure in seeing them do good, and also be helped by them to do good. This is what the Philosopher says in the *Ethics*.[58] For example, human beings need the aid of friends to act well, both in deeds of the practical life and in acts of the contemplative life.

And if we should be speaking about the perfect happiness that will be ours in our heavenly home, the company of friends is not absolutely necessary for happiness, since human beings have in God the entire fullness of their perfection. But the company of friends makes for the enhancement of happiness. And so Augustine says in his *Super Genesim*: "Only the eternity, truth, and love of the creator intrinsically help spiritual creatures to be happy. But if we may speak about spiritual creatures being extrinsically helped to be good, perhaps the mere fact that they see one another and rejoice in God about their companionship helps them."[59]

Reply to Obj. 1. The glory essential to happiness is the glory that human beings have in the company of God, not the glory that they have in the company of human beings.

Reply to Obj. 2. We understand the cited statement regarding the situation in which the good possessed is not completely sufficient. And we cannot say this in the case of the matter under consideration, since human beings have in God a sufficiency of every good.

Reply to Obj. 3. Perfection of love is essential to happiness with respect to loving God but not with respect to loving one's neighbor. And so, if there were to exist only one soul that enjoys God, that soul would be happy, although it has no neighbor to love. But loving one's neighbor, presupposing the existence of neighbors, results from loving God perfectly. And so friendship is disposed to accompany perfect happiness, as it were.

Notes

1. *Enarrationes in Psalmum 90, sermo* 2. PL 37:1170. Cf. *De Trinitate* I, 8. PL 42:832.
2. *Ethics* I, 9. 1099b16–17.
3. *Ethics* I, 7. 1097b7–21.
4. Q. 3, A. 8.
5. *Ethics* VII, 13. 1153b11.
6. Aristotle, *Ethics* VI, 5. 1140b13–16.
7. *Confessions* X, 23. PL 32:793.
8. Aristotle, *Ethics* X, 4. 1174b19–34.
9. *Sermo ad populum 117*. PL 38:663.
10. QQ. 79–82.
11. 1 Cor. 9:24.
12. 2 Tim. 4:7–8.
13. Q. 4, A. 2, *ad 3*.
14. Q. 3, A. 4.
15. *Retractationum* I, 4. PL 32:589.
16. Mt. 5:8.
17. Heb. 12:14.
18. Q. 3, A. 8.
19. Q. 3, AA. 2, 5.
20. *Ethics* VII, 13. 1153b16.
21. *Super Genesim* XII, 35. PL 34:483.
22. Ibid.
23. Ibid.

24. Rev. 14:13.
25. Q. 84, AA. 6, 7.
26. 2 Cor. 5:6.
27. 2 Cor. 5:7.
28. 2 Cor. 5:8.
29. Q. 84, A. 7.
30. Q. 12, A. 3.
31. *Super Genesim* XII, 35. PL 34:483.
32. Q. 75, A. 2.
33. Q. 2.
34. Q. 3, A. 8.
35. Q. 4, A. 5.
36. Jn. 13:17.
37. Is. 66:14.
38. *Ethics* I, 13. 1102a5–6.
39. *The City of God* XXII, 26. PL 41:794.
40. *Super Genesim* XII, 35. PL 34:483–84.
41. *Epistola 118* 3. PL 33:439.
42. Supp., QQ. 82–85.
43. Lk. 22:30.
44. Mt. 6:20.
45. Mt. 25:34.
46. *On the Consolation of Philosophy* III, 2. PL 63:724.
47. *De libero arbitrio* II, 19. PL 32:1268.
48. Mt. 5:12.
49. Ps. 73:25.
50. Ps. 73:28.
51. Aristotle, *Ethics* I, 13. 1102a5–6.
52. Q. 3, A. 5, *ad* 1.
53. Aristotle, *Ethics* X, 8. 1178a23–b7.
54. *Homilia in Evangelia 11*. PL 76:1114–15.
55. *De sermone Domini in monte* I, 5. PL 34:1237.
56. Probably a reference to Seneca, *Epistola ad Lucilium* 6.
57. Wis. 7:11.
58. *Ethics* IX, 9. 1169b8–-13.
59. *Super Genesim* VIII, 25. PL 34:391.

Question 5

On Attaining Happiness

[This question is divided into eight articles, four of which are included here.]

First Article

Can Human Beings Attain Happiness?

I proceed in this way to the first article: it seems that human beings cannot attain happiness.

Obj. 1. As rational nature is superior to sentient nature, so intellectual nature is superior to rational nature, as Denis makes clear in many places in his *De divinis nominibus.*[1] But irrational animals, which have only sentient nature, cannot attain the end of rational nature. Therefore, neither can human beings, who have a rational nature, attain the end of intellectual nature, that is, happiness.

Obj. 2. True happiness consists in the vision of God, who is pure truth. But it is inborn to human beings to perceive truth in material things, and so human beings "understand intelligible forms in sense images," as the *De anima* says.[2] Therefore, human beings cannot attain happiness.

Obj. 3. Happiness consists in attaining the highest good. But no one can attain the highest point without surmounting midpoints. Therefore, since the angelic nature is something in between God and human nature, and human beings cannot surmount the angelic nature, it seems that they cannot attain happiness.

On the contrary, the Psalm says: "Happy are the human beings whom you, O Lord, have instructed."[3]

I answer that happiness denotes attainment of the perfect good. Therefore, anyone capable of receiving the perfect good can attain happiness.

But human beings are evidently capable of receiving the perfect good, both because their intellect can apprehend the universal and perfect good, and because their will can desire that good. And so human beings can attain happiness.

The same conclusion is also evident because human beings are capable of the vision of God, as I maintained in the First Part,[4] and we say that perfect happiness indeed consists in such vision.

Reply to Obj. 1. Rational nature surpasses sentient nature in one way, and intellectual nature surpasses rational nature in another way. For rational nature surpasses sentient nature with respect to the object of knowledge, since the senses can in no way know the universal, which the power of reason knows. But intellectual nature surpasses rational nature with respect to the way of knowing the same intelligible truth. For intellectual nature understands truth immediately, while rational nature attains truth by rational inquiry, as is clear from what I have said in the First Part.[5] And so reason by a certain discursus attains what the intellect understands. And so a rational nature can attain the happiness that is the perfection of an intellectual nature, although in a different way than the angels do. For angels attained happiness immediately after they began to exist, while human beings attain happiness over the course of time. But sentient nature cannot at all attain such an end.

Reply to Obj. 2. The way of knowing intelligible truth by means of sense images is inborn to human beings in the condition of their present life. But another way of knowing is inborn to human beings after the condition of their present life is ended, as I have said in the First Part.[6]

Reply to Obj. 3. Human beings cannot surmount angels in natural rank, namely, to be by nature superior to angels. Nonetheless, human beings can surmount angels by intellectual activity when human beings understand that there is something superior to angels, and such a thing makes human beings happy. And human beings will be perfectly happy when they perfectly attain it.

Third Article

Can Human Beings Be Happy in This Life?

I proceed in this way to the third article: it seems that human beings can possess happiness in this life.

Obj. 1. The Psalm says: "Happy are those who journey blamelessly, those who walk in the law of the Lord."[7] But such happens in this life. Therefore, human beings can be happy in this life.

Obj. 2. Imperfect sharing in the highest good does not take away the essence of happiness; otherwise, one human being would not be happier than another. But human beings can in this life share in the highest good by knowing and loving God, however imperfectly. Therefore, human beings can be happy in this life.

Obj. 3. What people generally say, cannot be completely false, for it seems to be by nature that something is such for the most part, and nature does not entirely fail. But people generally hold that there is happiness in this life, as the Psalm makes clear: "They call happy the people who possess these things,"[8] namely, the goods of the present life. Therefore, human beings can be happy in this life.

On the contrary, the Book of Job says: "Human beings born of women, living a short time, are replete with afflictions."[9] But happiness excludes afflictions. Therefore, human beings cannot be happy in this life.

I answer that we can share in some kind of happiness in this life, but we cannot have perfect and true happiness in this life. And we can indeed consider this matter in two ways. First, indeed, by considering the general nature itself of happiness. For happiness, since it is a perfect and sufficient good, excludes every evil and fulfills every desire. But not every evil can be excluded in this life. For example, the present life is subject to many unavoidable evils, both to ignorance on the part of the intellect, and to disordered affection on the part of the appetite, and to many sufferings on the part of the body, as Augustine carefully develops in *The City of God*.[10] Likewise, too, our desire for good cannot be satisfied in this life. For human beings by nature desire that the goods they possess, perdure. But goods of the present life are transitory, since even the present life itself passes away, which life we by nature desire and would wish to perdure forever, since human beings by nature shun death. And so we cannot have true happiness in this life.

Second, by considering the thing in which happiness specifically consists, namely, the vision of God's essence, which human beings cannot attain in this life, as I have demonstrated in the First Part.[11]

And these considerations make evident that no human being can attain true and perfect happiness in this life.

Reply to Obj. 1. We call some human beings happy in this life, either because they hope to attain happiness in the future life, as the Letter to the Romans says that "we have been saved in this hope,"[12] or because they somewhat share in happiness by enjoying the highest good in some way.

Reply to Obj 2. Sharing in happiness can be imperfect in two ways. In one way, with respect to the object of happiness, which object we do not in fact behold in its essence. And such imperfection takes away the nature of true happiness. In the second way, sharing in happiness can be imperfect with respect to the very subject that shares in it, and the sharer indeed attains the very object of happiness as such, namely, God, but imperfectly with respect to the way in which God enjoys himself. And such imperfection does not take away the true nature of happiness. For, since happiness is an activity, as I have said before,[13] we consider the true nature of happiness by the object of happiness, which object specifies its activity, and not by its subject.

Reply to Obj. 3. Human beings reckon by an analogy to true happiness that there is some happiness in this life. And so human beings are not completely wrong in their reckoning.

Fifth Article

Can Human Beings by Their Natural Powers Attain Happiness?

I proceed in this way to the fifth article: it seems that human beings can attain happiness by their natural powers.

Obj. 1. Nature does not fail to provide necessary things. But nothing is so necessary for human beings as the means whereby they attain their ultimate end. Therefore, human nature does not lack such means. Therefore, human beings can attain happiness by their natural powers.

Obj. 2. Human beings seem to be more sufficient than irrational creatures, since human beings are more excellent. But irrational creatures can attain their ends by their natural powers. Therefore, much more can human beings attain happiness by their natural powers.

Obj. 3. Happiness is "perfect activity," according to the Philosopher.[14] But the same thing starts and finishes the very activity. Therefore, since imperfect activity, which is, as it were, the starting point of human activities, is subject to the natural power of human beings, the power whereby they are masters of their acts, it seems that human beings can by their natural power attain perfect activity, that is, happiness.

On the contrary, human beings are by nature the sources of their actions by means of their intellect and will. But the ultimate happiness prepared for the saints surpasses the intellect and will of human beings, for the Apostle says in the First Letter to the Corinthians: "Eye has not seen, nor has ear heard, nor has it arisen in the heart of human beings, what God has prepared for those who love him."[15] Therefore, human beings cannot attain happiness by their natural powers.

I answer that human beings can by their natural powers attain the imperfect happiness that they can possess in this life, in the same way in which they acquire virtue, in which activity happiness consists. And I shall speak about this later.[16] But the perfect happiness of human beings consists in the vision of God, as I have said before.[17] And to behold God essentially exceeds the nature both of human beings and of every creature, as I have demonstrated in the First Part.[18] For every creature knows by nature according to the modality of its substance. Just so, the *Liber de causis* says of the Intelligences that "they know things superior to themselves and things inferior to themselves according to the modality of their substance."[19] And every knowledge according to the modality of created substance falls short of beholding God's essence, which infinitely surpasses every created substance. And so neither a human being nor any creature can by its natural power attain the ultimate happiness.

Reply to Obj. 1. Nature does not fail to provide necessary things for human beings even though it has not given human beings the weapons and coverings that it has provided in the case of other animals, since nature gave human beings reason and hands, things by means of which human beings can acquire weapons and coverings for themselves. Just so, nature does not fail to provide necessary things for human beings even though it did not give human beings any source whereby they could attain happiness, since such was impossible. But nature did endow human beings with free choice, whereby they could direct themselves to God, who would make them happy. "For we can in some sense accomplish through ourselves what we can accomplish through friends," as the *Ethics* says.[20]

Reply to Obj. 2. A nature that can attain the perfect good, although the nature needs external help to do so, belongs to a more excellent state than a nature that cannot attain the perfect good but attains an imperfect good, although the nature needs no external help to do so. This is what the Philosopher says in the *De coelo.*[21] Similarly, a person who can attain a perfect state of health, albeit with the help of medicine, is more disposed to be healthy than a person who can without the help of medicine attain only an imperfect state of health. And so rational creatures, who can attain the perfect good of happiness even though they need God's help to attain it, are more perfect than irrational creatures, who are incapable of such a good even though they by their natural powers do attain an imperfect good.

Reply to Obj. 3. The same power can cause the perfect and the imperfect when both belong to the same species. But this is not necessarily the case if the perfect and the imperfect belong to different species, for not everything capable of causing the disposition of matter can produce the matter's ultimate perfection. And imperfect activity, which is subject to the natural power of human beings, belongs to a different species than the perfect activity that constitutes the happiness of human beings. This is so because the species of an activity depends on the activity's object. And so the argument is invalid.

Seventh Article

Are Any Good Deeds Necessary for Human Beings to Attain Happiness from God?

I proceed in this way to the seventh article: it seems that no deeds on the part of human beings are necessary to attain happiness from God. *Obj. 1.* God, since he is an efficient cause of unlimited power, does not require preexisting or predisposed matter for his causal activity; rather, he can at once produce the whole thing. But the deeds of human beings can be necessary for their happiness only as dispositions, since such deeds are not necessary for their happiness as its efficient cause, as I have said.[22] Therefore, God, who does not need predispositions for his causal activity, bestows happiness apart from previous deeds.

Obj. 2. As God directly causes the happiness of human beings, so also does he directly establish nature. But when he first established nature, he produced creatures apart from any previous disposition or action on their part; rather, he directly made every kind of creature perfect in its species. Therefore, it seems that he bestows happiness on human beings apart from any previous activities on their part.

Obj. 3. The Apostle says in the Letter to the Romans that happiness belongs to human beings "on whom God bestows righteousness without regard to their deeds."[23] Therefore, no deeds on the part of human beings are necessary in order for them to attain happiness.

On the contrary, the Gospel of John says: "If you know these things, you will be happy if you have done them."[24] Therefore, human beings by their actions attain happiness.

I answer that a rightly directed will is necessary for happiness, as I have said before,[25] since a rightly directed will is simply a will duly ordered to our ultimate end. And so a rightly directed will is necessary for us to attain our ultimate end, just as matter needs to be duly disposed in order to attain a form. But this does not prove that any activity by human beings need precede their happiness, for God could simultaneously cause their will to tend rightly toward their end, and their will to attain their end. Just so, for example, does he at times simultaneously dispose matter and introduce form. On the other hand, the ordination of his wisdom requires that he not do so, since, as the *De coelo* says, "of things constituted to possess the perfect good, one possesses that good without undergoing change, another by undergoing one change, another by undergoing many changes."[26] And to possess the perfect good without undergoing change belongs to the thing that by nature possesses it. And to possess happiness by nature belongs to God alone. And so it belongs to God alone that no previous activity bring him to a state of happiness.

And since happiness surpasses every created nature, no creature as such suitably attains happiness without undergoing change by activity, and creatures strive for happiness itself by activity. And angels, whom nature ordains as superior to human beings, God's wisdom ordained to attain happiness by undergoing the change of one meritorious action, as I have explained in the First Part.[27] And human beings attain their very happiness by undergoing many changes by activity, active movements that we call meritorious. And so also is happiness, according to the Philosopher, the reward of virtuous activities.[28]

Reply to Obj. 1. The activity of human beings is not a prerequisite for attaining happiness because of an inadequacy of God's power to make them happy, but that the order in things be observed.

Reply to Obj. 2. God at once produced perfect first creatures, without any previous disposition or activity on their part, because he established the first individuals of each species in such a way that they might propagate their natures to their progeny. And similarly, the soul of Christ, without any previous meritorious activity, was happy from the very first moment of his conception, since he, who is God and man, was to bring happiness to others, as the Apostle says in the Letter to the Hebrews that Christ is "the one who brought many sons to glory."[29] But this is unique in himself, since his merits assist baptized children to attain happiness, even though those children lack their own merits, because baptism makes them members of the Body of Christ.

Reply to Obj. 3. The Apostle is speaking about the righteousness of hope, which we have by the grace that makes us righteous, and such grace is indeed not bestowed on us because of our previous deeds.

For such grace is not the end point of a movement, as happiness is, but rather the starting point of the movement whereby we strive for happiness.

Notes

1. *De divinis nominibus* 4. PG 3:693–96.
2. Aristotle, *De anima* III, 7. 431b2.
3. Ps. 94:12.
4. Q. 12, A. 1.
5. Q. 58, A. 3. Q. 79, A. 8.
6. Q. 84, A. 7. Q. 89, A. 1.
7. Ps. 119:1.
8. Ps. 144:15.
9. Job 14:1.
10. *The City of God* XIX, 4–8. PL 41:627–35.
11. Q. 12, A. 11.
12. Rom. 8:24.
13. Q. 3, A. 2.
14. *Ethics* VII, 13. 1153b14–17.
15. 1 Cor. 2:9.
16. Q. 63.
17. Q. 3, A. 8.
18. Q. 12, A. 4.
19. *Liber de causis*, prop. 8.
20. Aristotle, *Ethics* III, 3. 1112b24–28.
21. *De coelo* II, 12. 292a22–24.
22. Q. 5, A. 6.
23. Rom. 4:6.
24. Jn. 13:17.
25. Q. 4, A. 4.
26. Aristotle, *De coelo* II, 12. 292a22–24.
27. Q. 62, A. 5.
28. *Ethics* I, 9. 1099b16–17.
29. Heb. 2:10.

Question 6

On Voluntary and Involuntary Things

[This question is divided into eight articles, six of which are included here.]

Third Article

Can Things Be Voluntary Without Any Act?

I proceed in this way to the third article: it seems that nothing can be voluntary without an act.

Obj. 1. We call things voluntary when they proceed from the will. But things proceed from the will by acts, at least acts of the will itself. Therefore, nothing can be voluntary without an act.

Obj. 2. As we say that persons will by acts of the will, so we say that persons do not will when acts of the will cease. But not willing causes things to be involuntary, and such is contrary to things being voluntary. Therefore, nothing can be voluntary when acts of the will cease.

Obj. 3. Knowledge belongs to the nature of something being voluntary, as I have said.[1] But we acquire knowledge by acts. Therefore, nothing can be voluntary without some act.

On the contrary, we call voluntary the things of which we are masters. But we are masters of our acting and nonacting, and of our willing and nonwilling. Therefore, as acting and willing are voluntary, so also are nonacting and nonwilling.

I answer that we call voluntary the things that proceed from the will. And we say that one thing proceeds from another in two ways. In one way, directly, namely, that one thing proceeds from the other because the latter causes the former; for example, heat causes things to become hot. In the second way, indirectly, because something does not act; for example, we attribute the sinking of a ship to its pilot if he stopped piloting the ship. But we should note that we do not always, because persons do not act, causally attribute the consequences of their inaction to them; rather, we attribute the consequences of inaction to such persons only when they have the ability and the duty to act. For example, we would not attribute the sinking of a ship to a pilot if the latter were unable to pilot the ship, or if he were not commissioned to pilot the ship, though the ship happened to sink for want of a pilot.

Therefore, since the will by willing and acting can, and sometimes ought, to prevent nonwilling and nonacting, we impute such nonwilling and nonacting to the will, as if the nonwilling and the nonacting proceeded from the will. And so something can be voluntary apart from any act, sometimes, indeed, with an internal act without an external act, as when the will wills not to act, and sometimes even without an internal act, as when the will does not will.

Reply to Obj. 1. We call something voluntary not only if it directly proceeds from the will as the efficient cause of the thing, but also if it indirectly proceeds from the will by reason of the will not willing.

Reply to Obj. 2. We predicate "not willing" in two ways. In one way, as we understand the words as one expression, as the participle of the verb "I am not willing." And so, as I mean "I will not to read" when I say, "I am not willing to read," so the expression, "not willing to read," means "willing not to read." And then not willing causes things to be involuntary. In the second way, we understand the term as a figure of speech. And then we do not assert an act of the will. And such not willing does not cause things to be involuntary.

Reply to Obj. 3. For things to be voluntary, cognitive acts are necessary in the same measure that acts of the will are, namely, in order that persons have the power to consider and to will and to act. And just as nonwilling and nonacting at the proper time are voluntary, so also is it voluntary not to consider whether to will and act.

Fourth Article

Can Force Coerce the Will?

I proceed in this way to the fourth article: it seems that force can coerce the will.

Obj. 1. Anything can be coerced by something more powerful. But something, namely, God, is more powerful than the human will. Therefore, at least God can coerce the human will.

Obj. 2. Everything acted upon, when affected by the cause acting upon it, is coerced by the cause. But the will is a power that is acted upon, for it is "something that, when itself moved, causes movement," as the *De anima* says.[2] Therefore, since the will is sometimes moved by the cause acting upon it, it seems that the will is sometimes coerced.

Obj. 3. Forced movement is contrary to nature. But movement of the will is sometimes contrary to nature, as is evident when the will is moved to commit sin, which action is contrary to nature, as Damascene says.[3] Therefore, the inclination of the will can be coerced.

On the contrary, Augustine says in *The City of God* that nothing done by the will is done necessarily.[4] But everything coerced is done necessarily. Therefore, nothing done by the will can be coerced. Therefore, the will cannot be coerced to act.

I answer that there are two kinds of acts of the will: one, indeed, that is directly its act, as the act produced by it, namely, the act of willing; the other acts of the will that are commanded by the will and executed by another power (e.g., walking and speaking, which are commanded by the will and executed by the power of locomotion). Therefore, with respect to acts that the will commands, the will can be subjected to force, since force can prevent external bodily members from executing commands of the will. But with respect to the will's very own acts, force cannot coerce the will.

And the reason for the latter is that acts of the will are simply inclinations that come from an internal, knowing source, just as appetites from nature are inclinations that come from sources that are internal but lack knowledge. And coerced or forced things come from external sources. And so it is contrary to the will's very act that it be coerced or forced, just as it is contrary to the nature of an inclination or movement from nature to be coerced or forced. For example, force can carry stones upward, but the stones' forced movement cannot be the product of their natural inclination. Also, similarly, force can carry human beings along, but it is contrary to the nature of force that the forced acts be products of the will of human beings.

Reply to Obj. 1. God, who is more powerful than the human will, can move the will, as the Book of Proverbs says: "The heart of the king is in God's hands, and God turns it whithersoever he has willed."[5] But if this were to be done by force, it would no longer be accompanied by an act of the will, nor would the will itself be inclined; rather, it would be something contrary to the will.

Reply to Obj. 2. Movements are not always forced when the things acted upon are affected by the causes that act upon them, but are forced when such movements occur in opposition to the internal inclinations of the things acted upon. Otherwise, all alterations and comings-to-be of elementary material substances would be contrary to nature and forced. But the alterations and comings-to-be of elementary material substances are from nature, since matter or the subjects of alterations or comings-to-be have from nature the capacity for such dispositions. And likewise, when desirable things move the will by the will's own inclinations, the movements of the will are voluntary, not forced.

Reply to Obj. 3. The things toward which the will in sinning inclines, although they are evil and objectively contrary to the rational nature of human beings, are nonetheless perceived as good and naturally agreeable, inasmuch as they are agreeable to human beings by reason of some sensual passion or bad habit.

Fifth Article

Does Force Cause Things to Be Involuntary?

I proceed in this way to the fifth article: it seems that force does not cause things to be involuntary.

Obj. 1. We speak about voluntary and involuntary things in terms of the will. But force cannot coerce the will, as I have demonstrated.[6] Therefore, force cannot cause things to be involuntary.

Obj. 2. Regret accompanies things that are involuntary, as Damascene[7] and the Philosopher[8] say. But persons are sometimes subjected to force and yet are not on that account regretful. Therefore, force does not cause things to be involuntary.

Obj. 3. Things that proceed from the will cannot be involuntary. But some forced things proceed from the will; for example, such is the case when persons of heavy weight stand up, and when persons twist their bodily members contrary to the members' natural suppleness. Therefore, force does not cause things to be involuntary.

On the contrary, the Philosopher[9] and Damascene[10] say that "force makes things involuntary."

I answer that force is directly contrary to things being voluntary, just as force is also directly contrary to things being from nature. For it is common to voluntary things and things from nature that both proceed from an internal source, while forced things proceed from an external source. And consequently, as force causes things contrary to nature in the case of things lacking knowledge, so force causes things contrary to the will in the case of knowing things. And we call things contrary to nature unnatural, and we similarly call things contrary to the will involuntary. And so force causes things to be involuntary.

Reply to Obj. 1. Involuntary things are contrary to voluntary things. And I have said before that we call voluntary both the act that the will itself directly causes, and the act that the will commands.[11] Therefore, with respect to acts that the will itself directly causes, force cannot coerce the will, as I have said before,[12] and so force cannot cause such acts to be involuntary. But with respect to acts that the will commands, the will can be subjected to force. And with respect to such acts, force makes the acts involuntary.

Reply to Obj. 2. As we call natural what proceeds from an inclination of nature, so we call voluntary what proceeds from an inclination of the will. And we say that things are from nature in two ways. In one way, in that nature as an active source produces something; for example, it is by nature that fire produces heat. In the second way, we say that things are from nature with respect to the sources acted upon, namely, in that things have an inclination from nature to receive causal action from an external source; for example, we say that the movements of heavenly bodies are natural because heavenly bodies have a capacity from nature for such movements, although something voluntary causes their movements. And we can likewise call things voluntary in two ways: in one way, regarding causal action, as in cases when persons will to do something; in the other way, regarding the condition of being acted upon, namely, when persons will to be subjected to causal action from another. And so nothing is absolutely forced when something external coerces action, if a willingness to be acted upon abides in those who are acted upon. This is so because, although the persons being acted upon contribute nothing to the action, they nonetheless contribute something by their willingness to be acted upon. And so we cannot call such things involuntary.

Reply to Obj. 3. As the Philosopher says in the *Physics*,[13] the movements of animals whereby animals sometimes move contrary to the natural inclinations of their body, while not natural to their body, are nonetheless natural to the animals, for whom it is natural that appetites cause their movements. And so such movements are forced in one respect, but not absolutely.

And we likewise need to say the same about the situation where persons twist their bodily members contrary to the members' natural disposition. For such movements are forced in one respect, namely, regarding particular bodily members, but not absolutely, regarding the very human beings.

Sixth Article

Does Fear Cause Things to Be Absolutely Involuntary?

I proceed in this way to the sixth article: it seems that fear causes things to be absolutely involuntary.

Obj. 1. As force regards things at present contrary to the will, so fear regards future evils contrary to the will. But force causes things to be absolutely involuntary. Therefore, fear also causes things to be absolutely involuntary.

Obj. 2. Things intrinsically such remain such no matter what is added to them. For example, things intrinsically hot, no matter what is added to them, still remain hot as long as they abide. But deeds done out of fear are intrinsically involuntary. Therefore, deeds are also involuntary when fear is present.

Obj. 3. Things conditionally such are such in some respect, but things unconditionally such are such absolutely. For example, things conditionally necessary are necessary in some respect, but something absolutely necessary is unconditionally necessary. But deeds done out of fear are absolutely involuntary, and they are only voluntary subject to a condition, namely, that the feared evils be avoided. Therefore, deeds done out of fear are absolutely involuntary.

On the contrary, Gregory of Nyssa[14] and also the Philosopher[15] say that such deeds done out of fear are "voluntary rather than involuntary."

I answer that, as the Philosopher says in the *Ethics*,[16] and Gregory of Nyssa the same in his work *De homine*,[17] such deeds done out of fear "are a mixture of something voluntary and something involuntary." For deeds done out of fear, absolutely speaking, are not voluntary, but they become voluntary in the concrete, namely, as done to avoid the evils feared.

But if we should consider the matter correctly, deeds done out of fear are voluntary rather than involuntary, since they are voluntary in an absolute sense, albeit involuntary in one respect. For we say that things exist absolutely insofar as they are actual, and we say things exist in some respect, not absolutely, insofar as they are only conceptual. And deeds done out of fear are actual in the way in which they are done. For deeds are actual in the way in which they exist here and now and under other individual conditions, since actualities exist in particular things, and particular things as such exist here and now. And so deeds done out of fear are voluntary as they actually exist here and now, namely, as they in the concrete case prevent the greater evil that was feared. For example, a ship's crew out of fear of danger voluntarily jettisons the ship's cargo during a storm. And so it is evident that the deed is absolutely voluntary. And so also does the deed have the nature of something voluntary, since the source of the deed is internal to the source.

But it is only conceptual that we understand deeds done out of fear as deeds contrary to the will, as deeds existing apart from the concrete case. And so such deeds are involuntary in one respect, that is, as we consider them apart from the concrete case.

Reply to Obj. 1. Deeds done out of fear and deeds done under compulsion differ not only with respect to whether the deeds are done in the present or the future, but also in that the will does not consent to deeds done under compulsion, and such deeds are completely contrary to the will's inclination. On the other hand, deeds done out of fear are voluntary, since the will inclines to them, albeit not for their own sake but because of something else, namely, to ward off feared evils. For it suffices for the nature of something to be voluntary that it be voluntary because of something else voluntary, since we will not only something that we will for its own sake as an end, but also something that we will for the sake of something else as the end. Therefore, the internal will evidently does nothing in the case of forced deeds, but the will does something in the case of deeds done out of fear. And so, as Gregory of Nyssa says,[18] we define forced action not only as action "whose source is external," but we add "with those subjected to force contributing nothing." For the will of those overcome by fear contributes something to the deeds done out of fear.

Reply to Obj. 2. Things predicated absolutely (e.g., hot and white) remain such irrespective of anything added. But things predicated relatively vary in relation to different things; for example, something large in relation to one thing is small in relation to something else. And we say that something is voluntary both for its very own sake (absolutely, as it were) and for the sake of something else (relatively, as it were). And so nothing prevents something that might not be voluntary in relation to one thing from being voluntary in relation to something else.

Reply to Obj. 3. Deeds done out of fear are unconditionally voluntary, that is, as they are actually done. But they are conditionally voluntary, that is, they would not be willed if no such fear were impending. And so we can by the argument of this objection rather draw the opposite conclusion.

Seventh Article

Does Concupiscence Cause Things to Be Involuntary?

I proceed in this way to the seventh article: it seems that concupiscence causes things to be involuntary.

Obj. 1. As fear is one kind of emotion, so also is concupiscence another kind. But fear in some way causes things to be involuntary. Therefore, concupiscence also does.

Obj. 2. As fearful persons out of fear act contrary to what they were intending to do, so persons lacking self-restraint, because of concupiscence, act contrary to what they were intending to do. But fear in some way causes things to be involuntary. Therefore, concupiscence also does.

Obj. 3. Knowledge is necessary for things to be voluntary. But concupiscence impairs knowledge, for the Philosopher says in the *Ethics* that "pleasure," or the lust for pleasure, "impairs the judgment of practical reason."[19] Therefore, concupiscence causes things to be involuntary.

On the contrary, Damascene says: "Involuntary deeds merit compassion or indulgence, and are done regretfully."[20] But none of these characteristics belong to deeds done out of concupiscence. Therefore, concupiscence does not cause things to be involuntary.

I answer that concupiscence does not cause things to be involuntary but rather causes voluntary things. For we call things voluntary because the will inclines toward them. And concupiscence inclines the will to will the objects of lust. And so concupiscence causes things to be voluntary rather than involuntary.

Reply to Obj. 1. Fear regards evil, and concupiscence regards good. But evil as such is contrary to the will, while good is consonant with the will. And so fear is more disposed to cause things to be involuntary than concupiscence is.

Reply to Obj. 2. The will of those who do things out of fear remains opposed to the things they do, absolutely considered. But those who, as persons lacking self-restraint, do things out of concupiscence, do not retain their previous will, the will whereby they rejected the objects of lust; rather, their will is altered to will what they previously rejected. And so deeds done out of fear are in one respect involuntary, but deeds done out of concupiscence are in no respect involuntary. For persons yielding to concupiscence act contrary to what they were previously intending, but not contrary to what they now will, while persons overcome by fear act contrary to what, as such, they even now will.

Reply to Obj. 3. If concupiscence were completely to eliminate knowledge, as happens in the case of those who are driven out of their mind by concupiscence, concupiscence would consequently eliminate things being voluntary. Nevertheless, things would not thereby be involuntary in the proper sense, since things are neither voluntary nor involuntary in the case of those who lack the use of reason. But knowledge is sometimes not completely eliminated in the case of deeds done out of concupiscence, since concupiscence does not completely take away the power to know but only active consideration about particular courses of action. And yet this very lack of consideration is voluntary, as we call voluntary things in the power of the will, for example, such things as not acting and not willing, and similarly even not considering. For the will can resist passion, as I shall say afterward.[21]

Eighth Article

Does Ignorance Cause Things to Be Involuntary?

I proceed in this way to the eighth article: it seems that ignorance does not cause things to be involuntary.

Obj. 1. "Involuntary things merit pardon," as Damascene says.[22] But sometimes deeds done out of ignorance do not merit pardon, as the First Letter to the Corinthians says: "If anyone does not acknowledge this [the command of the Lord], such a person will not be acknowledged."[23] Therefore, ignorance does not cause things to be involuntary.

Obj. 2. Ignorance accompanies every sin, as the Book of Proverbs says: "They err who do evil."[24] Therefore, if ignorance were to cause things to be involuntary, every sin would consequently be involuntary. And this is contrary to Augustine's statement that "every sin is voluntary."[25]

Obj. 3. "Regret accompanies involuntary things," as Damascene says.[26] But some deeds are done in ignorance and without regret; for instance, such is the case if a person, thinking to kill a deer, kills an enemy whom the person wants to kill. Therefore, ignorance does not cause things to be involuntary.

On the contrary, Damascene[27] and the Philosopher[28] say that "ignorance causes certain things to be involuntary."

I answer that ignorance has the power to cause things to be involuntary because ignorance deprives one of knowledge, which is a prerequisite for things to be voluntary, as I have said before.[29] Nevertheless, not every ignorance deprives persons of such knowledge. And so we need to note that ignorance is related to activity of the will in three ways: in one way, as accompanying the will's activity; in the second way, as a consequence of the will's activity; in the third way, as preceding the will's activity.

Ignorance indeed accompanies the will's activity when persons are ignorant about what they are doing, but would still do it even if they were to know what they were doing. For then ignorance does not induce the persons to will the deed, but the persons happen to do something and at the same time do not know what they have done. Such would be the case in the cited example[30] if the person were indeed to wish to kill an enemy but were to do so unwittingly, thinking to kill a deer. And such ignorance does not cause things to be involuntary, as the Philosopher says,[31] since it does not cause anything contrary to the will. But such ignorance does cause things not to be voluntary, since a person cannot actually will what is unknown.

And ignorance is a consequence of the will's activity if the very ignorance is voluntary. And this happens in two ways, corresponding to the two previously cited ways in which things are voluntary.[32] In one way, because an act of the will inclines to ignorance. For example, such is the case if a person wills not to know, in order to have an excuse for sinning, or in order not to be drawn away from sinning, as the Book of Job says: "We do not wish to know your ways."[33] And we call such ignorance affected. In the second way, we call ignorance of things that we can and should know voluntary, for it is in this way that we call nonaction and nonwilling voluntary, as I have said before.[34] Therefore, we speak of ignorance in this sense either when persons do not actually consider what they can and ought to consider (which ignorance results from evil choice), or when ignorance results from passion, or when ignorance results from habitual disposition. Or when persons do not take care to acquire the knowledge that they ought to possess. And it is in this way that we call ignorance of the general precepts of the law, which precepts one is obliged to know, voluntary, since such ignorance is the result of negligence, as it were. And since ignorance itself is voluntary in any of these ways, such ignorance cannot cause things to be absolutely involuntary. Nevertheless, such ignorance causes things to be involuntary in one respect, inasmuch as such ignorance precedes the will's inclination to do something, and the will would not have the inclination if one had knowledge.

And ignorance is antecedent to the will's activity when the ignorance is not voluntary and yet causes human beings to will what they otherwise would not will. Such is the case when human beings do not know some circumstance involved in their activity, a circumstance that they are not obliged to know, and they on that account do something that they would not do if they were to know the circumstance. For example, such is the case when someone, not knowing that a passerby is traveling along a road, after taking precautions, shoots an arrow that kills the passerby. And such ignorance causes things to be absolutely involuntary.

Reply to the Objections. And the foregoing makes clear the response to the objections. For the argument of the first objection was posed about the ignorance of things that one is obliged to know. And the argument of the second objection was posed about the ignorance of choice, which ignorance is somehow voluntary, as I have said.[35] And the argument of the third objection was posed about the ignorance that accompanies the will's activity.

Notes

1. Q. 6, AA. 1, 2.
2. Aristotle, *De anima* III, 10. 433b17–18.
3. *De fide orthodoxa* IV, 20. PG 94:1196.
4. *The City of God* V, 10. PL 41:152.
5. Prov. 21:1.
6. Q. 6, A. 4.
7. *De fide orthodoxa* II, 24. PG 94:953.
8. *Ethics* III, 1. 1111a32.
9. *Ethics* III, 1. 1109b35–1110a1.
10. See n. 7, supra.
11. Q. 6, A. 4.

12. Ibid.
13. *Physics* VIII, 4. 254b14–24.
14. Nemesius, *De natura hominis* 30. PG 40:721. St. Thomas wrongly attributes this work to Gregory of Nyssa.
15. *Ethics* III, 1. 1110a11–19, b1–9.
16. Ibid.
17. See n. 14, supra.
18. Nemesius, *De natura hominis* 30. PG 40:720. See comment in n. 14, supra.
19. *Ethics* VI, 5. 1140b11–16.
20. *De fide orthodoxa* II, 24. PG 94:953.
21. Q. 10, A. 3. Q. 77, A. 7.
22. *De fide orthodoxa* II, 24. PG 94:953
23. 1 Cor. 14:38.
24. Prov. 14:22.
25. *De vera religione* 14. PL 34:133.
26. See n. 22, supra.
27. Ibid.
28. *Ethics* III, 1. 1109b35–1110a1.
29. Q. 6, A. 1.
30. In the third objection.
31. *Ethics* III, 1. 1110b18–24.
32. Q. 6, A. 3.
33. Job 21:14.
34. Q. 6, A. 3.
35. In the body of the article.

Question 9

On What Moves the Will

[This question is divided into six articles, four of which are included here.]

First Article

Does the Intellect Move the Will?

I proceed in this way to the first article: it seems that the intellect does not move the will.

Obj. 1. Augustine comments on Ps. 119:20, "My soul craved to desire your ordinances": "The intellect flies ahead, desire follows sluggishly or not at all; we know what is good, and doing good deeds does not delight us."[1] But such would not be the case if the intellect were to move the will, since a moveable thing's movement results from the action of the cause moving the thing. Therefore, the intellect does not move the will.

Obj. 2. The intellect, in presenting desirable things to the will, is related to the will as the power of imagination presents desirable things to the sense appetites. But the power of imagination presenting desirable things does not move sense appetites. Rather, we are at times related to the things we imagine in the same way that we are related to the things presented to us in paintings—and the latter things do not move us, as the *De anima* says.[2] Therefore, the intellect likewise does not move the will.

Obj. 3. It does not belong to the same thing in the same respect to be the cause of motion and to be moved. But the will moves the intellect, for we are intellectually active when we will to be intellectually active. Therefore, the intellect does not move the will.

On the contrary, the Philosopher says in the *De anima* that "desirable things, when understood, cause movement without themselves being moved, but the will causes movement and is itself moved."[3]

I answer that things, insofar as they have potentiality for several actualities, need to be moved by something. For something actual is necessary to bring potential things to actuality, and this is to cause movement. But we find that powers of the soul have potentiality for different actualities in two ways: in one way, with respect to acting or not acting; in the second way, with respect to doing this or doing that. For example, the power of sight at times actually sees something and at other times does not, and the power of sight at times sees something white and at other times sees something black. Therefore, powers of the soul need something to move them in two respects, namely, with respect to exercising or performing acts, and with respect to determining acts. And the first of these regards the powers, which we find sometimes active and sometimes passive, and the other regards the objects that specify the powers' acts.

And an efficient cause moves the powers themselves. And since every efficient cause acts for an end, as I have demonstrated before,[4] ends are the source of the powers' movements. And so skills linked to ends, by the skills' power to command, activate skills linked to means, "as, for example, the skill of piloting governs the skill of shipbuilding," as the *Physics* says.[5] But good in general, which has the nature of end, is the object of the will. And so the will in this respect moves other powers of the soul to their acts, since we employ other powers of the soul when we will to do so. For the ends and perfections of all other powers of the soul are included in the will's object as particular goods, and skills or powers linked to a general end always activate skills or powers linked to particular ends included in the general end. For example, the commander of an army, whose goal as the army's common good, namely, the deployment of the entire army, by his power to command sets in motion one of his captains, whose goal is the deployment of a single company.

But the objects, by determining the powers' acts, move the powers by way of formal causality, the way in which objects specify the actions of things of nature, as, for example, heat specifies the action of heating. And the first formal cause is being and truth in general, which constitute the object of the intellect. And so it is by such kind of influence that the intellect, by presenting its object to the will, moves the will.

Reply to Obj. 1. The cited authority does not hold that the intellect does not move the will, but that the intellect does not move the will in a necessary way.

Reply to Obj. 2. As imagining forms without evaluating their suitability or harmfulness does not move sense appetites, so neither does understanding truth without considering goodness and desirability move the will. And so the practical, not the theoretical, intellect moves the will, as the *De anima* says.[6]

Reply to Obj. 3. The will moves the intellect with respect to performing the intellect's acts, since even truth itself, which is the perfection of the intellect, is included in universal good as a particular good. But with respect to specifying the will's acts, which regards the objects of the will, the intellect moves the will. For we understand even goodness itself as a particular aspect included in the universal notion of truth. And so it is evident that the same thing does not in the same respect cause motion and undergo motion.

Second Article

Do Sense Appetites Move the Will?

I proceed in this way to the second article: it seems that sense appetites cannot move the will.

Obj. 1. "Causing motion and being an efficient cause is more excellent than being acted upon," as Augustine says in his *Super Genesim.*[7] But sense appetites are inferior to the will, which is the intellectual appetite, just as the senses are inferior to the intellect. Therefore, sense appetites do not move the will.

Obj. 2. No particular power can produce a universal effect. But sense appetites are particular powers, since sense appetites result from particular sense perceptions. Therefore, sense appetites cannot cause the will's movement, which is universal because it results from the intellect's universal understanding.

Obj. 3. A cause of motion is not moved by what it moves, and so there is no reciprocal movement, as the *Physics* says.[8] But the will moves sense appetites, since sense appetites obey reason. Therefore, sense appetites do not move the will.

On the contrary, the Letter of James says: "Everyone is tempted when led away and enticed by concupiscence."[9] But concupiscence does not lead persons astray unless sense appetites, in which concupiscence resides, move the persons' will. Therefore, sense appetites move the will.

I answer that things apprehended under the aspect of good and fitting move the will as the will's object, as I have said before.[10] And that things seem good and fitting is the product of two factors, namely, the condition of the object proposed, and the condition of the subject to whom the object is proposed. For we predicate suitability relationally, and so suitability depends on both termini of the relation. And so the sense of taste, when differently disposed, perceives things differently, as agreeable or disagreeable. And so "each person perceives ends as the person is disposed," as the Philosopher says in the *Ethics*.[11]

And the emotions of sense appetites evidently cause human beings to be disposed in certain ways. And so, as emotions affect human beings, things seem to them suitable that do not seem so apart from their current emotional state; for example, things seem good to angry persons that do not seem good to composed persons. And it is in this way, as regards the object, that sense appetites move the will.

Reply to Obj. 1. Nothing prevents things that are more excellent absolutely and in themselves from being weaker in some respect. Thus the will, absolutely speaking, is more excellent than the sense appetites, but sense appetites excel the will in persons ruled by emotions, since such persons are subject to their emotions.

Reply to Obj. 2. The acts and choices of human beings concern particular things. And so sense appetites, by the very fact that they are powers regarding particular things, have considerable ability to dispose human beings to perceive things in this or that way in particular cases.

Reply to Obj. 3. As the Philosopher says in the *Politics*,[12] the will resides in the power of reason, and the power of reason by its power to command moves the irascible and concupiscible appetites. Reason indeed does not do so by "despotic rule," as masters move slaves to act, but by "kingly or political rule," as leaders rule free persons, who are nonetheless able to resist their leaders' commands. And so both irascible and concupiscible appetites can resist the will. And so nothing prevents them from sometimes moving the will.

Third Article

Does the Will Move Its Very Self?

I proceed in this way to the third article: it seems that the will does not move its very self.

Obj. 1. Every cause of motion, as such, is actual, and everything being moved has potentiality, for "motion is the actuality of something that has potentiality, insofar as the thing has potentiality."[13] But one and the same thing is not potential and actual in the same respect. Therefore, nothing moves its very self. Therefore, neither can the will move its very self.

Obj. 2. Moveable things are moved when causes of movement are present. But the will is always present to itself. Therefore, the will would always be in motion if the will itself were to move its very self. And such a conclusion is patently false.

Obj. 3. The intellect moves the will, as I have said.[14] Therefore, if the will moves its very self, it follows that two causes at the same time directly move the same thing, and this conclusion seems inappropriate. Therefore, the will itself does not move its very self.

On the contrary, the will is master of its own acts, and the will itself has the power to will or not to will. But such would not be the case if the will were not to have in its power the power to move its very self to will. Therefore, the will itself moves its very self.

I answer that, as I have said before,[15] it belongs to the will to move other powers of the soul by reason of the ends that are the will's object. But ends in the case of desirable things are like principles in the case of understandable things, as I have said before.[16] And the intellect, by knowing principles, evidently brings its very self from potentiality to actuality regarding knowledge of conclusions, and in this respect moves its very self. And the will, by willing ends, likewise moves its very self to will means to those ends.

Reply to Obj. 1. The will does not cause its own motion and undergo motion in the same respect. And so the will is not actual and potential in the same respect. But the will, in willing its end, brings itself from potentiality to actuality with respect to means, namely, actually to will the means.

Reply to Obj. 2. The power of the will is always actually present to the will, although the will itself does not always have the acts of the will whereby it wills ends. But the will moves its very self by such acts. And so it does not follow that the will is always moving its very self.

Reply to Obj. 3. The will does not move its very self in the same way that the intellect moves the will. Rather, the intellect in fact moves the will by reason of the will's objects, while the will, regarding performance of its acts, moves its very self by reason of the will's ends.

Sixth Article

Does Only God as External Cause Move the Will?

I proceed in this way to the sixth article: it seems that only God as external cause moves the will.

Obj. 1. Nature establishes that superior things move inferior things, as, for example, heavenly bodies move terrestrial bodies. But there are things superior to the will of human beings besides God, namely, angels. Therefore, angels as external causes can also move the will of human beings.

Obj. 2. Acts of the will result from acts of the intellect. But the intellect of human beings is brought to its acts not only by God but also by angels through their illuminations of the intellect, as Denis says.[17] Therefore, by the same reasoning, the will is also.

Obj. 3. God causes only good things, as the Book of Genesis says: "God saw all the things that he had made, and they were very good."[18] Therefore, if only God were to move the will of human beings, that will would never be moved to evil, although it is that will "by which human beings sin or live righteously," as Augustine says.[19]

On the contrary, the Apostle says in the Letter to the Philippians: "God is the one who acts in us to will and accomplish."[20]

I answer that movements of the will, just like the movements of nature, are from within. And although things that are not the cause of moved things' nature can move things of nature, yet only something that is in some way the cause of a thing's nature can cause the thing's natural movement. For example, human beings, who do not cause the nature of stones, throw stones up in the air, but this movement is not natural to stones, and only the cause of the stones' nature causes their natural movement. And so the *Physics* says that what causes things to come to be, causes the locomotion of heavy and light things.[21] Thus human beings, who have the power to will, may be moved by someone who is not their cause, but no external cause that is not the cause of their power to will can cause voluntary movements of the will.

And only God can cause the power to will. And this is demonstrable in two ways. First, indeed, because the will is a power of the rational soul, and only God by creation causes such a soul, as I have said in the First Part.[22] Second, it is also evident because the will is ordained for universal good. And so only God, who is universal good, can cause the power to will. And we call everything else good because it participates in God's goodness and is a particular kind of good. And particular causes do not impart universal inclinations. And so also no particular efficient cause can cause prime matter, which has potentiality for every kind of form.

Reply to Obj. 1. Angels are not so superior to human beings that they can cause the latter's power to will, in the way in which heavenly bodies cause the forms of nature, from which forms the natural movements of natural material substances result.

Reply to Obj. 2. Angels move the intellect of human beings regarding the intellect's object, which the power of angelic light presents to the human intellect for it to know. And so also can an external creature move the will, as I have said.[23]

Reply to Obj. 3. As the universal cause of motion, God moves the will of human beings to the universal object of the will, that is, the good. And human beings can will nothing apart from this universal movement. But human beings by their power of reason determine themselves to will this or that, and particular things are real or apparent goods.

And yet God sometimes specially moves certain individuals definitely to will something good, as in the case of those whom he by his grace moves, as I shall say later.[24]

Notes

1. Augustine, *Enarratio in Psalmum 118* 8. PL 37:1522.
2. Aristotle, *De anima* III, 3. 427b21–24.
3. *De anima* III, 10. 433b10–21.
4. Q. 1, A. 2.
5. Aristotle, *Physics* II, 2. 194b5–7.
6. Aristotle, *De anima* III, 9. 432b26–433a1; III, 10. 433a14–26.
7. *Super Genesim* XII, 16. PL 34:467.
8. Aristotle, *Physics* VIII, 5. 257a33–b13.
9. Jas. 1:14.
10. Q. 9, A. 1.
11. *Ethics* III, 5. 1114a32–b1.
12. *Politics* I, 2. 1254b5.
13. Aristotle, *Physics* III, 1. 201a10–11.
14. Q. 9, A. 1.
15. Ibid.
16. Q. 8, A. 2.
17. *Coelestia hierarchia* 4. PG 3:180.
18. Gen. 1:31.
19. *Retractationum* I, 9. PL 32:596.
20. Phil. 2:13.
21. Aristotle, *Physics* VIII, 4. 255b17–31.
22. Q. 90, AA. 1, 2.
23. Q. 9, A. 4.
24. Q. 109, A. 2.

Question 10

On the Way in Which the Will Is Moved

[This question is divided into four articles, all of which are included here.]

First Article

Does Nature Move the Will to Will Anything?

I proceed in this way to the first article: it seems that nature does not move the will to will anything.

Obj. 1. We contradistinguish natural efficient causes from voluntary efficient causes, as the beginning of the *Physics* makes clear.[1] Therefore, nature does not move the will to will anything.

Obj. 2. Things always possess what arises from nature; for example, fire always possesses heat. But the will does not always have some movement. Therefore, the will has no movement that arises from nature.

Obj. 3. A nature is determined to produce one thing. But the will is disposed to effect contrary things. Therefore, the will wills nothing by its nature.

On the contrary, movements of the will result from acts of the intellect. But the intellect by nature understands some things. Therefore, the will likewise by nature wills some things.

I answer that we speak about nature in many ways, as Boethius says in his *De duabus naturis*,[2] and the Philosopher says in the *Metaphysics*.[3] For example, we sometimes call the intrinsic causes in changeable things their nature. And such a nature consists both of matter and a material form, as the *Physics* makes clear.[4]

In another way, we call any substance or even any being a nature. And we accordingly say that characteristics substantially befitting things are natural to the things. And such characteristics are properties of the things. And in every kind of thing, we trace nonessential characteristics to essential characteristics, as the source of the nonessential characteristics. And so, in this way of understanding nature, the source of characteristics befitting things necessarily comes from nature. And this is clearly evident in the case of the intellect, for we by nature know the principles of the intellect's knowledge. Similarly, it is also necessary that the source of the will's movements be something that we by nature will.

And this is good in general, for which the will by nature strives, just as every power strives for its object. And this is also the will's final end itself, which is related to desirable things in the same way that the first principles of demonstration are related to intelligible things. And this includes absolutely everything that by nature befits the persons willing. For we by the will desire not only the things that belong to the power of the will, but also the things that belong to each power of the soul, and the things that belong to the whole human being. And so human beings by nature will both the will's object and other things that befit different powers of the soul, such as knowledge of truth, which befits the intellect, and existing and being alive and the like, which regard our natural constitution. And the object of the will includes all of these things as particular kinds of good.

Reply to Obj. 1. We contradistinguish the will from nature as we contradistinguish one kind of efficient cause from another, for nature causes certain things, and the will causes other things. And in addition to the way in which it befits a nature, which is determined to produce one thing, to cause, there is another way of causing that is proper to the will, which is the master of its activity. But the will in one respect necessarily shares in movements proper to nature, since the will is grounded in a nature, just as subsequent causes share in the causal activity that belongs to prior causes. For each thing's very existing, which is the product of nature, is prior to its willing, which is the product of the will. And so the will by nature wills something.

Reply to Obj. 2. What things of nature have by nature simply as a result of their form, as it were, they always have, as fire always has heat. But what things of nature have by nature as a result of matter, they sometimes have only potentially, not always actually. For form is actuality, and matter potentiality. And motion is "the actuality of something that has potentiality."[5] And so what belongs to motion, or what results from motion, is not always present in things of nature; for example, fire only moves upward when it is out of its proper place.[6] And the will, which is brought from potentiality to actuality when it wills something, likewise need not always will but need will only when disposed in a fixed way. On the other hand, God's will, which is pure actuality, is always actually willing.

Reply to Obj. 3. One produced thing, yet one proportioned to a nature, always accords with the nature. For a produced thing generically one accords generically with a nature, and a produced thing specifically one accords specifically with a nature, and something individual accords with an individuated nature. Therefore, since the will, just like the intellect, is an immaterial power, one universal thing, namely, the good, by nature accords with the will, just as one universal thing, namely, truth or being or the essential, accords with the intellect. And many particular goods are included in universal good, and the will is not determined to one of them.

Second Article

Do Objects of the Will Necessarily Move the Will?

I proceed in this way to the second article: it seems that objects of the will necessarily move the will.

Obj. 1. Objects of the will are related to the will as causes of motion are related to moveable things, as the *De anima* makes clear.[7] But causes of motion, if sufficient, necessarily move moveable things. Therefore, objects of the will can necessarily move the will.

Obj. 2. The will, just like the intellect, is an immaterial power, and both powers are ordained for universal objects, as I have said.[8] But objects of the intellect necessarily move the intellect. Therefore, objects of the will likewise necessarily move the will.

Obj. 3. Persons will things either as ends or means. But persons necessarily will an end, as it seems, since the end is like the principles in theoretical matters, and we necessarily assent to those principles. And an end is the reason why we will means, and so it seems that we likewise necessarily will means. Therefore, objects of the will necessarily move the will.

On the contrary, rational powers are disposed toward contrary things, as the Philosopher says.[9] But the will is a rational power, for the will is a faculty "in the power of reason," as the *De anima* says.[10] Therefore, the will is disposed toward contrary things. Therefore, the will is not moved necessarily to will one of the contrary things.

I answer that the will is moved in two ways: in one way, with respect to performing its acts; in the second way, with respect to specifying its acts, and objects do this. Therefore, no object moves the will necessarily in the first way, for persons are able not to think about any object and so also able not actually to will it.

But with respect to the second way of the will's movement, one object rather than another object necessarily moves the will. For, with respect to objects moving powers to act, we need to consider the reason why they do so. For example, visible things move the power of sight by reason of their actually visible colors. And so, when colors are presented to the power of sight, the colors necessarily move the power of sight to see, unless persons divert their sight—and this pertains to the performance of acts. And if something only partially actually colored were to present itself to the power of sight, the power of sight would not necessarily see such an object. For the power of sight could focus on the part of the very object that is not actually colored, and then the power of sight would not see the object itself. And good is the object of the will in the same way that actually colored things are the object of sight. And so, if an object universally good and good in every respect should present itself to the will, the will necessarily strives for it, if the will happens to will anything. For the will would have been unable to will the contrary. On the other hand, if an object not good in every respect should present itself to the will, the will will not necessarily be inclined to it.

And since lack of any good has an aspect of nongood, only the good that is complete and lacks nothing is the kind of good that the will cannot not will, and that good is happiness. And we can understand all other, particular goods, inasmuch as they lack some good, as nongoods. And so considered, they can be rejected or approved by the will, which can tend to the same thing variously considered.

Reply to Obj. 1. Only an object that completely possesses a nature capable of causing a power to act is a cause sufficient to move the power to do so. But a cause, if deficient in something, will not necessarily move a power to act, as I have said.[11]

Reply to Obj. 2. An object so constituted that it is always and necessarily true necessarily moves the intellect, but an object that can be true or false, namely, one contingently true, does not necessarily move the intellect.

Reply to Obj. 3. The will's final end necessarily moves the will, since that end is perfect good. And means ordained to that end, means without which we cannot possess the end, for example, existing and being alive and the like, also necessarily move the will. But persons willing their end do not necessarily will other things, things without which they can possess their end, just as persons assenting to principles do not necessarily assent to conclusions that do not contradict the principles.

Third Article

Do Lower Appetites Necessarily Move the Will?

I proceed in this way to the third article: it seems that the passions[12] of lower appetites necessarily move the will.

Obj. 1. The Apostle says in the Letter to the Romans: "For I do not do the good that I want to do; rather, I do the evil that I despise."[13] And he says this because of concupiscence, which is one of the passions. Therefore, passions necessarily move the will.

Obj. 2. "Ends appear to each person as the person is disposed," as the *Ethics* says.[14] But it is not within the will's power immediately to cast emotions aside. Therefore, it is not within the will's power not to will the things toward which the emotions incline.

Obj. 3. Universal causes are only linked to particular effects by particular causes, and so universal principles do not move us except by means of our evaluation of particulars, as the *De anima* says.[15] But as universal principles are related to evaluation of particulars, so is the will related to sense appetites. Therefore, the will is moved to particular things only by means of sense appetites. Therefore, if emotions dispose sense appetites toward particular things, the will cannot be moved to the opposite.

On the contrary, the Book of Genesis says: "Your desires will be under your control, and you will be masters over them."[16] Therefore, lower appetites do not necessarily move the will.

I answer that, as I have said before,[17] the passions of sense appetites move the will regarding the objects moving the will, namely, inasmuch as human beings disposed in certain ways by their emotions judge things to be agreeable and good that they would not judge to be such apart from their present emotions. And emotions may so affect human beings in two ways. In one way, so that reason is completely constrained, with the consequence that human beings do not have the use of reason. For example, this happens in the case of those whom raging anger or lustful desire drives mad or insane, just as bodily disorders may do. (Indeed, such emotions do not occur apart from bodily changes.) And there is the same incapacity to reason in the case of such persons as there is in the case of irrational animals (who necessarily follow the impulses of their emotions), since there is in such persons no movement of reason and consequently no movement of the will.

But emotions at times do not completely engross reason, and the judgment of reason remains to some degree free. And there accordingly remains some movement of the will. Therefore, to the degree that reason remains free and not subject to passion, to that degree the will does not necessarily tend to the things to which the emotions incline. And so either human beings have no movement of the will, and passion alone rules, or the movement of their will, if there be such movement, does not necessarily result from passion.

Reply to Obj. 1. Although the will may not be able to prevent the movement of concupiscence from arising (about which the Apostle says in the Letter to the Romans: "I do," that is, sensually desire, "the evil that I despise"), the will is able not to will to desire lustfully, or not to consent to concupiscence. And so movements of the will do not necessarily result from movements of concupiscence.

Reply to Obj. 2. Although human beings have a dual nature, namely, the intellectual and the sensual, they are indeed sometimes simply of one kind regarding the entire soul. This is so either because the sensual part of human beings is completely subject to reason, as happens in the case of the virtuous, or, conversely, because the passions completely engross reason, as happens in the case of the insane. But sometimes, although passion clouds reason, part of reason nonetheless remains free. And such persons accordingly can either completely resist their passions or keep themselves from following their passions. For human beings so disposed perceive things in one way by reason and in another way by passion, since different parts of the soul dispose human beings in different ways.

Reply to Obj. 3. Both the universal good conceived by reason and goods perceived by the senses move the will. And so the will can be moved to particular goods without any passion of sense appetites. For we will and do many things dispassionately, simply by choice, as is most evident in those cases when reason resists passion.

Fourth Article

Does the External Cause of the Will's Movement, God, Move the Will in a Necessary Way?

I proceed in this way to the fourth article: it seems that God moves the will in a necessary way.

Obj. 1. Irresistible efficient causes necessarily move things. But God, since he has unlimited power, cannot be resisted, and so the Letter to the Romans says: "Who can resist his will?"[18] Therefore, God moves the will in a necessary way.

Obj. 2. The will is necessarily moved in what it wills by nature, as I have said.[19] But "natural to everything is what God effects in it," as Augustine says in his *Contra Faustum*.[20] Therefore, the will necessarily wills everything to which God moves the will.

Obj. 3. Things are possible if they presuppose no impossible consequence. But there is an impossible consequence if we should hold that the will may not will that to which God moves the will, since God's causal action would consequently be ineffective. Therefore, the will cannot not will that to which God moves the will.

On the contrary, the Book of Sirach says: "God formed human beings in the beginning and left them in the hand of their own counsel."[21] Therefore, God does not move the will of human beings in a necessary way.

I answer that "it belongs to God's providence to preserve the nature of things, not to destroy them," as Denis says in his *De divinis nominibus*.[22] And so he moves everything according to its condition, so that, by his causal motion, necessary causes produce necessary effects, and contingent causes produce contingent effects. Therefore, since the will is an efficient cause undetermined to effect one thing but indeterminately disposed to effect many things, God moves the will in such a way that the will is not determined to effect one thing; rather, God moves the will in such a way that the will's movement remains contingent and only necessary in the case of the things to which nature moves the will.

Reply to Obj. 1. God's will extends both to the deeds done by the things he moves, and the way in which deeds are done befitting the things' nature. And so it would be more contrary to God's causal motion if he were to move the will in a necessary way (which way does not belong to the will's nature) than if he were to move the will in a free way (since free movement belongs to the will's nature).

Reply to Obj. 2. Each thing has by nature what God effects in it to be natural for it. For things befit each thing as God wills that things befit the thing. And he does not will that whatever he effects in things be natural to them, for example, that the dead should rise again. But he does will that it is natural for every kind of thing to be subject to his power.

Reply to Obj. 3. If God moves the will to something, it is incompatible with the assertion that the will would not be moved to that thing. Nonetheless, it is not unconditionally impossible. And so it does not follow that God moves the will in a necessary way.

Notes

1. Aristotle, *Physics* II, 1. 192b8–20.
2. *De duabis naturis* 1. PL 64:1341.
3. *Metaphysics* IV, 4. 1014b16–1015a19.
4. Aristotle, *Physics* II, 1. 193a28–31.
5. Aristotle, *Physics* III, 1. 201a10.

6. The "proper" place of fire in Aristotelian cosmology is in the highest heavenly body, the sphere of pure fire.
7. Aristotle, *De anima* III, 10. 433b11–12.
8. Q. 10, A. 1, *ad* 3.
9. *Metaphysics* VIII, 2. 1046b4–7.
10. Aristotle, *De anima* III, 9. 432b5.
11. In the body of the article.
12. See Glossary, s.v. "Emotion."
13. Rom. 7:15.
14. Aristotle, *Ethics* III, 5. 1114a32–b1.
15. Aristotle, *De anima* III, 11. 434a16–21.
16. Gen. 4:7.
17. Q. 9, A. 2.
18. Rom. 7:15.
19. Q. 10, A. 2, *ad* 3.
20. *Contra Faustum* XXVI, 3. PL 42:480.
21. Sir. 15:14.
22. *De divinis nominibus* 4. PG 3:733.

Question 12

On Intention

[This question is divided into five articles, four of which are included here.]

First Article

Is Intention an Act of the Intellect or an Act of the Will?

I proceed in this way to the first article: it seems that intention is an act of the intellect and not an act of the will.

Obj. 1. The Gospel of Matthew says: "If your eyes shall be pure, your whole body will be full of light."[1] And eyes means intention, as Augustine says in his *De sermone Domini*.[2] But eyes, since they are the instruments of sight, signify a cognitive power. Therefore, intention is the act of a cognitive power and not the act of an appetitive power.

Obj. 2. Augustine says in the same place that the Lord called intention light when the Lord said: "If the light in you is darkness," etc.[3] But light belongs to knowledge. Therefore, intention does too.

Obj. 3. Intention designates an ordination to an end. But ordination belongs to the power of reason. Therefore, intention belongs to the power of reason and not to the power of the will.

Obj. 4. Acts of the will concern either ends or means. But we call acts of the will concerning ends volition or enjoyment, and we call acts of the will concerning means choice. And intention differs from these. Therefore, intention is not an act of the will.

On the contrary, Augustine says in his *De Trinitate* that "the will's intention unites the power of sight to visible material substances, and likewise unites images in the power of memory to the gaze of the soul's internal thinking process."[4] Therefore, intention is an act of the will.

I answer that intention signifies tending toward something, as the word itself indicates. And both the action of the cause that moves a thing and the movement of the moveable thing tend toward something. But the tendency of the thing's movement toward something results from the action of the cause moving the thing. And so intention belongs first and foremost to the cause that moves a thing to an end. And so we say that builders and everyone in authority move others under their command to what builders and those in authority intend. And the will moves all other powers of the soul to ends, as I have maintained before.[5] And so intention in the strict sense is evidently an act of the will.

Reply to Obj. 1. Eyes signify intention metaphorically, not to indicate that intention should belong to knowledge, but to indicate that intention presupposes knowledge, which presents to the will an end toward which the will moves. For example, we look ahead with our eyes to see whither we should move our bodies.

Reply to Obj. 2. We call intention light because light is visible to one who intends something. And so we also call actions darkness if human beings know what they intend, but do not know what results from their action, as Augustine explains in the same place.

Reply to Obj. 3. The will indeed does not appoint the order of things, but the will nonetheless tends toward something by the ordination of reason. And so the word "intention" designates an act of the will on the supposition that reason ordains something for an end.

Reply to Obj. 4. Intention is the act of the will in relation to an end. But the will is related to an end in three ways. In one way, absolutely, and then we call the will volition; for example, we absolutely will health or anything like it. In the second way, we consider an end as the will comes to rest in its possession, and the will's enjoyment is so related to the end. In the third way, we consider an end as the terminus of the means to the very end, and the will's intention is so related to the end. For example, we say that we intend health not only because we will health, but because we will to achieve health by means of something else.

Second Article

Does Intention Only Concern the Final End of Human Beings?

I proceed in this way to the second article: it seems that intention only concerns the final end of human beings.

Obj. 1. Prosper says in his *Sententiarum*: "The intention of the heart is a cry to God."[6] But God is the final end of the human heart. Therefore, intention always concerns the final end of human beings.

Obj. 2. Intention concerns ends as the termini of the will's movements, as I have said.[7] But a terminus has the nature of something final. Therefore, intention always concerns the final end of human beings.

Obj. 3. As intention concerns ends, so also does enjoyment. But enjoyment always concerns the final end of human beings. Therefore, so does intention.

On the contrary, there is only one final end of human acts of volition, namely, happiness, as I have said before.[8] Therefore, human beings would not have different intentions if intention were to concern only the final end of human beings. And such a conclusion is patently false.

I answer that intention is related to an end as the terminus of the will's movement, as I have said.[9] But we can understand the terminus of a movement in two ways: in one way, as the absolutely final terminus itself, in which the movement comes to rest, and this is the terminus of the entire movement; in the second way, as an intermediate terminus, which completes or terminates one phase of the movement and begins another phase. For example, when A moves to C through B, C is the final terminus, and B is an intermediate terminus. And intention can concern both. And so intention need not always concern the final end of human beings, although intention always concerns an end.

Reply to Obj. 1. We call the intention of the heart a cry to God, not to indicate that God is always the object of our intention, but to indicate that he knows our intention.

Or the intention of the heart is a cry to God because, when we pray, we direct our intention to God, and such an intention indeed has the nature of a cry.

Reply to Obj. 2. A terminus has the nature of something final, not always final with respect to the whole movement but sometimes final with respect to a phase of the movement.

Reply to Obj. 3. Enjoyment implies resting in an end, and such a state of rest belongs only to the final end. But intention implies movement toward an end, not rest. And so there is no comparable argument.

Third Article

Can One Intend Two Things at the Same Time?

I proceed in this way to the third article: it seems that one cannot intend two things at the same time.

Obj. 1. Augustine says in his *De sermone Domini* that human beings cannot at the same time strive for God and their bodily convenience.[10] Therefore, by like reasoning, neither can they strive for any other two things at the same time.

Obj. 2. Intention denotes the will's movement to a terminus. But one movement in the same phase cannot have several termini. Therefore, the will cannot intend many things at the same time.

Obj. 3. Intention presupposes an act of reason or the intellect. But "we cannot understand several things at the same time," as the Philosopher says.[11] Therefore, we likewise cannot intend several things at the same time.

On the contrary, crafts imitate nature. But nature by one means strives to produce two advantages; "for example, the tongue is ordained both for taste and for speech," as the *De anima* says.[12] Therefore, by like reasoning, crafts and reason can ordain one thing for two ends. And so one can intend several things at the same time.

I answer that we can understand any two things in two ways: either as two things related to one another or as two things independent of one another. And it is evident from what I have previously explained[13] that human beings can simultaneously intend many things if the things are related to one another. For intention concerns both our final end and intermediate ends, as I have said.[14] And persons simultaneously intend both proximate and ultimate ends; for example, persons simultaneously intend to take medicine and to restore health.

But if we understand two things as independent of one another, then too human beings can intend several things. And this is indicated by the fact that human beings choose one thing over another, since one thing is better than another. And one of the reasons why one thing is better than another is because one thing is useful for more things than the other is, and so human beings can choose one thing over another because the chosen thing is useful for more things. And so human beings evidently intend several things at the same time.

Reply to Obj. 1. Because the same human being cannot have several final ends, as I have previously demonstrated,[15] Augustine understands that human beings cannot simultaneously strive for God and their temporal convenience as final ends.

Reply to Obj. 2. One movement in one and the same phase can have several termini if one terminus is related to the other. On the other hand, one movement in one and the same phase cannot have several termini independent of one another. And yet we should note that reason can understand really different things as one. And intention is the will's movement to something preordained by reason, as I have said.[16] And so reason can understand several really distinct things as one terminus of intention, as reason conceives the things to be one. Reason can conceive several really distinct things as one either because two particular things mix to form an integrated whole, as heat and cold in proper proportion mix to produce health, or because two particular things are included in something common that may be what is intended. For instance, acquiring wine and clothing is included in wealth as something common to both, and so nothing prevents those who intend to acquire wealth from intending to acquire wine and clothing.

Reply to Obj. 3. We may understand several things at the same time insofar as they are in some respect one, as I have said in the First Part.[17]

Fourth Article

Do We Intend an End and Will Means to That End by the Same Act?

I proceed in this way to the fourth article: it seems that we do not intend an end and will means to that end by one and the same movement of the will.

Obj. 1. Augustine says in his *De Trinitate* that "there is one act of the will whereby one wills to see a window in order to see the window, and there is another act of the will whereby one wills to see passersby through the window."[18] But it belongs to intention that I should will to see passersby through the window, while it belongs to willing means to that end that I should will to see the window. Therefore, intending ends is one movement of the will, and willing means to ends is a different movement of the will.

Obj. 2. Objects differentiate acts. But ends and means are different objects. Therefore, intending ends is one movement of the will, and willing means to ends is another.

Obj. 3. We call the willing of means choosing. But choosing and intending are not the same thing. Therefore, the will does not by one and the same act intend ends and will means.

On the contrary, means are related to ends as midpoints are related to the endpoints of movements. But things of nature have movements that pass through midpoints to endpoints. Therefore, free-willing things have one and the same movements that intend ends and will means.

I answer that we can in two ways consider the will's movement to ends and means. In one way, as the will is moved to ends and means independently and in themselves. And then there are absolutely two movements of the will, one to the end and one to the means.

In the second way, we can consider the will's movement to ends and means as the will is moved to means because of the end. And then one and the same movement of the person's will tends toward an end and the means. For example, when I say, "I will to take medicine for the sake of my health," I designate only one and the same movement of my will. And this is so because the end is the reason why I will the means. And the same act fastens on its object and the reason for the object; similarly, the same act of sight perceives color and light, as I have said before.[19] And it is likewise in the case of the intellect. For the intellect considers principles and conclusions by different acts if it considers each independently, but there is only one act of the intellect in assenting to conclusions because of principles.

Reply to Obj. 1. Augustine is speaking about the act of seeing a window, and the act of seeing passersby through a window, as the will is independently moved to will each.

Reply to Obj. 2. Ends as things and means to the ends are different objects of the will. But ends and means constitute one and the same object of the will insofar as ends are the reason why means are willed.

Reply to Obj. 3. We can conceptually distinguish the beginning and end of movements that are one and the same in the things in motion, as the *Physics* says about the movements of ascent and descent.[20] Therefore, the will chooses means insofar as its movements are borne to means as ordained to ends. But we call the will's movements to ends, insofar as the ends are acquired by means, intention. And a sign of the latter is the fact that we can intend ends even though means to attain the ends have not yet been determined, and means are the object of choice.

Notes

1. Mt. 6:22.
2. *De sermone Domini in monte* II, 13. PL 34:1289.
3. Mt. 6:23.
4. *De Trinitate* XI, 4, 8, and 9. PL 42:990, 994, 996.
5. Q. 9, A. 1.
6. *Sententiarum* 100. PL 51:441.
7. Q. 12, A. 1, *ad* 4.
8. Q. 1, A. 7.
9. Q. 12, A. 1, *ad* 4.
10. *De sermone Domini in monte* II, 14 and 17. PL 34:1290, 1294.
11. *Topics* II, 10. 114b34–35.
12. Aristotle, *De anima* II, 8. 420b17–18.
13. Q. 12, A. 2.
14. Ibid.

15. Q. 1, A. 5.
16. Q. 12, A. 1, *ad* 3.
17. Q. 12, A. 10. Q. 58, A. 2. Q. 85, A. 4.
18. *De Trinitate* XI, 6. PL 42:992.
19. Q. 8, A. 3, *ad* 2.
20. Aristotle, *Physics* III, 3. 202a18–21.

Question 13

On Choice, the Act of the Will Regarding Means to Ends

[This question is divided into six articles, five of which are included here.]

First Article

Is Choice an Act of the Will or of the Power of Reason?

I proceed in this way to the first article: it seems that choice is an act of the power of reason and not of the will.

Obj. 1. Choice implies a comparison by means of which we choose one thing over another. But comparing belongs to the power of reason. Therefore, choice belongs to the power of reason.

Obj. 2. It belongs to the power of reason to reason deductively and to draw conclusions. But it belongs to the power of reason to reason deductively about practical matters. Therefore, since choice is a conclusion about a practical matter, as it were, as the *Ethics* says,[1] it seems that choice is an act of the power of reason.

Obj. 3. Ignorance pertains to cognitive power and not to the will. But there is some "ignorance in choice," as the *Ethics* says.[2] Therefore, it seems that choice pertains to the power of reason and not to the will.

On the contrary, the Philosopher says in the *Ethics* that choice is "the desire for things in our power."[3] But desire is an act of the will. Therefore, choice is likewise an act of the will.

I answer that the word "choice" implies an aspect that belongs to the power of reason or the intellect, and an aspect that belongs to the will. For the Philosopher says in the *Ethics* that choice consists in "understanding with desire" or "desire with understanding."[4] But whenever two things combine to form a unit, one of them is a quasi-form in relation to the other. And so Gregory of Nyssa says that choice "consists neither in desire as such nor only in deliberation, but in a combination of the two. For just as we say that animals are composed of souls and bodies, and that animals are neither bodies as such nor only souls, but both, so also do we say that choice is a combination of desire and deliberation."[5]

And with respect to the soul's acts, we need to note that acts belonging essentially to one power or disposition get their form or species from a higher power or disposition, insofar as the higher power or disposition ordains the lower. For example, if a person should perform an act of bravery out of love of God, the act indeed belongs to courage with respect to the act's subject matter, but to love with respect to the act's form. And reason in one way evidently precedes willing and ordains the will's acts, namely, as the will strives for its object by an ordination of reason, since cognitive powers make their objects manifest to appetitive powers. Therefore, the acts whereby the will strives for things presented to it as good indeed belong materially to the will and formally to the power of reason, since reason ordains the will to ends. And the substance of such acts is disposed as matter subject to the order imposed by a higher power. And so choice is substantially an act of the will and not an act of the power of reason, since movements of the soul toward chosen goods effect choice. And so choice is evidently an act of the appetitive power.

Reply to Obj. 1. Choice implies a previous comparison, not that choice essentially consists in the comparison itself.

Reply to Obj. 2. Conclusions even about practical matters belong to the power of reason, and we call such conclusions decisions or judgments, and choice results from them. And so conclusions seem to belong to choice as their product.

Reply to Obj. 3. We say that ignorance belongs to choice, not that choice itself is knowledge, but because persons choosing do not know what they are going to choose.

Third Article

Does Choice Concern Only Means or Also Sometimes
Ends Themselves?

I proceed in this way to the third article: it seems that choice does not concern only means.

Obj. 1. The Philosopher says in the *Ethics* that "virtue causes persons to choose rightly, and everything caused to be done for the sake of virtue belongs to other powers and not to virtue."[6] But that for the sake of which something is done is an end. Therefore, choice concerns ends.

Obj. 2. Choice implies the preference of one thing over another. But as we can prefer one means over another, so also can we prefer one end over another. Therefore, choice can concern ends as well as means.

On the contrary, the Philosopher says in the *Ethics* that "volition concerns ends, and choice concerns means."[7]

I answer that choice results from decisions or judgments, which are like the conclusions of practical syllogisms, as I have already said.[8] And so the things that stand as the conclusions of practical syllogisms are subject to choice. But in practical matters, ends stand as principles and not as conclusions, as the Philosopher says in the *Physics*.[9] And so ends as such are not subject to choice.

But in the case of theoretical matters, nothing prevents the principles of one demonstration or way of knowing from being the conclusions of other demonstrations or ways of knowing (although indemonstrable first principles cannot be the conclusions of any demonstration or way of knowing). Just so, something functioning in one activity as an end may also be ordained to something as means. And something functioning as an end is in this way subject to choice. For example, health is the end of doctors' activity, and so this end is not subject to their choice; rather, doctors' exercise of choice presupposes that health is the final cause of their choosing means. But bodily health is ordained for the soul's good, and so bodily health or sickness is subject to choice by those responsible for the soul's health. For example, the Apostle says in the Second Letter to the

Corinthians: "For when I am weak, then I am strong."[10] The final end of human beings, however, is in no way subject to their choice.

Reply to Obj. 1. Virtues' characteristic ends are ordained for happiness as the final end of human beings. And it is thus that we can choose those ends.

Reply to Obj. 2. There is only one final end of human beings, as I have previously maintained.[11] And so we can choose between ends whenever there are several ends, insofar as they are ordained for a further end.

Fourth Article

Does Choice Concern Only Our Deeds?

I proceed in this way to the fourth article: it seems that choice concerns other things besides human acts.

Obj. 1. Choice concerns means. But means includes not only our acts but also the instruments of our acts, as the *Physics* says.[12] Therefore, choice concerns other things besides human acts.

Obj. 2. We distinguish practical action from theoretical contemplation. But choice plays a role even in theoretical contemplation, namely, as we choose one opinion over another. Therefore, choice concerns other things besides human acts.

Obj. 3. Persons are chosen for some offices, both civil and ecclesiastical, by electors who do nothing in regard to the persons chosen. Therefore, choice concerns other things besides human acts.

On the contrary, the Philosopher says in the *Ethics* that "persons choose only the deeds that they think that they themselves are to do."[13]

I answer that choice concerns means in the same way that intention concerns ends. And ends are either actions or things. And if the ends are things, there needs to be intervening human actions. This is so either because human beings cause the things that are the ends, as, for example, doctors cause health, which is their end (and we for this reason also say that causing health is the doctors' end), or because human beings in some way use or enjoy the things that are the ends, as, for example, money or its possession is the goal of the greedy. And we need to speak in the same way about the means. For the means need to be either actions, or things with intervening human actions, whereby human beings cause or use the means. And it is in the foregoing way that choice always concerns human acts.

Reply to Obj. 1. Instruments are ordained for ends, since human beings use instruments for ends.

Reply to Obj. 2. In theoretical contemplation itself, there are acts of the intellect assenting to these or those opinions. And we contra-distinguish external action from theoretical contemplation.

Reply to Obj. 3. The electors of bishops and civic leaders choose to appoint the very officials to such positions of honor. Otherwise, the choice would not belong to the electors if there were no action on their part in the appointment of bishops or civic leaders. And like-wise, whenever we say that someone chooses one thing over another, such preference involves some action on the part of the person who chooses.

Fifth Article

Does Choice Concern Only Things That Are Possible?

I proceed in this way to the fifth article: it seems that choice does not concern only things that are possible.

Obj. 1. Choice is an act of the will, as I have said.[14] But "there is willing of impossible things," as the *Ethics* says. [15] Therefore, there is also choice of impossible things.

Obj. 2. Choice concerns our deeds, as I have said.[16] Therefore, it does not matter at all, with respect to choice, whether we should choose something absolutely impossible or something impossible for us. But it is frequently the case that we cannot accomplish what we have chosen, and so such things are impossible for us. Therefore, choice concerns impossible things.

Obj. 3. Human beings try to do things only by choosing to do so. But blessed Benedict says that those subject to a religious superior should try to do impossible things if their religious superior happens to command such things.[17] Therefore, there can be choice of impossible things.

On the contrary, the Philosopher says in the *Ethics* that "there is no choice of impossible things."[18]

I answer that our choices are always related to our actions, as I have said.[19] But the things we do are possible for us to do. And so we need to say that choice concerns only things that are possible.

Similarly, we choose something because it conduces to an end. But one cannot attain an end by means of something that is impossible. And one indication of this is the fact that human beings in the course of deliberating disband if they come upon something impossible for them to accomplish, as if they were unable to go on.

This point is also clearly evidenced by the process of reasoning that precedes choice. For means, which are the object of choice, are related to ends in the same way that conclusions are related to principles. But possible principles obviously do not imply necessary conclusions. And so ends are possible only if the means thereto are possible. And no one is moved to the impossible. And so no one would strive for an end except because the means thereto seem possible. And so impossible things are not subject to choice.

Reply to Obj. 1. Willing is in between understanding and external action, for the intellect presents its object to the will, and the will itself causes external action. Therefore, since the will's movements proceed from the soul to things, we consider the source of the will's movements in relation to the intellect, which understands things as generally good, and we consider the end or completion of the will's acts in relation to external actions, which are the means whereby persons strive to attain things. And so we consider the completion of the will's acts insofar as there are good things for persons to do. And these things are possible. And so complete willing concerns only things that are possible, that is, things that are good for the persons who will them. And incomplete willing concerns things that are impossible, and some call such willing velleity, namely, that persons would will such things if the things were possible. But choice denotes acts of the soul already determined to what persons are to do. And so choice in no way concerns anything but possible things.

Reply to Obj. 2. Since the will's object is the good understood by the intellect, we necessarily judge about the will's object as the intellect understands it. And so, just as willing sometimes concerns something that the intellect understands to be good, although the thing is not really good, so choice sometimes concerns something that the intellect understands to be possible for the one choosing, although the thing is impossible for the person.

Reply to Obj. 3. Benedict makes this statement in this way to indicate that persons subject to a religious superior ought not to decide by their own judgments whether something is possible, and that in every instance they ought to rely on their superior's judgment.

Sixth Article

Do Human Beings Choose Necessarily or Freely?

I proceed in this way to the sixth article: it seems that human beings choose necessarily.

Obj. 1. Ends are related to objects of choice as principles are related to the conclusions that follow from the principles, as the *Ethics* makes clear.[20] But principles necessarily lead to conclusions. Therefore, ends necessarily move persons to choose.

Obj. 2. Choice results from judgments of reason about things to be done, as I have said.[21] But reason necessarily judges about some things, since the judgments' premises are necessary. Therefore, it seems that choice also necessarily results from necessary premises.

Obj. 3. Human beings are not moved to one thing rather than another if the two things are completely equal. For example, if hungry persons have within their grasp two separate, equally distant portions of equally appetizing food, they are no more moved to one portion than to the other, as Plato said.[22] And Plato ascribes the reason for this to the earth's immobility at the center of the universe, as the *De coelo* relates.[23] But far less can persons choose things understood to be of less worth than they can choose things understood to be of equal worth. Therefore, if two or more things should be presented to a person's will, and one of these seems to be of greater worth than the others, the person cannot choose any of the others. Therefore, a person necessarily chooses the good that seems to be more excellent. But every choice concerns whatever seems better in some way. Therefore, human beings always choose necessarily.

On the contrary, choice is the act of a rational power, and such a power is disposed toward contrary things, as the Philosopher says.[24]

I answer that human beings do not choose necessarily. And this is so because things that can not-exist, do not not exist necessarily. And from the twofold power that human beings possess, we can understand the reason why they are able to choose or not choose. For human beings can will and can not will, can act and can not act; they can also will this or will that, and do this or do that. And we understand from human beings' very power of reason why they can. For the will can strive for whatever reason can understand as good. And reason can understand as good not only willing and acting but also nonwilling and not acting. And also, in the case of every particular good, reason can consider the aspect of good and the deficiency of good (which deficiency has the aspect of evil), and can accordingly understand every such good as something to be chosen or to be shunned.

But the perfect good, that is, happiness, is the only good that reason cannot understand under the aspect of evil or of any deficiency. And so human beings necessarily will their happiness, nor can they will not to be happy, or will to be unhappy.

And since choice concerns means and not ends, as I have already said,[25] choice does not concern the perfect good (i.e., happiness) but other goods that are particular. And so human beings choose freely and not necessarily.

Reply to Obj. 1. Conclusions do not always necessarily follow from principles but do so only if the principles cannot be true unless the conclusions are true. And it likewise need not be the case that ends always make it necessary for human beings to choose a means, since some means are such that the ends could be attained without recourse to the means. Or if the means are necessary to attain the ends, we do not always so regard the means.

Reply to Obj. 2. Reason's decisions or judgments about what we should do concern contingent things, things that we can do. And conclusions in such matters do not necessarily follow from principles

that are absolutely necessary, but from principles that are hypothetically necessary (e.g., If one runs, one moves).

Reply to Obj. 3. If two things equal in one respect are presented to
a person, nothing prevents the person from considering a superior
characteristic regarding one of them, or the person's will from being
inclined to that very one rather than the other.

Notes

1. Aristotle, *Ethics* VII, 3. 1147a24–b1. Cf. III, 3. 1113a4, 11.
2. Aristotle, *Ethics* III, 1. 1110b31.
3. *Ethics* III, 3. 1113a11.
4. *Ethics* VI, 2. 1139b4–5.
5. Nemesius, *De natura hominis* 33. PG 40:733. St. Thomas wrongly attributes this
   work to Gregory of Nyssa.
6. *Ethics* VI, 12. 1144a6–11.
7. *Ethics* III, 2. 1111b26–27.
8. Q. 13, A. 1, *ad* 2.
9. *Physics* II, 9. 200a15–24.
10. 2 Cor. 12:10.
11. Q. 1, A. 5.
12. Aristotle, *Physics* II, 3. 194b32–195a3.
13. *Ethics* III, 2. 1111b25–26.
14. Q. 13, A. 1.
15. Aristotle, *Ethics* III, 2. 1111b20–22.
16. Q. 13, A. 4.
17. *Regula ad monachos 68.* PL 66:917.
18. *Ethics* III, 2. 1111b20–21.
19. Q. 13, A. 4
20. Aristotle, *Ethics* VII, 8. 1151a16–17.
21. Q. 13, A. 1, *ad* 2.
22. *Timaeus* 63A. *Phaedo* 108E. Cf. Averroes, *In De coelo* II, comm. 90.
23. Aristotle does not say that Plato so reasoned. *De coelo* II. 295b12, 25.
24. *Metaphysics* VIII, 2. 1046b8.
25. Q. 13, A. 3.

Question 14

On the Deliberation Preceding Choice

[This question is divided into six articles, five of which are included here.]

First Article

Is Deliberation an Inquiry?

I proceed in this way to the first article: it seems that deliberation is not an inquiry.

Obj. 1. Damascene says that "deliberation is desire."[1] But inquiring does not belong to desire. Therefore, deliberation is not an inquiry.

Obj. 2. Inquiring belongs to discursive reasoning, and so inquiry is inappropriate for God, whose way of knowing is not discursive, as I have maintained in the First Part.[2] But we ascribe deliberation to God, for the Letter to the Ephesians says that "he does everything according to the deliberation of his will."[3] Therefore, deliberation is not an inquiry.

Obj. 3. Inquiry concerns doubtful things. But counsel is given about things that are undoubtedly good, as the Apostle says in the First Letter to the Corinthians: "Now, I have no command from the Lord about virgins, but I offer my counsel."[4] Therefore, consultation is not an inquiry.

On the contrary, Gregory of Nyssa says: "Every deliberation is indeed an inquiry, but not every inquiry is a deliberation."[5]

I answer that choice results from judgments of reason about things to be done, as I have said.[6] And we find a great deal of uncertainty in practical matters, since actions deal with contingent particulars, and contingent particulars are uncertain because they can vary. But reason does not produce judgments about doubtful and uncertain things without a preceding inquiry. And so reason needs to inquire before judging about what is to be chosen, and we call such an inquiry deliberation. And the Philosopher consequently says that choice is "our desire for something about which we have already deliberated."[7]

Reply to Obj. 1. If the acts of two powers are interrelated, there exists in the acts of each power something that belongs to the other power, and so each power can designate the acts of the other power. But acts of reason directing means to ends, and acts of the will striving for the means at the direction of reason, are evidently interrelated. And so both something proper to reason, namely, an ordination of means to ends, is evidently present in the acts of the will that are choices, and something proper to the will is evidently present in deliberation, which consists of acts of reason. Something proper to the will is present in deliberation as the subject matter under deliberation, since deliberation concerns what human beings will to do, and also as the cause of deliberation, since human beings are moved to deliberate about means because human beings will ends. And therefore, as the Philosopher says in the *Ethics* that "choice is understanding with desire,"[8] in order to show that both the intellect and the will work together in choice, so Damascene says the "deliberation is desire with inquiry,"[9] in order to show that deliberation somehow belongs both to the will, concerning which and on account of which the inquiry is made, and to reason, which makes the inquiry.

Reply to Obj. 2. We need to understand things that we predicate of God, without any of the deficiencies that we find in ourselves. For example, we know conclusions by reasoning discursively from causes to effects, but the knowledge we predicate of God denotes the sure knowledge that the first cause has about every effect without recourse to discursive reasoning. And we likewise attribute deliberation to God in reference to the sure knowledge contained in his decisions or judgments, sure knowledge that we attain by means of deliberative inquiry. But such inquiry does not exist in God, and so we attribute no such inquiry to him. And Damascene accordingly says that "God does not deliberate, for deliberating belongs to those who lack knowledge."[10]

Reply to Obj. 3. Nothing prevents things that wise and spiritual persons regard as most certainly good from nonetheless being doubtful in the opinion of most people, especially carnal persons. And so counsels are given about such things.

Third Article

Does Deliberation Concern Only Our Deeds?

I proceed in this way to the third article: it seems that deliberation does not concern only our deeds.

Obj. 1. Deliberation implies a comparison. But it is possible for ordinary people to make comparisons even about things that cannot be changed and are not caused by us, for example, the natures of things. Therefore, deliberation does not concern only our deeds.

Obj. 2. Human beings sometimes seek counsel about things prescribed by law, and so also we speak about counselors-at-law. And yet making laws does not belong to those who seek such counsel. Therefore, consultation does not concern only our deeds.

Obj. 3. We also speak of certain persons consulting about future events, even though such events do not lie within our power. Therefore, consultation does not concern only our deeds.

Obj. 4. If human beings were to deliberate only about their deeds, no one would deliberate about things to be done by others. But this conclusion is clearly false. Therefore, deliberation does not concern only our deeds.

On the contrary, Gregory of Nyssa says: "We deliberate about things that lie in our power and can be done by us."[11]

I answer that deliberation in the strict sense implies a conference involving several people. And even the word itself indicates this, for we speak about deliberation as if it were a group session,[12] since many persons sit together in order to deliberate together. And we should note that we need to consider many conditions or circumstances about contingent particulars in order to know anything with certainty. And while one person cannot easily consider such conditions or circumstances, several persons assess them with greater certainty, since one person takes note of something that does not occur to another person. On the other hand, we consider necessary and universal things in a more absolute and purer way, so that a single person can rather suffice to consider such things. And so deliberative inquiry, properly speaking, pertains to contingent particulars. And true knowledge about such things does not rank as high as knowledge desirable in itself, such as knowledge of universal and necessary things. Rather, we seek knowledge about contingent particulars insofar as such knowledge is useful for action, since actions concern contingent particulars. And so deliberation, properly speaking, concerns our deeds.

Reply to Obj. 1.   Deliberation does not imply any kind of comparison, but implies a comparison about things to be done, for the reason I have already stated.[13]

Reply to Obj. 2. Things prescribed by law, although not the product of any activity by the persons seeking counsel, nonetheless direct the persons' activity, since legal mandates are one reason why persons do things.

Reply to Obj. 3. Consultation concerns not only deeds but things related to actions. And we consequently speak of there being consultation about future events insofar as known future events induce human beings to do or shun things.

Reply to Obj. 4. We seek deliberation about the deeds of others insofar as others are one with us. We are united to others either by a bond of affection, as, for example, one is as solicitous about a friend's concerns as one is about one's own concerns. Or else we are united to another in an instrumental way, for a chief cause and an instrumental cause are one cause, as it were, since the chief cause acts by means of the instrumental cause. And so masters deliberate about what their slaves are to do.

Fourth Article

Does Deliberation Concern Everything That We Do?

I proceed in this way to the fourth article: it seems that deliberation concerns everything that we are to do.

Obj. 1. Choice is "the desire for something about which we have already deliberated," as I have said.[14] But choice concerns everything that we do. Therefore, deliberation likewise concerns everything that we do.

Obj. 2. Deliberation implies an inquiry by reason. But we proceed by an inquiry of reason in everything that we do not do under the impulse of passion. Therefore, deliberation concerns everything that we do.

Obj. 3. The Philosopher says in the *Ethics* that "we by deliberation inquire about the means to accomplish things most suitably and in the best way if those things can be accomplished by more than one means, and we by deliberation inquire about the manner to accomplish things if those things can be accomplished by only one means."[15] But we by one or many means accomplish everything that we do. Therefore, deliberation concerns everything that we do.

On the contrary, Gregory of Nyssa says that "there is no deliberation about the activities accomplished by training or skill."[16]

I answer that deliberation is a type of inquiry, as I have said.[17] And we are accustomed to inquire about doubtful things, and so also reasoning by inquiry, which reasoning we call argumentation, "induces certainty about things hitherto in doubt."[18] And things related to human activity may be beyond doubt in two ways. In one way, because things come to fixed ends in fixed ways, as happens in the case of skills that have fixed ways of operating; for example, scribes do not deliberate about how they should draw letters of the alphabet, since their craft determines how they should do so. In the second way, because it matters little whether things are done in this way or that, and things that help or hinder little with respect to attaining ends, are trivial. And reason understands trivial things as if they were nothing. And so, as the Philosopher says,[19] we do not deliberate about two kinds of things, even though the things are ordained to ends, namely, trivial things and things that need to be done in fixed ways. Actions proper to skills are instances of the latter "except in the case of such imprecise skills as medicine, business, and the like," as Gregory of Nyssa says.[20]

Reply to Obj. 1. By reason of judgments or decisions, choice presupposes deliberation. And so deliberative inquiry is unnecessary when judgments or decisions are evident without inquiry.

Reply to Obj. 2. Reason makes no inquiry about evident things but judges immediately. And so there need not be deliberative inquiry about everything that reason does.

Reply to Obj. 3. When we can accomplish things by only one means but in different ways, we can have doubts, just as we can have doubts when we can accomplish things by several means. And so there is need to deliberate. On the other hand, there is no need to deliberate when both the means and the method of using the means are fixed.

Fifth Article

Is the Process of Deliberation Analytic?

I proceed in this way to the fifth article: it seems that the process of deliberation is not analytic.

Obj. 1. Deliberation concerns our deeds. But our actions proceed synthetically, namely, from simple things to composite things, rather than analytically. Therefore, the process of deliberation is not always analytic.

Obj. 2. Deliberation is an inquiry by reason. But reasoning more appropriately begins with prior things and arrives at subsequent things. Therefore, since the past is prior to the present, and the present is prior to the future, it seems that our process of deliberation should go from the present and the past to the future. But such a process is not analytic. Therefore, we do not follow an analytic process in deliberation.

Obj. 3. Deliberation concerns only things that we can do, as the *Ethics* says.[21] But whether something is possible for us depends on what we can or cannot do to achieve it. Therefore, deliberative inquiry needs to begin with things at hand.

On the contrary, the Philosopher says that "persons who deliberate, seem to inquire and analyze."[22]

I answer that every inquiry needs to begin from some source. And if this source indeed be both prior in knowledge and prior in reality, the process of inquiry is synthetic rather than analytic, for to go from causes to effects is a synthetic process of inquiry, since causes are more elementary than effects. But if the source is prior in knowledge and subsequent in reality, the process of inquiry is analytic, as when we judge about evident effects by analyzing the effects in terms of their root causes. And the source in deliberative inquiry is an end, which is indeed prior in intention but subsequent in reality. And accordingly, deliberative inquiry needs to be analytic, namely, to start with what we intend to obtain in the future, and to continue until we reach a decision about what we are to do right away.

Reply to Obj. 1. Deliberation indeed concerns our actions. But we understand the nature of our actions by their ends. And so the order of reasoning about our actions is the opposite of the order of acting.

Reply to Obj. 2. Reason begins with conceptually prior things, but not always with temporally prior things.

Reply to Obj. 3. We would not seek to know whether a means to an end is possible unless the means were suitable for attaining the end. And so we need to inquire whether the means is suitable to conduce to the end before we consider whether the means is possible.

Sixth Article

Is the Process of Deliberation Endless?

I proceed in this way to the sixth article: it seems that the process of deliberative inquiry is endless.

Obj. 1. Deliberation is an inquiry about particulars, in which actions consist. But the number of particulars is unlimited. Therefore, deliberative inquiry is endless.

Obj. 2. Both considering what we are to do, and considering how we are to remove obstacles, are subject to deliberative inquiry. But every human action can be hindered, and some acts of human reason can remove the obstacles. Therefore, there is an endless quest to remove the obstacles.

Obj. 3. The inquiry of demonstrative sciences does not go on indefinitely, since such inquiry arrives at self-evident principles that are absolutely certain. But we cannot find such certitude in the case of contingent particulars, which can vary and are uncertain. Therefore, the process of deliberative inquiry is endless.

On the contrary, "no one is moved to something that the person cannot attain," as the *De coelo* says.[23] But one cannot pass through what is unlimited. Therefore, no one would begin to deliberate if deliberative inquiry were endless. And this conclusion is evidently false.

I answer that deliberative inquiry is actually limited in two respects, namely, in respect to its source and in respect to its term. For we understand two sources of deliberative inquiry. One source, by the very nature of practical things, is proper to deliberative inquiry, and this source is the end. And deliberation does not concern ends; rather, we presuppose ends as the source of deliberation, as I have said.[24]

We take the second source from a different kind of thing, as it were, just as one demonstrative science presupposes certain things from another demonstrative science and does not make inquiry about those things. And such sources presupposed by deliberative inquiry comprise everything perceived by the senses (e.g., that this particular thing is bread or iron) and everything known in a universal way by theoretical or practical sciences (e.g., that God forbids adultery, or that human beings cannot survive without suitable nourishment). And deliberators do not make inquiry about these sources.

And the term of deliberative inquiry is something in our immediate power to accomplish. For just as ends by their nature cause deliberative inquiry, so means by their nature conclude deliberative inquiry. And so what presents itself as the first thing to be done, by its nature brings deliberative inquiry to a final conclusion, at which deliberative inquiry ceases.

Nothing, however, prevents deliberation from being potentially endless insofar as an unlimited number of things present themselves as things for deliberation to inquire about.

Reply to Obj. 1. The number of particulars is only potentially and not actually unlimited.

Reply to Obj. 2. Although human actions can be impeded, there is sometimes no obstacle at hand. And so we need not always deliberate about removing obstacles.

Reply to Obj. 3. Although we cannot understand contingent particulars as absolutely certain, we can nonetheless understand them as certain as they are presently, as we appropriate them for our actions.

For example, it is not necessary that Socrates sit, but it is necessary that Socrates be sitting while he sits. And we can know with certainty that Socrates is sitting.

Notes

1. *De fide orthodoxa* II, 22. PG 94:945.
2. Q. 14, A. 7.
3. Eph. 1:11.
4. 1 Cor. 7:25.
5. Nemesius, *De natura hominis* 34. PG 40:736. St. Thomas errs in attributing this work to Gregory of Nyssa.
6. Q. 13, A. 1, *ad* 2, and A. 3.
7. *Ethics* III, 3. 1113a11.
8. *Ethics* VI, 2. 1139b4.
9. See n. 1, supra.
10. See n. 1, supra.
11. Nemesius, *De natura hominis* 34. PG 40:736. See comment in n. 5, supra.
12. St. Thomas here dubiously derives the Latin word for deliberation (*consilium*) from *considium*, a sitting together.
13. In the body of the article.
14. Q. 14, A. 1.
15. *Ethics* III, 3. 1112b16–18.
16. Nemesius, *De natura hominis* 34. PG 40:737. See comment in n. 5, supra.
17. Q. 14, A. 1.
18. Cf. Cicero, *De inventione* I, 34.
19. *Ethics* III, 3. 1112b9–11.
20. Nemesius, *De natura hominis* 34. PG 40:740. See comment in n. 5, supra.
21. Aristotle, *Ethics* III, 3. 1112a30–31.
22. *Ethics* III, 3. 1112b20.
23. Aristotle, *De coelo* I, 7. 274b17–18.
24. Q. 14, A. 2.

Question 15

On Consent, the Act of the Will Related to Means

[This question is divided into four articles, two of which are included here.]

First Article

Is Consent an Act of Appetitive Power or Cognitive Power?

I proceed in this way to the first article: it seems that consent belongs only to the cognitive part of the soul.

Obj. 1. Augustine in his *De Trinitate* ascribes consent to higher reason.[1] But reason denotes cognitive power. Therefore, the act of consent belongs to cognitive power.

Obj. 2. To consent is to sense in conjunction with something else. But sensing belongs to cognitive power. Therefore, consenting belongs to cognitive power.

Obj. 3. As assenting means the inclination of the intellect toward something, so also does consenting. But assenting belongs to the intellect, which is a cognitive power. Therefore, consenting belongs to cognitive power.

On the contrary, Damascene says in his *De fide orthodoxa* that "there is no decision," that is, consent, "if one should judge and not love" something.[2] But loving something belongs to appetitive power. Therefore, consent also does.

I answer that consenting implies an inclination of the senses toward something. And it belongs to the external senses to know things physically present. (For it is the power of imagination that knows the likenesses of material things even when the things to which the likenesses belong are physically absent.) And the intellect knows universal natures, which it can know without difference both when individual things are physically present and when individual things are physically absent. And because acts of the will are inclinations toward the things themselves, those very inclinations, as they cleave to the things, by analogy get a name from sense perception, as if they acquire some knowledge of the things to which they cleave, as they take pleasure in the things. And so also the Book of Wisdom says: "Learn about the Lord in goodness."[3] And consenting is accordingly an act of appetitive power.

Reply to Obj. 1. As the *De anima* says, "the will resides in the power of reason."[4] And so, when Augustine ascribes consent to reason, he understands reason to include the will.

Reply to Obj. 2. "Sensing" in the proper sense belongs to cognitive power, but "sensing" in a sense analogous to sense knowledge belongs to appetitive power, as I have said.[5]

Reply to Obj. 3. Assenting is, as it were, sensing in relation to something else, and so assenting implies a separation from its object. But consenting is sensing with something else, and so consenting implies a union with its object. And so we more properly say that the will, to which it belongs to strive for things themselves, consents. And we more properly say that the intellect, whose activity does not consist in movements toward things but rather the converse, as I have said in the First Part,[6] assents. Nonetheless, we are accustomed to substitute one term for the other.

We can also say that the intellect assents inasmuch as the will moves it.

Third Article

Does Consent Concern Ends or Means?

I proceed in this way to the third article: it seems that consent concerns ends.

Obj. 1. What causes things to be such is even more such. But we consent to means because of ends. Therefore, we consent to ends more than we consent to means.

Obj. 2. Intemperate actions constitute the end of intemperate persons, just as virtuous actions constitute the end of virtuous persons. But intemperate persons consent to their human acts. Therefore, consent can concern ends.

Obj. 3. To desire means is to choose, as I have said.[7] Therefore, if consent were to concern only means, consent would seem not to differ from choice in any respect. And this conclusion is clearly disproved by Damascene, who says that "choice occurs after the disposition" that he called decision.[8] Therefore, consent does not concern only means.

On the contrary, Damascene says in the same place that "decision," or consent, occurs "when human beings dispose and love the things decided by deliberation."[9] But deliberation concerns only means. Therefore, consent concerns only means.

I answer that consent denotes the inclination of an appetitive movement toward something that preexists in the power of one so inclining. And there is a sequence in doing things. We indeed need first to conceive an end, then to desire the end, then to deliberate about the means, then to desire the means. And the will by nature strives for the final end. And so the inclination of the appetitive movement toward the understood final end has the nature of pure volition and not the nature of consent.

And things subsequent to the final end, as means, are subject to deliberation, and so consent can concern them, since appetitive movements are attached to the things decided by deliberation. And appetitive movements toward ends are not attached to deliberation, but rather deliberation is attached to appetitive movements themselves, since deliberation presupposes desire of ends. But desire of means presupposes the decisions of deliberation. And so the inclinations of appetitive movements toward the decisions of deliberation constitute consent in the proper sense. And so, since deliberation concerns only means, consent in the proper sense concerns only means.

Reply to Obj. 1. We know conclusions scientifically by means of principles, although we do not know the principles scientifically but in a higher way, namely, by understanding. Just so we consent to means because of ends, although we do not consent to ends but do something more important, namely, will the ends.

Reply to Obj. 2. Intemperate persons consider the pleasure in their deeds rather than the deeds themselves to be their end, and they consent to their actions because of the attendant pleasure.

Reply to Obj. 3. Choice adds to consent a relationship with respect to the preference of one thing over another, and so there still remains a choice after consent. For we may by deliberation find that several means conduce to an end, and we consent to each when we approve of each, and we by choosing prefer one of the several approved means over the others. But if we should find only one means of which we approve, there is only a conceptual and not a real difference between consent and choice, so that we speak of consent insofar as we approve the means in order to do something, and we speak of choice insofar as we prefer the approved means over those of which we disapprove.

Notes

1. *De Trinitate* XII, 12. PL 42:1007.
2. *De fide orthodoxa* II, 22. PG 94:945.
3. Wis. 1:1.
4. Aristotle, *De anima* III, 9. 432b5.
5. In the body of the article.
6. I, Q. 16, A. 1. Q. 27, A. 4. Q. 59, A. 2.
7. Q. 13, A. 1.
8. *De fide orthodoxa* II, 22. PG 94:945.
9. Ibid.

Question 17

On the Acts Commanded by the Will

[This question is divided into nine articles, six of which are included here.]

First Article

Is Commanding an Act of Reason or an Act of the Will?

I proceed in this way to the first article: it seems that commanding is an act of the will rather than an act of reason.

Obj. 1. Commanding is a movement, for Avicenna says that there are four kinds of movement, namely, "one that perfects, one that disposes, one that commands," and "one that deliberates."[1] But it belongs to the will to move every other power of the soul, as I have said before,[2] Therefore, commanding is an act of the will.

Obj. 2. As it belongs to subjects to be commanded, so it belongs to those who are most free to command. But freedom is rooted most of all in the will. Therefore, it belongs to the will to command.

Obj. 3. Actions immediately result from commands. But actions do not immediately result from acts of reason, since one who decides that something ought to be done, does not do so at once. Therefore, commanding is an act of the will and not of reason.

On the contrary, both Gregory of Nyssa[3] and also the Philosopher[4] say the "the will obeys the power of reason." Therefore, it belongs to the power of reason to command.

I answer that commanding is an act of reason, although commanding presupposes an act of the will. And to prove this, we need to note that an act of reason may precede an act of the will, or vice versa, since acts of the will and acts of reason can be moved to act upon one another, namely, as reason reasons about willing, and the will wills to reason. And since subsequent acts retain the power of prior acts, there may at times be some acts of the will that retain some of the power of acts of reason, as I have said about application of the will[5] and about choice.[6] And conversely, there may be some acts of reason that retain some of the power of acts of the will.

And commanding is indeed essentially an act of reason, for it is by indicating or giving commands that those commanding order those commanded to do things. And so to order things in some communicative way belongs to reason. And reason can indicate or give commands in two ways. In one way, simply, and we indeed express such an indication by a verb in the indicative mood, as when one person may say to another, "This is what you should do." And reason sometimes gives a command to someone by impelling the person to do it, and we express such an indication by a verb in the imperative mood, as when one person says to another, "Do this." And the primary power that causes the movement of other powers of the soul to perform their acts is the will, as I have said before.[7] Therefore, since secondary causes only cause movement by primary causes, the will's power consequently causes the very fact that reason by commanding moves other powers of the soul. And so we conclude that commanding is an act of reason, although commanding presupposes an act of the will. And it is by the will's power that the commands of reason move other powers to perform their acts.

Reply to Obj. 1. Commanding is not any kind of movement but one by some declarative indication to another. And such movement belongs to an act of reason.

Reply to Obj. 2. Freedom is rooted in the will as its subject but in reason as its cause. For the will can freely move itself to different things, since reason conceives good in different ways. And so philosophers define free will as "a free decision issuing from reason,"[8] as if to say that reason causes freedom.

Reply to Obj. 3. The argument of this objection proves that commands are not simply acts of reason, but acts of reason accompanied by movements, as I have said.[9]

Fifth Article

Do We Command Acts of the Will?

I proceed in this way to the fifth article: it seems that we do not command acts of the will.

Obj. 1. Augustine says in his *Confessions*: "The soul commands the soul to will, and yet the soul does not will."[10] But willing is an act of the will. Therefore, we do not command acts of the will.

Obj. 2. Only one fit to understand commands is fit to be commanded. But the will is not fit to understand commands, since the will differs from the intellect, to which understanding belongs. Therefore, we do not command acts of the will.

Obj. 3. If some acts of the will are commanded, like reasoning leads to the conclusion that every act of the will is. But if every act of the will is commanded, there necessarily results an endless regression. For an act of the will precedes the act of reason that commands, as I have said,[11] and if that act of the will is likewise commanded, another act of reason in turn precedes this command, and so on endlessly. And an infinite regression is inappropriate. Therefore, we do not command acts of the will.

On the contrary, everything in our power is subject to our command. But acts of the will are especially in our power, for we say that all our actions are in our power inasmuch as they are freely determined. Therefore, we command acts of the will.

I answer that commands are simply acts of reason that by a causal movement ordain things to be done, as I have said.[12] And reason can evidently ordain in the case of acts of the will. For just as reason can judge that it is good to will things, so reason can ordain things by commanding that human beings should will things. And so acts of the will can evidently be commanded.

Reply to Obj. 1. As Augustine says in the same place, the soul already wills when it completely commands itself to will, but it may sometimes command and not will, since it sometimes does not completely command. And commands may be incomplete because different considerations impel reason to command or not to command. And so reason wavers between the two outcomes and does not completely command.

Reply to Obj. 2. In the case of bodily members, each acts for the whole body and not for itself alone; for example, eyes see for the whole body. So also in the case of the soul's powers, each acts for the whole soul and not for itself alone. For example, the intellect understands not only for itself but for all the soul's powers, and the will wills not only for itself but for all the soul's powers. And so human beings, as endowed with intellect and will, command acts of the will for human beings themselves.

Reply to Obj. 3. Because commands are acts of reason, the acts subject to reason are commanded. But the first act of the will results from a natural drive or a higher cause, as I have said,[13] and not from an ordination of reason. And so there is no need to regress endlessly.

Sixth Article

Do We Command Acts of Reason?

I proceed in this way to the sixth article: it seems that we cannot command acts of reason.

Obj. 1. It seems inappropriate that something should command its very self. But reason commands, as I have said before.[14] Therefore, we do not command acts of reason.

Obj. 2. What is such by essence differs from what is such by sharing. But powers whose acts reason commands, share in reason, as the *Ethics* says.[15] Therefore, we do not command acts of the power that is by essence reason.

Obj. 3. We command acts that lie within our power. But knowing and judging truth, which are acts of reason, sometimes do not lie within our power. Therefore, we cannot command acts of reason.

On the contrary, we can do by our command what we can do by our free choice. But we perform acts of reason by freely choosing to do so, for Damascene says that "human beings by free choice inquire and investigate and judge and dispose."[16] Therefore, we can command acts of reason.

I answer that, since reason is reflexively conscious of itself, it can ordain things related to its own acts, just as it can ordain things related to the acts of other powers of the soul. And so reason can command even its own acts.

But we need to note that we can consider acts of reason in two ways. In one way, with respect to performing the acts. And so considered, acts of reason can always be commanded, as when we tell someone to pay attention and think. In the second way, with respect to objects of the acts, and we note two acts of reason in this respect. First, indeed, the act whereby reason understands truth about something. And such is not within our power to command, for it occurs by the power of illumination, whether natural or supernatural. And so, with respect to such an object, acts of reason do not lie within our power and cannot be commanded. And there is another act when reason assents to what it understands.

Therefore, if the things reason understands are such that the intellect by nature assents to them (for example, first principles), it does not lie within our power whether to assent or dissent in the case of such things. Rather, nature ordains assent, and so, properly speaking, the assent is not subject to our command. But some understood things do not convince the intellect to such an extent that the intellect cannot for some reason assent or dissent, or at least withhold assent or dissent. And the very assent or dissent in the case of such things lies within our power and is subject to our command.

Reply to Obj. 1. Reason commands its very self in the same way that the will also moves its very self, as I have said before that the will does,[17] namely, as each of these powers is reflexively conscious of its acts and goes from one act to another.

Reply to Obj. 2. Because objects subject to acts of reason differ, nothing prevents reason from sharing in its very self, as, for example, knowledge of conclusions shares in knowledge of principles.

Reply to Obj. 3. The response to the third objection is evident from what I have said.[18]

Seventh Article

Do We Command Acts of Sense Appetites?

I proceed in this way to the seventh article: it seems that we do not command acts of sense appetites.

Obj. 1. The Apostle says in the Letter to the Romans: "For I do not do the good that I will to do."[19] And a gloss explains that human beings will not to desire things, and yet they do desire them.[20] But desiring is the act of a sense appetite. Therefore, the acts of sense appetites are not subject to our command.

Obj. 2. Regarding change of form, corporeal matter obeys God alone, as I have maintained in the First Part.[21] But the acts of sense appetites involve certain bodily transformations, namely, those of warming or chilling. Therefore, the acts of sense appetites are not subject to human command.

Obj. 3. The senses and the power of imagination perceive the characteristic things that move sense appetites. But it sometimes does not lie within our power to perceive things by the senses or the power of imagination. Therefore, the acts of sense appetites are not subject to our command.

On the contrary, Gregory of Nyssa says that "things obedient to reason are of two kinds, the concupiscible and the irascible,"[22] and those things belong to sense appetites. Therefore, the acts of sense appetites are subject to the command of reason.

I answer that acts are subject to our command insofar as they lie within our power, as I have said before.[23] And so we need to consider how the acts of sense appetites lie within our power in order to understand how such acts are subject to our command. And we need to note that sense appetites differ from the intellectual appetite, which we call the will, in that sense appetites are the powers of bodily organs, while the will is not such a power. And every act of powers that utilize bodily organs depends not only on the soul's power but also on the disposition of the bodily organs. For example, seeing depends on the power of sight and on the condition of the eyes, which condition helps or hinders vision. And so also the acts of sense appetites depend both on the power of sense appetites and the disposition of the body.

And what happens regarding the soul's powers results from apprehension. And the understanding of reason, which concerns the universal, governs the perception of imagination, which concerns the particular, just as universal active powers govern particular active powers. And so the acts of sense appetites are in this respect subject to the command of reason. But the condition and disposition of the body is not subject to the command of reason. And so the movements of sense appetites are in this respect impeded from being totally subject to the command of reason.

And also perceptions by the power of imagination or the senses may at times suddenly arouse movements of the sense appetites. And then such movements are beyond the command of reason, although reason could have prevented them if it had foreseen them. And so the Philosopher says in the *Politics* that reason does not govern the concupiscible and irascible appetites by "despotic rule," which is the rule of masters over slaves; rather, reason governs such appetites by "political or kingly rule," which is the rule over free persons, who are not totally subject to commands.[24]

Reply to Obj. 1. The fact that human beings will not to desire and yet do desire arises from the disposition of the body, which prevents sense appetites from totally following the command of reason. And so also the Apostle adds in the same place: "I perceive another law in my bodily members, a law contrary to the law of my mind."[25]

And this condition may also be due to sudden movements of concupiscence, as I have said.[26]

Reply to Obj. 2. The condition of the body is related to sense appetites in two ways. In one way, as an antecedent condition, as, for example, a person is in some way disposed toward this or that emotion. In the second way, as a consequent condition, as, for example, when a person gets hot as a result of anger. Thus an antecedent condition is not subject to a command of reason, since the condition results either from nature or from a previous movement that cannot be stilled right away. But a consequent condition results from a command of reason, since the condition results from pulsation of the heart, and different acts of sense appetites affect the heart in different ways.

Reply to Obj. 3. Since external, sensible things are necessary for sense perception, it lies within our power to perceive things sensibly only when sensible things are physically present, and the presence of such things sometimes does not lie within our power. For it is when things are physically present that human beings can use their senses if they should so wish, unless there is an impediment regarding a bodily organ.

And perception by the power of imagination is subject to the ordination of reason in proportion to the strength or weakness of the power of imagination. For human beings may not be able to imagine the things that reason contemplates, either because such things cannot be imagined, as immaterial things cannot, or due to the weakness of the power of imagination, and such weakness results from the indisposition of a bodily organ.

Eighth Article

Do We Command Acts of the Vegetative Soul?

I proceed in this way to the eighth article: it seems that acts of the vegetative soul are subject to the command of reason.

Obj. 1. Sense powers are more excellent than powers of the vegetative soul. But powers of the sensory soul are subject to the command of reason. Therefore, far more are powers of the vegetative soul.

Obj. 2. We call human beings worlds in miniature,[27] since human souls are in bodies as God is in the world. But God is in the world in such a way that everything in it obeys his commands. Therefore, everything in human beings, even the powers of their vegetative soul, likewise obey the command of reason.

Obj. 3. Praise and blame arise in the case of acts subject to the command of reason. But praise and blame, and virtue and vice, arise in the case of the nutritive and reproductive powers, as is evidently the case in gluttony and sexual lust and their contrary virtues. Therefore, acts of those powers are subject to the command of reason.

On the contrary, Gregory of Nyssa says that "the powers of nutrition and reproduction are things over which reason cannot prevail."[28]

I answer that some acts issue from natural appetites, and others from animal appetites and the intellectual appetite, for every efficient cause seeks an end in a particular way. And natural appetites do not result from any cognition, as animal appetites and the intellectual appetite do. And reason commands by way of cognitive power. And so reason can command the acts that issue from the intellectual appetite and animal appetites, but not the acts that issue from natural appetites. And that is why Gregory of Nyssa says that "we call the powers of nutrition and reproduction natural powers."[29] And so acts of the vegetative soul are not subject to the command of reason.

Reply to Obj. 1. The more immaterial an act is, the more excellent it is, and the more it is subject to the command of reason. And so the very fact that powers of the vegetative soul do not obey reason shows that they are the lowest powers belonging to human beings.

Reply to Obj. 2. We note the similarity between the body and the world in one respect, namely, in that the human soul moves the body as God moves the world. But we do not note a similarity in every respect. For example, the human soul did not create the body out of nothing, as God created the world, and the world is subject to his command because he created it.

Reply to Obj. 3. Virtue and vice, praise and blame, are not due to the very acts of the nutritive and reproductive powers, that is, the acts of digesting food and producing human bodies, but to acts of the sensory part of the soul, acts ordained for acts of the reproductive and nutritive powers. For example, in desiring the pleasure of food and sex and in making use of them, whether properly or improperly.

Ninth Article

Do We Command the Acts of Our External Bodily Members?

I proceed in this way to the ninth article: it seems that our bodily members, regarding their acts, are not subject to the command of reason.

Obj. 1. Bodily members are evidently further removed from reason than powers of the vegetative soul are. But powers of the vegetative soul do not obey reason, as I have said.[30] Therefore, far less do our bodily members.

Obj. 2. The heart is the source of animal movements. But the heart's pulsation is not subject to reason, for Gregory of Nyssa says that "reason cannot prevail over the power of pulsation."[31] Therefore, the movements of our bodily members do not obey reason.

Obj. 3. Augustine says in *The City of God*: "Our sex organs are at times aroused unsuitably and apart from any desire, and they at other times fail to be aroused when there is desire, and the body's desire is cold despite the heat of the soul's desire."[32] Therefore, the movements of our bodily members do not obey reason.

On the contrary, Augustine says in his *Confessions*: "The soul commands our hands' movements, and our hands are so ready to obey that we can scarcely distinguish the soul's command from the hands' obedience."[33]

I answer that our bodily members are organs of powers of the soul. And so the bodily members are disposed to obey reason in the way in which the powers of the soul are disposed to obey reason. Therefore, since our sense powers are subject to the command of reason, and our powers from nature are not, every movement of bodily members by our sense powers is subject to the command of reason, and bodily members' movements resulting from the powers of nature are not.

Reply to Obj. 1. Bodily members do not move themselves; rather, the soul's powers move them. And some powers of the soul are closer to reason than the powers of the vegetative soul are.

Reply to Obj. 2. In things belonging to the intellect and the will, the first things we find are things from nature, things from which other things are derived. For example, we derive our knowledge of conclusions from our knowledge of the principles that nature makes known to us, and we derive our choice of means from our willing the end that we by nature desire. So also the source of bodily movements is from nature and the heart's pulsation. And so the heart's pulsation is from nature and not from the will, since the heart's pulsation results as a property of our life, which the union of soul and body produces. (Similarly, the movements of heavy and light things result from the things' substantial forms, and so the cause of the things' coming-to-be causes their movements, as the Philosopher says in the *Physics*.[34]) And we consequently call the heart's pulsation vital. And so Gregory of Nyssa says that, as the reproductive and nutritive powers do not obey reason, neither does the power of pulsation, and the power of pulsation is vital.[35] And he calls the power of pulsation the heart's pulse, which pulsating blood vessels manifest.

Reply to Obj. 3. As Augustine says in *The City of God*,[36] punishment of sin is responsible for the fact that arousal of our sex organs does not obey reason. That is to say, the soul, for its insubordination to God, suffers the punishment of insubordination especially in the bodily members by which original sin is transmitted to posterity.

But because the sin of our first parents caused our nature to be left to itself, and the supernatural gift bestowed by God on human beings to be withdrawn, as I shall say later,[37] we accordingly need to consider the ground in nature why the arousal of our sex organs in particular does not obey reason. And Aristotle in the *De animalium motione* says that "the heart's pulsation and the arousal of sex organs are involuntary," and he assigns the following reason why the movements of these bodily members do not obey reason.[38] Mental perceptions arouse our sex organs, namely, as the intellect and the power of imagination represent things that result in emotions of the soul, and the emotions result in movements of these bodily members. Nonetheless, these bodily members are not stirred at the command of reason or the intellect, since natural changes, namely, those of heat and cold, are undoubtedly necessary for the members to be stirred, and natural changes are indeed not subject to the command of reason. This happens especially in the case of these two bodily members because each is, as it were, a sort of distinct living thing, since each is a source of life, and a source of life is by its power the entire living thing. For the heart is the source of sense powers, and the semen's power, which is by its power the whole living thing, comes from the sex organs. And so these bodily members have their characteristic movements from nature, since sources need to be from nature, as I have said.[39]

Notes

1. *Sufficientia* I, 10. *De anima*, part 1, chap. 5.
2. Q. 9, A. 1.
3. Nemesius, *De natura hominis* 16. PG 40:672. St. Thomas errs in attributing this work to Gregory of Nyssa.
4. *Ethics* I, 13. 1102b25–33.
5. Q. 16, A. 1.
6. Q. 13, A. 1.
7. Q. 9, A. 1.
8. Cf. Boethius, *In librum Aristotelis De interpretatione* III. PL 64:492.
9. In the body of the article.
10. *Confessions* VIII, 9. PL 32:758.
11. Q. 17, A. 1.
12. Ibid.
13. Q. 9, A. 4.
14. Q. 17, A. 1.
15. Aristotle, *Ethics* I, 13. 1102b25–1103a10.
16. *De fide orthodoxa* II, 22. PG 94:945.
17. Q. 9, A. 3.
18. In the body of the article.
19. Rom. 7:15.
20. Cf. Augustine, *Contra Iulianum* III, 26. PL 44:734.
21. I, Q. 65, A. 4. Q. 91, A. 2. Q. 110, A. 2.
22. Nemesius, *De natura hominis* 16. PG 40:672. On the attribution, see n. 3, supra.
23. Q. 17, A. 5, in the section "On the contrary."
24. *Politics* I, 2. 1254b5.
25. Rom. 7:23.
26. In the body of the article.
27. Aristotle, *Physics* VIII, 2. 252b26–27.
28. Nemesius, *De natura hominis* 22. PG 40:692–93. On the attribution, see n. 3, supra.
29. Ibid.
30. Q. 17, A. 8.
31. Nemesius, *De natura hominis* 22. PG 40:693. On the attribution, see n. 3, supra.
32. *The City of God* XIV, 16. PL 41:425.
33. *Confessions* VIII, 9. PL 32:758.
34. *Physics* VIII, 4. 255b17–31.
35. See n. 31.
36. *The City of God* XIV, 17 and 20. PL 41:425, 428.
37. Q. 85, A. 1, *ad* 3.
38. *De animalium motione* 11. 703b6.
39. In the reply to *Obj. 2*.

Question 18

On the Goodness and Malice of Human Acts in General

[This question is divided into eleven articles, seven of which are included here.]

First Article

Is Every Human Act Good, or Are Some Human Acts Evil?

I proceed in this way to the first article: it seems that every human act is good, and none evil.

Obj. 1. Denis says in his *De divinis nominibus* that bad things act through the power of good things.[1] But the power of good things does not cause bad things. Therefore, no action is bad.

Obj. 2. Things act only insofar as they are actual. But things are bad insofar as their potentiality lacks actuality, and not insofar as they are actual. And things are good insofar as actuality perfects their potentiality, as the *Metaphysics* says.[2] Therefore, nothing acts insofar as it is bad, and everything acts insofar as it is good. Therefore, every action is good, and no action is bad.

Obj. 3. Bad things can cause only by chance, as Denis makes clear in his *De divinis nominibus*.[3] But an intrinsic effect belongs to every action. Therefore, every action is good, and no action is bad.

On the contrary, the Lord says in the Gospel of John: "Everyone who does evil, hates the light."[4] Therefore, some actions of human beings are evil.

I answer that we need to speak about good and bad in the case of actions as we speak about good and bad in the case of things, since each thing produces the same kind of action as the thing itself is. And in the case of things, each has as much good as it has existing, for "good" and "being" are convertible terms, as I have said in the First

Part.⁵ But only God possesses the entire fullness of his existing in an undivided and uncomposed way, while all other things possess in different ways the fullness of existing proper to them. And so in the case of some things, they may possess existing in some respect and yet lack something regarding the fullness of existing proper to them. For example, for the fullness of human existing, there needs to be a composite that possesses all the powers of the soul and the means of knowledge and locomotion. And so human beings who lack any of these things lack part of the fullness of their proper existing. Therefore, human beings have as much goodness as they have existing, and they lack goodness as much as they lack part of the fullness of existing, and we call such a lack bad. For example, it is good for a blind man to be alive, and it is bad for him to lack the power to see. And we could not call him good or bad if he were not to possess any being or goodness at all.

But the very fullness of a thing's existing belongs to the nature of good. Therefore, if a thing should lack part of its proper fullness of existing, we will call the thing good in one respect, inasmuch as it is a being, and not absolutely good. (Nonetheless, we could call the thing a being absolutely and a nonbeing in some respect, as I have said in the First Part.⁶)

Therefore, we need to say that every human action is good inasmuch as it shares in existing, and it lacks goodness, and we call the action evil, inasmuch as it lacks part of the proper fullness of existing for human action. Such is the case when human action lacks either the measure determined by reason or the proper place or some such thing.

Reply to Obj. 1. Bad things act through the power of good things that are deficient. For there would be no being and could be no action if there were nothing good in a cause's power. And there would be nothing bad if there were nothing deficient in a cause's power. And so also the caused action is a deficient good, that is, good in some respect and bad in an absolute sense.

Reply to Obj. 2. Nothing prevents something from being actual in some respect, and so it would be able to act, and being deprived of actuality in another respect, and so it may cause defective action. For example, a blind man actually possesses the power to take steps, and so he can walk, but he walks defectively as he stumbles along, since he lacks the vision to direct his walking.

Reply to Obj. 3. Bad action can have an intrinsic effect insofar as the action has some goodness and reality. For example, adultery causes human begetting because adultery involves the sexual union of a man and a woman, and not because adultery lacks the ordination of reason.

Second Article

Are the Actions of Human Beings Good or Bad by
Reason of Their Objects?

I proceed in this way to the second article: it seems that human actions are not good or bad by reason of their objects.

Obj. 1. The objects of actions are things. But "evil consists in sinners' use of things rather than in things," as Augustine says in his *De doctrina Christiana.*[7] Therefore, human actions are not good or bad by reason of their objects.

Obj. 2. We relate objects to actions as the subject matter of the actions. But the goodness of things does not derive from their matter but rather from their form, which is their actuality. Therefore, the goodness and malice of human acts do not derive from the acts' objects.

Obj. 3. We relate the objects of active powers to actions as effects to causes. But the goodness of causes does not depend on their effects; rather, the converse is true. Therefore, human actions are not good or bad by reason of their objects.

On the contrary, the prophet Hosea says: "They became as detestable as the things they loved."[8] But human beings became detestable to God because of the wickedness of their actions. Therefore, the bad objects that human beings love cause the wickedness of their actions. And like reasoning applies to the goodness of human actions.

I answer that we note that human actions, just like other things, are good or bad by reason of the fullness of their existing, or the lack thereof, as I have said.[9] But the chief thing that seems to belong to the fullness of things' existing is what gives the things their species. And as forms give things of nature their species, so objects give actions their species; for example, goals specify movements. And so, as we note the chief goodness of things of nature by reason of their forms, so also we note the chief goodness of moral acts by reason of their befitting objects. And so also some call the objects good by reason of their kind (e.g., using one's own property). And the chief evil in the case of things of nature is when the things they produce do not attain their specific form (e.g., when human beings beget something other than a human being). Just so, the chief evil in the case of moral actions consists of something regarding the actions' objects (e.g., taking property that belongs to another). And we call such objects evil by reason of their kind, understanding kind as species in the same manner of speaking as we understand humankind to mean the whole human species.

Reply to Obj. 1. Although external things are good in themselves, they nonetheless do not always have the requisite proportion to this or that particular action. And so external things do not have the nature of good as we consider them as objects of such acts.

Reply to Obj. 2. Objects are not the source matter of actions but the matter with which actions are concerned, and objects as they specify actions in a way have the nature of form.

Reply to Obj. 3. The objects of human actions are sometimes not the objects of active powers. For example, appetitive powers are in one respect passive, inasmuch as desirable objects move our appetites, and yet appetitive powers are sources of human actions.

Similarly, the objects of active powers sometimes do not have the nature of effects, but the objects are such only after they have already been transformed. For example, digested food is an effect of the nutritive power, but we relate food not yet digested to the nutritive power as the matter on which the power acts. And because an object is somehow the effect of an active power, the object is consequently the goal of the power's action, and the object consequently gives the action its form and species, since goals specify movements.

And also, although the goodness of effects does not cause actions to be good, we nonetheless call actions good because they are able to produce good effects. And so the very proportion of actions to their effects is the reason why the actions themselves are good.

Third Article

*Do Circumstances Determine Whether
Human Actions Are Good or Bad?*

I proceed in this way to the third article: it seems that circumstances do not determine whether human actions are good or bad.

Obj. 1. Circumstances, as being outside actions, surround actions, as I have said.[10] But "good and evil are in things themselves," as the *Metaphysics* says.[11] Therefore, circumstances do not determine whether human actions are good or bad.

Obj. 2. We especially consider the goodness or malice of human acts in moral instruction. But circumstances, as accidents of human acts, seem to be beyond the scope of practical skills, since "no practical skill takes notice of things that are by chance," as the *Metaphysics* says.[12] Therefore, circumstances do not determine whether human actions are good or bad.

Obj. 3. We do not ascribe properties to things by reason of accidents. But good and evil are properties of human actions, since human actions can be good or bad by reason of their kind, as I have said.[13] Therefore, circumstances do not determine whether human actions are good or bad.

On the contrary, the Philosopher says in the *Ethics* that virtuous persons act as they ought, and when they ought, and according to other circumstances.[14] Therefore, vicious persons, in the case of every vice, act when they ought not, where they ought not, and so forth regarding other circumstances. Therefore, human actions are good or bad according to circumstances.

I answer that we do not find in the case of things of nature that the entire fullness of their due perfection derives from their substantial form, which gives them their species; rather, additional accidents contribute a great deal. In the case of human beings, for example, shape, color, and the like contribute a great deal to the fullness of human perfection. And evil results if any such accident falls short of a suitable form. So also is it in the case of human action. For the entire fullness of an action's goodness does not consist in the action's species; rather, additional things as accidents contribute something to an action's goodness. And such additional things are the action's requisite circumstances. And so human actions will be bad if they lack anything necessary as a requisite circumstance.

Reply to Obj. 1. Circumstances are outside actions inasmuch as circumstances do not belong to the essence of actions. Nonetheless, circumstances belong to actions as accidents. So also the accidents in things of nature do not belong to the essence of those things.

Reply to Obj. 2. Not every accident is related by chance to the subject in which it inheres; rather, some accidents are related to their subjects intrinsically, and practitioners in every skill take such accidents into consideration. And we thus consider the circumstances of actions in moral instruction.

Reply to Obj. 3. The terms "good" and "being" are convertible. Therefore, just as we predicate being regarding substances and accidents, so also do we ascribe good to things both regarding their essential existing and regarding their accidental existing, both in the case of things of nature and in the case of moral actions.

Fourth Article

Do Ends Determine Whether Human Actions Are Good or Bad?

I proceed in this way to the fourth article: it seems that ends do not determine whether human actions are good or bad.

Obj. 1. Denis says in his *De divinis nominibus* that "nothing acts looking for evil."[15] Therefore, no human action would be evil if ends were to make them good or bad. And this conclusion is patently false.

Obj. 2. The goodness of an action is something in the action. But ends are extrinsic causes. Therefore, we do not call human actions good or bad by reason of their ends.

Obj. 3. A good action may be ordained for a bad end, as, for example, when one gives alms to gain renown. And conversely, a bad action may be ordained for a good end, as, for example, when one steals to give to the poor. Therefore, ends do not make human actions good or bad.

On the contrary, Boethius says in his *De diffentia topicorum* that "actions whose ends are good, are themselves good, and actions whose ends are bad, are themselves bad."[16]

I answer that things have the same disposition regarding goodness and existing. For there are some things whose existing does not depend on another, and it suffices in their case to consider their very existing unconditionally. And there are other things whose existing depends on another, and so we need to consider their existing in relation to the cause on which they depend. And as the existing of a thing depends on its efficient cause and its form, so the goodness of the thing depends on its end. And so in the case of the divine Persons of the Trinity, whose goodness does not depend on another, we do not consider any aspect of their goodness from an end. But human actions, and other things whose goodness depends on something else, have the aspect of goodness from the ends on which they depend, in addition to the unqualified goodness that exists in them.

Therefore, we can consider four kinds of goodness in human actions. We consider one kind of goodness, indeed, by the kind of thing they are, namely, as action, for they have as much goodness as they partake of action and being, as I have said.[17] And we consider a second kind of goodness by the species of human action, which we take from the suitable objects of human action. We consider a third kind of goodness by the circumstances of human action, the actions' accidents, as it were. And we consider a fourth kind of goodness by the ends of human action, the actions' relationship to the cause of their goodness, as it were.

Reply to Obj. 1. The good that persons look for in actions is not always a real good, but that good is sometimes a real good and sometimes an apparent good. And bad actions accordingly sometimes result from bad ends.

Reply to Obj. 2. Although ends are extrinsic causes, a due proportion and a relation to the very ends are inherent in human actions.

Reply to Obj. 3. Nothing prevents a human action having one of the aforementioned kinds of goodness[18] from lacking another kind of goodness. And so human actions that are good by reason of their species or their circumstances may be ordained for bad ends, and vice versa. Nonetheless, no human action is unqualifiedly good unless it is good in all of the aforementioned ways. For "a single defect causes evil, and an uncorrupted cause causes good," as Denis says in his *De divinis nominibus*.[19]

Eighth Article

Are Some Human Acts by Their Species Morally Indifferent?

I proceed in this way to the eighth article: it seems that no human act is by its species morally indifferent.

Obj. 1. Evil is "the deprivation of good," according to Augustine.[20] But privations and possessions are direct contraries, according to the Philosopher.[21] Therefore, there are some human acts that are by their species morally indifferent, things in between good and evil, as it were.

Obj. 2. Ends or objects specify human acts, as I have said.[22] But every object and every end have the character of being good or bad. Therefore, every human act is by its species good or bad. Therefore, no human act is by its species morally indifferent.

Obj. 3. We call human acts good that have the due completeness of goodness, and we call human acts bad that lack some of such due completeness, as I have said.[23] But every human act necessarily either possesses the entire fullness of its goodness or lacks something. Therefore, every human act is necessarily by its species morally good or bad, and no human act is morally indifferent.

On the contrary, Augustine says in his *De sermone Domini* that "there are some intermediate deeds that we can perform with a good or bad will, and it is rash to judge about them."[24] Therefore, some human acts are by their species morally indifferent.

I answer that, as I have said,[25] every act is specified by its object, and human acts, which we call moral acts, are specified by objects related to the source of the acts, that is, reason. And so there will be specifically good human acts if the objects of the acts comprise things befitting the ordination of reason (e.g., giving alms to the needy). And there will be specifically bad human acts if the objects of the acts comprise things contrary to the ordination of reason (e.g., stealing, which is the taking of property belonging to another). But the objects of human acts may not comprise anything belonging to the ordination of reason (e.g., picking up straw from the ground, going to the country, and the like). And such human acts are by their species morally indifferent.

Reply to Obj. 1. There are two meanings of deprivation. One is the meaning that consists of the consequence of being deprived, and this meaning of deprivation takes away the whole of something and leaves nothing. For example, blindness entirely takes away the power of sight, and darkness entirely takes away light, and death entirely takes away life. And there can be nothing in between deprivation in this sense and a contrary possession with respect to a proper subject.

And the other meaning of deprivation consists of the condition of being deprived. For example, sickness deprives a person of health, not that sickness entirely takes away health, but that sickness is a path, as it were, to the total loss of health, which death brings about. And so this meaning of deprivation, since it lets something remain, is not always directly opposed to a contrary possession. And evil deprives a person of good in this way, since evil does not take away the whole good but leaves some, as Simplicius says in his commentary.[26] And so there can be something in between good and evil.

Reply to Obj. 2. Every object or end has some goodness or badness, at least from nature, but this does not always imply moral goodness or malice, which we judge in relation to reason, as I have said.[27] And we are presently treating of moral goodness or malice.

Reply to Obj. 3. Not every property of a human act belongs to its species. And so, although a human act may not contain in its specific nature everything that belongs to the fullness of its goodness, it is not thereby either specifically bad or specifically good. Similarly, human beings are not by their species either virtuous or vicious.

Ninth Article

Are Any Human Acts, Individually Considered, Morally Indifferent?

I proceed in this way to the ninth article: it seems that some human acts, individually considered, are morally indifferent.

Obj. 1. Every species may or can include individuals. But some human acts can by their species be morally indifferent, as I have said.[28] Therefore, individual human acts can be morally indifferent.

Obj. 2. Individual human acts produce like habitual dispositions, as the *Ethics* says.[29] But some habitual dispositions are morally indifferent. For the Philosopher says in the *Ethics* that some persons (e.g., the placid and the prodigal) are not evil,[30] and yet they are evidently not good, since they draw away from virtue. And so such persons are by habitual disposition morally indifferent. Therefore, some individual human acts are morally indifferent.

Obj. 3. Moral good belongs to virtue, and moral evil belongs to vice. But human beings at times may not ordain for virtuous or vicious ends acts that are by their species morally indifferent. Therefore, individual human acts may be morally indifferent.

On the contrary, Gregory says in a homily: "Idle words lack the benefit of rectitude or the ground of just necessity or pious benefit."[31] But idle words are evil, since "Human beings will render account for them on the day of judgment," as the Gospel of Matthew says,[32] and words grounded in just necessity or pious benefit are good. Therefore, every word is either good or evil. Therefore, by like reasoning, every other human act is also either good or evil. Therefore, no individual human act is morally indifferent.

I answer that some human acts, considered as species, may be morally indifferent, but the acts, considered as individual acts, are either morally good or morally bad. And this is so because, as I have said,[33] moral acts are good both by reason of their objects, which specify the acts, and by reason of their circumstances, which are the acts' accidents, as it were. Similarly, some things belong to individual human beings as individual accidents, and such things do not belong to the individual human beings by reason of their species.

And every individual human act needs to have some circumstance, at least regarding the intended end that causes the act to be good or bad. For, since it belongs to reason to ordain, acts that issue from reason by deliberation, if they are not ordained for appropriate ends, are by that very fact contrary to reason and have the character of being evil. And if the acts are ordained for appropriate ends, they are in accord with the ordination of reason and so have the character of being good. And acts are necessarily either ordained or not ordained for appropriate ends. And so every act of human beings that issues from reason by deliberation, considered as individual, is necessarily morally good or morally bad.

And if human acts do not issue from reason by deliberation but from some fancy (e.g., when men stroke their beard, or persons move their hands or feet), such acts are not, properly speaking, moral or human acts, since acts have that character from reason. And so such acts will be morally indifferent, being outside the class of moral acts, as it were.

Reply to Obj. 1. There may be several ways in which human acts are morally indifferent. In one way, such that acts by their species require that they be morally indifferent. And this objection so argues. And yet no human act by its species is morally indifferent in this way, since there is no object of a human act such that an end or circumstance could not ordain it either for good or for evil.

In the second way, we may call human acts morally indifferent by reason of their species because their species do not cause them to be good or evil. And so they can be good or evil by reason of something else. Similarly, the species of being human does not require that human beings be white or black, and neither does it require that they not be white or black. For whiteness or blackness can be added to human beings from other sources than those that constitute the species.

Reply to Obj. 2. The Philosopher says that human beings who harm other human beings are evil in the strict sense. And he accordingly says that prodigal persons are not evil, since they harm no one other than themselves. And it is likewise in the case of all others who do not harm their neighbors. But we are here in a general sense calling evil everything that is contrary to right reason. And every individual human act is accordingly good or evil, as I have said.[34]

Reply to Obj. 3. Every end intended by deliberative reason, belongs to the good of some virtue or to the evil of some vice. For example, what persons do to sustain their bodies or to give their bodies rest, is ordained for the good of virtue in those who so ordain their bodies. And the same is evident in other cases.

Tenth Article

Do Circumstances Constitute Moral Acts in Species of Good or Evil?

I proceed in this way to the tenth article: it seems that circumstances cannot constitute species of good or evil acts.

Obj. 1. Objects specify human acts. But circumstances differ from objects. Therefore, circumstances do not specify human acts.

Obj. 2. Circumstances are related to acts as accidents of the acts, as I have said.[35] But accidents do not constitute species. Therefore, circumstances do not constitute species of good or evil.

Obj. 3. One thing does not have more than one species. But one thing has more than one circumstance. Therefore, circumstances do not constitute moral acts in species of good or evil.

On the contrary, place is a circumstance. But place constitutes moral acts in species of evil; for example, it is a sacrilege to steal something from a sacred place. Therefore, circumstances constitute moral acts in species of good or evil.

I answer that as forms of nature constitute the species of things of nature, so forms as conceived by reason constitute the species of moral acts, as is evident from what I have said before.[36] And a nature is determined to attain one thing, and its process of doing so cannot go on endlessly. Therefore, it necessarily reaches a final form, from which we understand its specific difference—besides which there can be no other specific difference. And that is why we cannot in the case of things of nature understand accidents as differences constituting the things' species.

But the process of reason is not determined to attain one thing, and, given anything attained, reason can always go further. And so what reason in one act understands as a circumstance added to the object that specifies the act, reason, ordaining, can then understand as the specifying object's chief characteristic. For example, a property's character of belonging to another specifies the act of taking such property, since that is why we classify the act in the species of theft. And if we were additionally to consider the character of where or when an act took place, we shall consider place or time as a circumstance. But because reason can also ordain regarding place, time, and the like, reason may understand the characteristic of place regarding the act's object as contrary to the ordination of reason. For example, reason ordains that one should not do wrong in a sacred place. And so stealing property from a sacred place adds a particular contrariety to the ordination of reason. And so place, which we hitherto considered to be a circumstance, we presently consider as the object's chief characteristic contrary to reason. And so whenever a circumstance regards a particular ordination of reason, whether the circumstance be in accord with, or contrary to, the ordination of reason, the circumstance necessarily specifies the moral act, whether as good or evil.

Reply to Obj. 1. We consider circumstances, insofar as they specify human acts, as characteristics of the acts' objects, as I have said before,[37] and as if specific differences of the objects.

Reply to Obj. 2. Circumstances, while they retain such a nature, do not specify human acts, since they have the character of accidents. But inasmuch as they become the chief characteristics of the acts' objects, they accordingly specify the acts.

Reply to Obj. 3. Not every circumstance constitutes moral acts in species of good or evil, since not every circumstance implies accord or discord with reason. And so, although individual human acts involve many circumstances, the acts do not necessarily belong to several species. Nonetheless, it is not inappropriate that a single moral act belong to several moral species, even disparate species, as I have said.[38]

Notes

1. *De divinis nominibus* 4. PG 3:717.
2. Aristotle, *Metaphysics* VIII, 9. 1051a4–19.
3. *De divinis nominibus* 4. PG 3:732.
4. Jn. 3:20.
5. I, Q. 5, AA. 1, 3. Q. 17, A. 4, *ad* 2.
6. I, Q. 5, A. 1, *ad* 1.
7. *De doctrina Christiana* III, 12. PL 34:73.
8. Hos. 9:10–11.
9. Q. 18, A. 1.
10. Q. 7, A. 1.
11. Aristotle, *Metaphysics* V, 4. 1027b25–29.
12. Aristotle, *Metaphysics* V, 2. 1026b2–12.
13. Q. 18, A. 2.
14. *Ethics* II, 3. 1104b18–28.
15. *De divinis nominibus* 4. PG 3:716.
16. *De differentia topicorum* II. PL 64:1189.
17. Q. 18, A. 1.
18. The four kinds described in the body of the article.
19. *De divinis nominibus* 4. PG 3:729.
20. *Enchiridion* 11. PL 40:236.
21. *Categories* 10. 13a3–17.
22. Q. 18, A. 6. Q. 1, A. 3.
23. Q. 18, A. 1.
24. *De sermone Domini in monte* II, 18. PL 34:1296.
25. Q. 18, AA. 2, 5.
26. *Super librum Praedicamentorum* 10.
27. In the body of the article.
28. Q. 18, A. 8.
29. Aristotle, *Ethics* II, 1. 1103b21–22.
30. *Ethics* IV, 1. 1121a16–21, 25–27.
31. *Homiliarum in Evangelia* I, 6. PL 76:1098.
32. Mt. 12:36.
33. Q. 18, A. 3.
34. In the body of the article.
35. Q. 7, A. 1.
36. Q. 18, A. 5.
37. In the body of the article.
38. Q. 18, A. 7, *ad* 1. Q. 1, A. 3, *ad* 3.

Question 19

On the Goodness and Malice of Interior Acts of the Will

[This question is divided into ten articles, six of which are included here.]

First Article

Does the Will's Goodness Depend on the Will's Object?

I proceed in this way to the first article: it seems that the will's goodness does not depend on the will's object.

Obj. 1. Good is the only object of the will, since evil is "beyond the power of the will," as Denis says in his *De divinis nominibus*.[1] Therefore, if we were to judge the will's goodness by the will's object, every act of the will would consequently be good, and no act of the will would be bad.

Obj. 2. We first find good in ends, and so the goodness of ends, as such, does not depend on anything else. But "good action, and never making things," is the end of human acts, as the Philosopher says in the *Ethics*.[2] For making things is always ordained for the things made as the end of making things. Therefore, the goodness of acts of the will does not depend on any object.

Obj. 3. Everything produces other things like itself. But the will's object is good by reason of its goodness from nature. Therefore, the will's object cannot bestow moral goodness on the will. Therefore, the will's goodness does not depend on the will's object.

On the contrary, the Philosopher says in the *Ethics* that justice is the disposition whereby persons will just things.[3] And every virtue, by like reasoning, is the disposition whereby persons will good things. But a good will is one in accord with virtue. Therefore, the will is good because persons will what is good.

I answer that good and evil intrinsically differentiate the will's acts. For good and evil belong intrinsically to the will. (Similarly, truth and falsity belong intrinsically to reason, and the difference between truth and falsity intrinsically distinguishes acts of reason, since we call one opinion true and another opinion false.) And so good and bad acts of the will are specifically different acts. And objects specifically differentiate human acts, as I have said.[4] And so we in the strict sense direct our attention to the good or evil in human acts by reason of the acts' objects.

Reply to Obj. 1. An apparent good and not a real good is sometimes the will's object. And an apparent good indeed has the character of good but not of one absolutely suitable to be desired. And consequently, acts of the will are not always good but sometimes evil.

Reply to Obj. 2. Although action can in a way be the final end of human beings, such action is nonetheless not an act of the will, as I have said before.[5]

Reply to Obj. 3. Reason presents a good to the will to be the will's object. And the object, inasmuch as it is subject to the ordination of reason, belongs to the category of moral acts and causes the moral goodness of the will's acts. For reason is the source of human and moral acts, as I have said before.[6]

Second Article

Does the Will's Goodness Depend Exclusively on the Will's Object?

I proceed in this way to the second article: it seems that the will's goodness does not depend exclusively on the will's object.

Obj. 1. Ends have a closer relation to the will than to other powers. But the acts of other powers derive their goodness both from their objects and from their ends, as is evident from what I have previously said.[7] Therefore, acts of the will also derive their goodness both from their objects and from their ends.

Obj. 2. The goodness of human acts derives both from their objects and from their circumstances, as I have said before.[8] But different circumstances may cause a difference in the goodness or badness of the will's acts; for example, that persons will when they should, and where they should, and as much as they should, and how they should—or as they should not. Therefore, the goodness of the will depends not only on the will's object but also on circumstances.

Obj. 3. Ignorance of circumstances excuses the will from malice, as I have maintained before.[9] But such would be the case only if the will's goodness or badness were to depend on circumstances. Therefore, the will's goodness or badness depends on circumstances and not only on the will's object.

On the contrary, circumstances as such do not specify acts, as I have said before.[10] But good and evil specifically differentiate acts of the will, as I have said.[11] Therefore, the will's goodness or badness depends exclusively on the will's object and not on circumstances.

I answer that things in any genus, as much as they are prior, are simpler and consist of fewer things; for example, the first material substances are simple things. And so we find that the first things in any genus are in some way simple things and consist of only one thing. But the goodness and badness of human acts originate from the will's acts. And so we note the will's goodness and badness by that one thing, while we may note the goodness and badness of other acts by various things.

And the one thing that is the source in any genus is such intrinsically and not by chance, since we trace everything that is such by chance to something that is such intrinsically. And so the will's goodness depends exclusively on the one thing that intrinsically causes the goodness in the will's act, namely, its object, and not on circumstances, which are accidents of the will's acts.

Reply to Obj. 1. Ends are objects of the will and not the objects of other powers. And so the goodness deriving from the object does not differ from the goodness that derives from the end in the case of the will's acts, as the one goodness differs from the other in the case of other powers' acts. (There may by chance be an exception inasmuch as one end depends on another end, and one act of the will depends on another act of the will.)

Reply to Obj. 2. If we suppose that one act of the will is good, no circumstance can make the will bad. Therefore, we can understand in two ways the statement that persons will good things when they should not or where they should not. In one way, such that we relate the circumstance to the things willed. And then the will's object is not good, since willing to do something when one should not do it is not to will what is good. In the second way, such that we relate the circumstance to the act of willing. And then it is impossible that persons would will something good when they should not, since human beings should always will what is good. (There may by chance be an exception inasmuch as persons, by willing particular goods, are at the same time prevented from willing goods that they should will. And then evil does not occur because the persons will the particular goods, but because they do not will the other goods.) And we need to speak similarly about other circumstances.

Reply to Obj. 3. Ignorance of circumstances excuses the will from malice insofar as we understand circumstances in regard to the things willed, namely, inasmuch as persons do not know the circumstances of the acts that they will.

Third Article

Does the Will's Goodness Depend on Reason?

I proceed in this way to the third article: it seems that the will's goodness does not depend on reason.

Obj. 1. Prior things do not depend on subsequent things. But good belongs to the will before it belongs to reason, as is evident from what I have previously said.[12] Therefore, the will's goodness does not depend on reason.

Obj. 2. The Philosopher says in the *Ethics* that the practical intellect's goodness consists in "truth in accord with right desire."[13] But right desire is a good act of the will. Therefore, the goodness of practical reason depends on the will's goodness rather than the converse.

Obj. 3. A cause of motion does not depend on the thing that it moves; rather, the converse is true. But the will moves reason and other powers, as I have said before.[14] Therefore, the will's goodness does not depend on reason.

On the contrary, Hilary says in his *De Trinitate*: "Any persistence in submitting to desires when the will is not subject to reason, is intemperate."[15] But the will's goodness consists in the will being temperate. Therefore, the will's goodness depends on the will being subject to reason.

I answer that the will's goodness depends in the strict sense on the will's object, as I have said.[16] But reason presents the object to the will. For understood objects are objects proportioned to the will, while sensible or imaginary goods are objects proportioned to sense appetites and not to the will. This is because reason understands, and the will strives for, universal good, while sense powers perceive, and sense appetites strive for, only goods that are particular. And so the will's goodness depends on reason in the same way that the will's goodness depends on the will's object.

Reply to Obj. 1. Good under that aspect, that is, the aspect of being desirable, belongs to the will before it belongs to reason. But good under the aspect of true nonetheless belongs to reason before it belongs to the will under the aspect of being desirable, since something good cannot be an object of the will's desire unless reason first understands that good.

Reply to Obj. 2. The Philosopher is speaking in the cited text about the practical intellect as the latter deliberates and reasons about means to ends, since it is in this way that practical wisdom makes the practical intellect perfect. And right reason in the case of means to ends consists in the accord of reason with desires for appropriate ends. And yet the very desire for an appropriate end presupposes right understanding about the end, and such understanding is the product of reason.

Reply to Obj. 3. The will moves reason in one way, and reason moves the will in another way, namely, by the will's object, as I have said before.[17]

Fourth Article

Does the Will's Goodness Depend on the Eternal Law?

I proceed in this way to the fourth article: it seems that the human will's goodness does not depend on the eternal law.

Obj. 1. One thing has one rule and measure. But the human will's rule, on which that will's goodness depends, is right reason. Therefore, the human will's goodness does not depend on the eternal law.

Obj. 2. "Measures and the things they measure, are the same kind of thing," as the *Metaphysics* says.[18] But the eternal law and the human will are different kinds of things. Therefore, the eternal law cannot measure the human will, and so the human will's goodness does not depend on the eternal law.

Obj 3. A measure ought to be most certain. But we do not know the eternal law. Therefore, the eternal law cannot measure our will, and so our will's goodness does not depend on the eternal law.

On the contrary, Augustine says in his *Contra Faustum* that "sin is anything done, said, or desired contrary to the eternal law."[19] But the will's malice is the root of sin. Therefore, since wickedness is contrary to goodness, the will's goodness depends on the eternal law.

I answer that, when causes are subordinated to one another, effects depend more on the primary cause than on the secondary causes, since secondary causes act only in the power of the primary cause. But the fact that human reason rules the human will and measures that will's goodness derives from the eternal law, that is, God's reason. And so the Psalm says: "Many ask, 'Who reveals to us what is good?' The light of your countenance is marked upon us, O Lord."[20] This is as if to say: "The light of our reason can reveal to us what is good, and rule our will, inasmuch as the light of our reason is the light of your countenance." And so the human will's goodness evidently depends much more on God's eternal law than on human reason, and we need to have recourse to eternal reason when human reason is insufficient.

Reply to Obj. 1. One thing does not have several proximate measures, but one thing can have several measures if one measure is subordinated to another.

Reply to Obj. 2. Proximate measures and the things they measure are the same kind of thing, but remote measures and the things they measure are different kinds of things.

Reply to Obj. 3. Although we do not know the eternal law as it exists in God's mind, we nonetheless come to know it to some degree either by our natural power of reason, which is derived from the eternal law as that law's own image, or by some kind of supplementary revelation.

Fifth Article

Is the Will Evil If It Wills Contrary to Erroneous Reason?

I proceed in this way to the fifth article: it seems that the will is not evil if it wills contrary to erroneous reason.

Obj. 1. Reason is the rule of the human will insofar as reason derives from the eternal law, as I have said.[21] But erroneous reason does not derive from the eternal law. Therefore, erroneous reason is not the rule of the human will. Therefore, the will is not evil if it wills contrary to erroneous reason.

Obj. 2. The command of a subordinate official does not oblige a subject to obey if the command happens to be contrary to the command of a higher authority, as Augustine says.[22] For example, a subject is not obliged to obey if a provincial governor should command something that the emperor prohibits. But erroneous reason at times presents to the will something contrary to the command of a higher authority, namely, God, whose power is supreme. Therefore, the judgment of erroneous reason does not oblige persons to obey. Therefore, the will is not evil if it wills contrary to erroneous reason.

Obj. 3. We trace every bad will to a species of evil. But we cannot trace a will that wills contrary to erroneous reason to a species of evil. For example, if reason erroneously tells a person to fornicate, we cannot trace the person's willing not to do so to any species of evil. Therefore, the will is not evil if it wills contrary to erroneous reason.

On the contrary, as I have said in the First Part,[23] conscience simply directs one's knowledge to an action. And knowledge is in the power of reason. Therefore, the will that wills contrary to erroneous reason wills contrary to conscience. But every such willing is evil, for the Letter to the Romans says: "Everything not of faith," that is, everything contrary to conscience, "is sin."[24] Therefore, the will is evil if it wills contrary to erroneous reason.

I answer that to ask if the will is evil when it acts contrary to erroneous reason is the same as to ask if erroneous conscience obliges persons to obey. This is so because conscience is in some way a judgment of reason, since conscience directs one's knowledge to an action, as I have said in the First Part.[25]

And on this matter, some thinkers have distinguished three kinds of acts: some acts are indeed good by their nature, some acts are morally indifferent, and some acts are evil by their nature.[26] Therefore, they say that there is no error in reason or conscience if reason or conscience should tell a person to do something that is good by its nature. Similarly, there is no error if reason or conscience should tell a person not to do something that is evil by its nature, for the same power of reason commands persons to do good and forbids them to do evil. But if reason or conscience should tell a person that human beings are obliged by precept to do something intrinsically evil, or that human beings are prohibited from doing something intrinsically good, reason or conscience will be in error. And reason or conscience will likewise be in error if it should tell someone that something as such morally indifferent (e.g., picking up straw from the ground) is forbidden or commanded. Therefore, they say that reason or conscience, when it errs about morally indifferent things, whether by command or injunction, obliges one to obey, so that the will will be evil if it wills contrary to erroneous reason, and there will be sin. On the other hand, reason or conscience, when it errs by commanding something intrinsically evil, or when it errs by forbidding something intrinsically good and necessary for salvation, does not oblige persons to obey. And so the will in such cases is not evil if it wills contrary to erroneous reason or conscience.

But such an explanation is unsound. For the will that wills contrary to erroneous reason or conscience in morally indifferent things is somehow evil because of the will's object on which the will's goodness or malice depends. And this is not because of the object by reason of its own nature, but because reason happens to understand the object as an evil to be done or shunned. And the will's object is what reason presents to the will, as I have said.[27]

Therefore, by tending toward something that reason proposes as evil, the will takes on the character of evil. And this happens not only in the case of morally indifferent things but also in the case of things intrinsically good or evil. For not only can morally indifferent things happen to take on the character of good or evil, but good things can likewise take on the character of evil, or evil things the character of good, because reason so understands them.

For example, abstaining from fornication is something good, although the will tends toward this good only insofar as reason so presents it. Therefore, if erroneous reason presents such abstinence as evil, the will tends toward it as something evil. And so the will will be evil because it wills something evil, indeed not something intrinsically evil but something that happens to be evil because reason so understands it. And similarly, belief in Christ is intrinsically good and something necessary for salvation, but the will tends toward that good only insofar as reason so presents it. And so the will tends toward belief in Christ as something evil if reason so presents it, not because such belief is intrinsically evil, but because it happens to be evil due to the way reason understands it.

And so the Philosopher says in the *Ethics* that "an intemperate person is, strictly speaking, one who does not follow right reason, but those who do not follow erroneous reason, by chance are also intemperate."[28] And so we need to say without qualification that every will that wills contrary to reason, whether reason be correct or erroneous, is always evil.

Reply to Obj. 1. Although the judgments of erroneous reason are not derived from God, erroneous reason nonetheless presents its judgments as true and so derived from God, who is the source of all truth.

Reply to Obj. 2. The statement of Augustine is appropriate when we know that a subordinate official commands something contrary to the command of a higher authority. But if a subject were to believe that the emperor commands what the provincial governor commands, the subject would scorn the emperor's command if the subject scorned the provincial governor's command. And similarly, human beings would not be obliged to follow reason if they were to know that human reason commanded something contrary to God's command, although reason would not then be completely in error. But if reason presents something to the will as God's command, to scorn the dictate of reason would then be the same as to scorn God's command. *Reply to Obj. 3.* Whenever reason understands something to be evil, reason understands it under some aspect of evil, for example, evil because contrary to God's command, or because of scandal, or for some such reason. And then we trace such a bad will to such a species of evil.

Sixth Article

Is the Will Good If It Wills in Accord with Erroneous Reason?

I proceed in this way to the sixth article: it seems that the will is good if it wills in accord with erroneous reason.

Obj. 1. As a will that wills contrary to reason tends toward what reason judges to be evil, so a will that wills in accord with reason tends toward what reason judges to be good. But the will is evil if it wills contrary to reason, even erroneous reason. Therefore, the will is good if it wills in accord with reason, even erroneous reason.

Obj. 2. A will is always good if it is in accord with God's commands and the eternal law. But the understanding of reason, even erroneous reason, presents the eternal law and God's commands to us. Therefore, the will is good even if it wills in accord with erroneous reason.

Obj. 3. The will is evil when it wills contrary to erroneous reason. Therefore, if the will is also evil when it wills in accord with erroneous reason, it seems that the will is evil whenever the person willing reasons erroneously. And so such human beings will be caught in a dilemma and necessarily sin, and this is inappropriate. Therefore, the will is good when it wills in accord with erroneous reason.

On the contrary, the will of those who killed the Apostles was evil. And yet the will of those killers was in accord with erroneous reason, as the Gospel of John says: "The hour is coming, and then all those who kill you, will think that they are offering service to God."[29] Therefore, the will can be evil when it wills in accord with erroneous reason.

I answer that, as the previous question is the same as to ask if an erroneous conscience obliges persons, so the present question is the same as to ask if an erroneous conscience excuses persons. But the present question depends on what I previously said about ignorance. For I have previously said that ignorance sometimes causes and sometimes does not cause things to be involuntary.[30] And acts have moral good and evil insofar as they are voluntary, as is evident from what I have previously explained.[31] Therefore, the ignorance that causes things to be involuntary evidently takes away the character of moral good and evil, while the ignorance that does not cause things to be involuntary evidently does not take away that character. I have also said before that the ignorance that is in some way voluntary, whether directly or indirectly, does not cause things to be involuntary.[32] And I call that ignorance directly voluntary toward which acts of the will tend. And I call that ignorance indirectly voluntary that is due to negligence, because persons do not will to know what they are obliged to know, as I have said before.[33]

Therefore, if reason or conscience should err voluntarily, whether directly or due to negligence, because persons err about things that they are obliged to know, then such an error of reason or conscience does not excuse the will that wills in accord with the reason or conscience erring in this way from being evil. But if the error that causes something to be involuntary comes from ignorance of a particular circumstance, without any negligence on the person's part, then such an error of reason or conscience excuses the person, and so the person's will is not evil when it wills in accord with erroneous reason. For example, if erroneous reason should tell a man that he ought to have intercourse with someone else's wife, the will in accord with such an erroneous reason is evil, since the error springs from ignorance of God's law, which he is obliged to know. But if his reason should err in thinking that the woman lying with him is his wife, and he should will to have intercourse with her when she seeks from him the right of a wife to intercourse with her husband, his will is excused and so is not evil. This is because the error springs from ignorance of the circumstance. And such ignorance excuses the person and causes the evil deed to be involuntary. *Reply to Obj. 1.* As Denis says in his *De divinis nominibus,* "an uncorrupted cause causes good, and single defects cause evil."[34] And so, for us to call evil the things toward which the will inclines, it suffices either that the things be evil by their nature, or that we understand them to be evil. But for the things to be good, they need to be good in both ways.

Reply to Obj. 2. The eternal law cannot err, but human reason can. And so the will is not always correct when it wills in accord with human reason, nor is such a will always in accord with the eternal law.

Reply to Obj. 3. As unsuitable consequences necessarily result from an unsuitable antecedent in the case of syllogistic arguments, so unsuitable consequences necessarily result from an unsuitable supposition in the case of moral things. For example, supposing that persons seek vainglory, they will sin whether they on that account do or omit to do what they are obliged to do. And yet they are not caught in a dilemma, since they can abandon their evil intention. And similarly, supposing an error of reason or conscience that springs from inexcusable ignorance, evil in the will necessarily results. And yet persons so erring are not caught in a dilemma, since they can draw away from their error, because their ignorance is voluntary and can be overcome.

Notes

1. *De divinis nominibus* 4. PG 3:732.
2. *Ethics* VI, 5. 1140b6–7.
3. *Ethics* V, 1. 1129a6–9.
4. Q. 18, A. 5.
5. Q. 1, A. 1, *ad* 2.
6. Q. 18, A. 5.
7. Q. 18, A. 4.
8. Q. 18, A. 3.
9. Q. 6, A. 8.
10. Q. 18, A. 10, *ad* 2.
11. Q. 19, A. 1.
12. Q. 9, A. 1.
13. *Ethics* VI, 2. 1139a29–31.
14. Q. 9, A. 1.
15. *De Trinitate* X, 1. PL 10:344.
16. Q. 19, AA. 1, 2.
17. Q. 9, A. 1.
18. Aristotle, *Metaphysics* IX, 1. 1053a24–30.

19. *Contra Faustum* XXII, 27. PL 42:418.
20. Ps. 4:6.
21. Q. 19, A. 4.
22. *Sermo ad populum 62* 8. PL 38:421.
23. Q. 79, A. 13.
24. Rom. 14:23.
25. Q. 79, A. 13.
26. St. Bonaventure, *In librum Sententiarum* II, dist. 39, A. 1, Q. 3. Alexander of Hales, *Summa theologiae* II–II, n. 388.
27. Q. 19, A. 3.
28. *Ethics* VII, 9. 1151a29–b4.
29. Jn. 16:2.
30. Q. 6, A. 8.
31. Q. 19, A. 2.
32. Q. 6, A. 8.
33. Ibid.
34. *De divinis nominibus* 4. PG 3:729.

Question 20

On the Goodness and Malice of External Human Acts

[This question is divided into six articles, one of which is included here.]

Second Article

Do External Acts' Entire Goodness and Malice Depend on the Will's Goodness?

I proceed in this way to the second article: it seems that external acts' entire goodness and malice depend on the will's goodness.

Obj. 1. The Gospel of Matthew says: "A good tree cannot produce bad fruit, nor can a bad tree produce good fruit."[1] But a gloss says that "tree" signifies the will, and "fruit" signifies external acts.[2] Therefore, it cannot be the case that the interior will is good, and external acts are bad—or vice versa.

Obj. 2. Augustine says in his *Retractationum* that persons sin only in their willing.[3] Therefore, if there is no sin in willing, there is no sin in external acts. And so external acts' entire goodness or malice depends on the will.

Obj. 3. The good and evil of which we are speaking are the specific differences in moral acts. But specific differences intrinsically divide genera, as the Philosopher says in the *Metaphysics*.[4] Therefore, it seems that we understand the good and evil in moral acts only regarding the will, since acts are moral because they are voluntary.

On the contrary, Augustine says in his *Contra mendacium* that "no good end, as it were, and no good will can cause certain things to be done rightly."[5]

I answer that, as I have already said,[6] we can consider two kinds of goodness or malice in external acts: one by reason of the acts' requisite matter and circumstances; the second by reason of the acts' relation to ends. And the whole goodness or malice in the relation of acts to ends indeed depends on the will. But the goodness or malice in the requisite matter and circumstances depends on reason, and the will's goodness depends on such goodness insofar as the will tends toward that very goodness.

And as I have said before,[7] we need to consider that a single defect suffices to make things evil, but a single good does not suffice, and integral goodness is required, in order to make things good in every respect. Therefore, if the will is good by reason of its own object and the end, it follows that the external act is good. But the will's goodness by reason of intending good ends does not suffice to make external acts good; rather, external acts are evil if the will is evil either by reason of the will intending evil ends or by reason of the will willing evil acts.

Reply to Obj. 1. We need to understand the good will signified by the good tree as a will that is good by reason of the acts that it wills, and by reason of the ends that it intends.

Reply to Obj. 2. Persons sin when they will evil ends, and also when they will evil acts.

Reply to Obj. 3. We do not only call interior acts of the will voluntary, but we also call external acts voluntary, insofar as external acts issue from the will and reason. And so the specific differences of good and evil can belong both to internal acts and to external acts.

Notes

1. Mt. 7:18.
2. Augustine, *Contra Iulianum* I, 8. PL 44:667.
3. *Retractationum* I, 9. PL 32:596.
4. *Metaphysics* VI, 12. 1038a9–18.
5. *Contra mendacium* 7. PL 40:528.
6. Q. 20, A. 1.
7. Q. 19, A. 6, *ad* 1.

Question 24

On the Good and Evil in the Soul's Emotions

[This question is divided into four articles, one of which is included here.]

First Article

Can We Find Moral Good and Evil in the Soul's Emotions?

I proceed in this way to the first article: it seems that no emotion of the soul is morally good or evil.

Obj. 1. Moral good and evil are peculiar to human beings, for "we in a proper sense call moral acts human acts," as Ambrose says in his *Super Lucam.*[1] But emotions are not peculiar to human beings; rather, emotions are also common to other animals. Therefore, no emotion of the soul is morally good or evil.

Obj. 2. The good or evil of human beings consists of "being in accord with reason" or "being in discord with reason," as Denis says in his *De divinis nominibus.*[2] But emotions reside in sense appetites and not in reason, as I have said before.[3] Therefore, emotions do not belong to the good or evil of human beings, and such good is moral good.

Obj. 3. The Philosopher says in the *Ethics* that "we are neither praised nor blamed because of our emotions."[4] But we are praised or blamed because of moral good or evil. Therefore, emotions are not morally good or evil.

On the contrary, Augustine, speaking about the soul's emotions, says in *The City of God*: "Those things are evil if love is evil, and good if love is good."[5]

I answer that we can consider the soul's emotions in two ways: in one way, as such; in the second way, as subject to the command of reason and to the will. Therefore, if we consider emotions in themselves, namely, as they are indeed movements of irrational appetites, then they have no moral good or evil, which depends on reason, as I have said before.[6] But if we consider emotions as subject to the command of reason and to the will, then they have moral good or evil. For sense appetites are more closely connected to reason itself and the will than external bodily members are. And yet the movements and acts of external bodily members are morally good or evil insofar as those movements and acts are voluntary. And so much more can we also call emotions themselves, insofar as they are voluntary, good or evil. And we call them voluntary either because the will commands them, or because the will does not forbid them.

Reply to Obj. 1. Those emotions, considered as such, are common to human beings and other animals, but they are peculiar to human beings insofar as reason commands them.

Reply to Obj. 2. We call even lower appetitive powers rational insofar as "they share in some way in reason," as the *Ethics* says.[7]

Reply to Obj. 3. The Philosopher says that we are not praised or blamed because of emotions considered as such, but he does not exclude the possibility that emotions are praiseworthy or blameworthy insofar as reason ordains them. And so he adds: "For example, we do not praise or blame those who are fearful or angry, but we do praise or blame those who are fearful or angry in a particular way," that is, in accord with reason or in discord with reason.

Notes

1. *Super Lucam*, prologue, n. 7. PL 15:1532.
2. *De divinis nominibus* 4. PG 3:733.
3. Q. 22, A. 3.
4. *Ethics* II, 5. 1105b31–1106a2.
5. *The City of God* XIV, 7. PL 41:410.
6. Q. 18, A. 5.
7. Aristotle, *Ethics* I, 13. 1102b13–14.

Question 26

On the Soul's Emotions in Particular, and First on Love

[This question is divided into four articles, one of which is included here.]

Fourth Article

*Do We Appropriately Divide Love into the Love of
Friendship and the Love of Desire?*

I proceed in this way to the fourth article: it seems that we do not appropriately divide love into the love of friendship and the love of desire.

Obj. 1. "Love is an emotion, while friendship is an enduring disposition," as the Philosopher says in the *Ethics*.[1] But an enduring disposition cannot be the subdivision of an emotion. Therefore, we do not appropriately distinguish love by the love of desire and the love of friendship.

Obj. 2. We do not distinguish things by other species of the same genus, as for example, "human being" and "animal" are not species of the same genus.[2] But desire and love are species of the same genus, since they are different kinds of emotion. Therefore, we cannot distinguish love by desire.

Obj. 3. As the Philosopher says in the *Ethics*,[3] there are three kinds of friendship: "the useful, the pleasurable, and the worthy." But desire belongs to useful and pleasurable friendships. Therefore, we should not distinguish desire from friendship.

On the contrary, we say that we love some things because we desire them. For example, "we say that persons love wine because of the sweetness in it that they desire," as the *Topics* says.[4] But we have no friendship with wine and the like, as the *Ethics* says.[5] Therefore, the love of desire is one thing, and the love of friendship is another.

I answer that "to love is to will good for someone," as the Philosopher says in the *Rhetoric*.[6] Therefore, movements of love strive for two things, namely, the good that one wills for someone, whether one's self or another, and the person for whom one wills the good. Therefore, persons have love of desire for the good that they will for another, and they have love of friendship for the one for whom they will the good.

And this division has an order of priority. For what one loves with a love of friendship, one loves without qualification and as such, while what one loves with a love of desire, one does not love without qualification and as such but for the other. For as things possessing existing are beings in an unqualified sense, while things that exist in something else are beings in a qualified sense, so the good convertible with being indeed possesses its very goodness without qualification, while the good of the other is good in a qualified sense. And so the love whereby one loves something that is the good of oneself is love in an unqualified sense, while the love whereby one loves something that is the good of another is love in a qualified sense.

Reply to Obj. 1. We do not distinguish love by friendship and desire; rather, we distinguish love by the love of friendship and the love of desire. For we in a proper sense call friends those for whom we will some good, and we say that desiring is what we will for ourselves.

Reply to Obj. 2. And the foregoing makes clear the answer to the second objection.

Reply to Obj. 3. In friendships of the useful and pleasurable kinds, persons indeed will some good for friends, and the character of friendship is in this respect preserved in such friendships. But because the good of another further concerns one's own pleasure or utility, useful and pleasurable friendships, since they conduce to love of desire, in this respect lack the true character of friendship.

Notes

1. *Ethics* VIII, 5. 1157b28–29.
2. The point of the example is that the genus "animal" can be subdivided into the species "rational animal" and "irrational animal," while "human being," "rational animal," cannot be subdivided by other species of the genus "animal" (e.g., "dog" or "cat").
3. *Ethics* VIII, 3. 1156a7–10.
4. Aristotle, *Topics* II, 3. 111a3–4.
5. Aristotle, *Ethics* VIII, 2. 1155b29–31.
6. *Rhetoric* II, 4. 1380b35–36.

Question 27

On the Causes of Love

[This question is divided into four articles, one of which is included here.]

Third Article

Does Likeness Cause Love?

I proceed in this way to the third article: it seems that likeness does not cause love.

Obj. 1. The same thing does not cause contrary things. But likeness causes hate, for the Book of Proverbs says that "the proud are always contending with one another,"[1] and the Philosopher says in the *Ethics* that "potters quarrel with one another."[2] Therefore, likeness does not cause love.

Obj. 2. Augustine says in his *Confessions* that "persons love in others what they themselves would not wish to be; for example, persons who would not wish to be actors love those who are actors."[3] But this would not happen if likeness were to be the peculiar cause of love, for human beings would then love in others what they themselves possessed or wished to possess. Therefore, likeness does not cause love.

Obj. 3. All human beings love what they need, even if they happen not to possess it; for example, sick persons love health, and paupers love riches. But persons are unlike health or riches insofar as they need or lack such things. Therefore, unlikeness as well as likeness causes love.

Obj. 4. The Philosopher says in the *Rhetoric* that "we love those who are generous to us regarding money and health, and everyone likewise loves those who attend to friendships regarding the dead."[4] But not everyone is generous to us regarding money and health, or attends to friendships regarding the dead. Therefore, likeness does not cause love.

On the contrary, the Book of Sirach says: "Every living thing loves its own kind."[5]

I answer that likeness, strictly speaking, causes love. But we should consider that we note the likeness of things in two ways. In one way, because every like thing actually possesses the same thing; for example, we call two things that possess whiteness like things. In the second way, because one thing possesses potentially and by an inclination what something else possesses actually; for example, if we should say that a heavy material substance situated out of its proper place is like such a substance situated in its proper place. Or also insofar as potentialities are like actualities themselves, for actualities are in some way in potentialities themselves.

Therefore, the first way of likeness causes a love of friendship or benevolence. For two things alike in possessing, as it were, the same form, are by that fact somehow one in that form. For example, two human beings are the same in being specifically human, and two white persons are the same in being white. And so the affection of one person extends to another as the other is one with himself or herself, and persons will good for others just as they do for themselves. And the second way of likeness causes a love of desire or a friendship of utility or pleasure. This is so because everything with potentiality, inasmuch as it is such, by its nature seeks to actualize its potentiality, and things endowed with powers of sensing and knowing take pleasure in doing so.

And I have said before that those who love with a love of desire, when they will the good that they desire, in a proper sense love their very selves.[6] But all love themselves more than others, because persons are substantially one with themselves, whereas they are one with others in likeness of form. And so, if persons should be prevented from gaining the good that they love, by those like them in sharing form, the others become hateful to them, not because the others are like them, but because the others prevent them from gaining their own good. And the reason why "potters quarrel with one another" is because they diminish one another's profits. And the reason why "the proud are contending" is because they diminish one another's standing, which they desire.

Reply to Obj. 1.   And this makes clear the answer to the first objection.

Reply to Obj. 2.   We find a proportional likeness even in the fact that persons love in another what they do not love in themselves, for those persons themselves are related to what they love in themselves, in the way in which the other is related to what the persons love in the other. For example, if a good singer loves one who writes well, we note a proportional likeness in such a love insofar as each possesses what is appropriate for the person with respect to the person's skill.

Reply to Obj. 3.   Persons who love what they need are like what they love, as potentialities are like actualities, as I have said.[7]

Reply to Obj. 4.   By the same likeness of potentiality to actuality, persons who are not generous love those who are, inasmuch as the former expect from the latter something that they desire. And the same reasoning applies in the case of persons persevering in friendship toward those who do not. For the friendship in both cases seems to be because of utility.

Or, granted that some human beings do not possess such virtues by way of complete habitual disposition, they nonetheless possess the virtues by way of principles of reason, in which way those lacking virtue love what is virtuous, as conformed to their natural power of reason.

Notes

1. Prov. 13:10.
2. *Ethics* VIII, 1. 1155a35–b1.
3. *Confessions* IV, 14. PL 32:702.
4. *Rhetoric* II, 4. 1381a20–21.
5. Sir. 13:14.
6. Q. 26, A. 4.
7. In the body of the article.

Question 28

On the Effects of Love

[This question is divided into six articles, two of which are included here.]

First Article

Is Union an Effect of Love?

I proceed in this way to the first article: it seems that union is not an effect of love.

Obj. 1. Absence is contrary to union. But love is compatible with absence, for the Apostle says in the Letter to the Galatians (speaking of himself, as a gloss says[1]): "Strive for good in things always and not only when I am with you."[2] Therefore, union is not an effect of love.

Obj. 2. Every union is either intrinsically such (for example, forms are intrinsically united to matter, and accidents are intrinsically united to the subjects in which they inhere, and parts are intrinsically united to a whole and one another in order to constitute the whole) or the result of a generic or specific or accidental likeness. But love does not cause an intrinsic union; otherwise, we would never love intrinsically different things. And love does not cause a union by likeness; rather, such a likeness causes love, as I have said.[3] Therefore, union is not an effect of love.

Obj. 3. The senses actually perceiving become the things actually perceived, and the intellect actually understanding becomes the things actually understood. But those actually loving do not become the things actually beloved. Therefore, union is an effect of knowledge rather than an effect of love.

On the contrary, Denis says in his *De divinis nominibus* that every love is "a force that unifies."[4]

I answer that lovers are united to the beloved in two ways. One kind of union is indeed in an external way, as, for example, when the beloved is in the company of the lover. The second kind of union is by way of affection. And we indeed need to consider this way by the lover's prior understanding, since movements of the will follow understanding. And since there are two kinds of love, namely, the love of desire and the love of friendship, each kind of love results from an understanding of the beloved's unity with the lover. For persons, when they love something by desiring it, conceive that thing as part of their well-being. Similarly, persons, when they love someone with a love of friendship, will good for the other just as they will good for themselves. And so persons conceive the other as another self, since they will good for the other just as they will good for themselves. And so we call a friend "another self."[5] And Augustine says in his *Confessions*: "A certain person rightly said that his friend was half of his soul."[6]

Therefore, love is the efficient cause of the first kind of union, since love moves lovers to desire and seek the company of the beloved as fitting for them and belonging to them. And love is the formal cause of the second kind of union, since love itself is such a union or bond. And so Augustine says in his *De Trinitate* that love is, as it were, "a living source that unites, or seeks to unite, two things, namely, the lover and the beloved."[7] For the expression "unites" refers to the union of affection, without which there is no love, while the expression "seeks to unite" pertains to an external union.

Reply to Obj. 1. The argument of this objection holds in the case of an external union, which is indeed necessary to cause pleasure. But there is desire when the beloved is physically absent, and there is love whether the beloved is absent or present.

Reply to Obj. 2. Union is related to love in three ways. For one kind of union causes love. And this union is indeed an intrinsic union with respect to the love whereby persons love themselves, and a union of likeness with respect to the love whereby persons love other things, as I have said.[8]

And a second kind of love is essentially love itself and the product of a common bond of affection. And this union resembles an intrinsic union, inasmuch as lovers in a love of friendship are disposed toward the beloved as they are disposed toward themselves, while lovers in a love of desire are disposed toward the beloved as something that belongs to them.

And a third kind of union is the effect of love. And this union is an external union, one that lovers seek regarding the beloved. And such a union indeed exists in a way suitable to love. For, as the Philosopher relates in the *Politics*, "Aristophanes said that lovers desire that the two of them become one."[9] But since "this would result in both lovers or the other lover being destroyed," they seek a fitting and becoming union, namely, that they engage in common enterprise, and converse with one another, and be united in other such ways.

Reply to Obj. 3. Knowledge results from known things being united to knowers by the things' likenesses. But love causes the very things loved to be somehow united to lovers, as I have said.[10] And so love effects a greater union than knowledge does.

Second Article

Is Mutual Indwelling an Effect of Love?

I proceed in this way to the second article: it seems that love does not cause mutual indwelling, namely, that the lover be in the beloved, and vice versa.

Obj. 1. What is in something else is contained in it. But the same thing cannot contain something else and be contained in it. Therefore, love cannot cause mutual indwelling, that the beloved be in the lover, and the lover in the beloved.

Obj. 2. Nothing can penetrate the inner parts of a whole except by dividing the whole. But it belongs to reason to divide things that are really united, and not to the will, which is the subject in which love inheres. Therefore, mutual indwelling is not an effect of love.

Obj. 3. If love causes the lover to be in the beloved, and the beloved to be in the lover, then the beloved is united to the lover in the same way that the lover is united to the beloved. But the very union of the lover and the beloved is love, as I have said.[11] Therefore, it follows that the lover is always loved by the beloved, and this is obviously false. Therefore, mutual indwelling is not an effect of love.

On the contrary, the First Letter of John says: "Who abides in love, abides in God, and God in him."[12] But this love is the love of God. Therefore, by like reasoning, every love causes the beloved to be in the lover, and the lover to be in the beloved.

I answer that we can understand mutual indwelling as an effect of love, both with respect to the power of understanding and with respect to the power of desiring. For we say with respect to the power of understanding that the beloved is in the lover because the beloved abides in the understanding of the lover, as the Letter to the Philippians says: "Because I have you in my heart."[13] And we say that the lover is in the beloved by way of understanding, because the lover does not rest content with a superficial grasp of the beloved, but strives to search out particulars that belong to the beloved's innermost being, and then to enter into the inner things of the beloved. In this vein, the First Letter to the Corinthians says of the Holy Spirit, who is God's love, that "he searches out everything, even the depths of God."[14]

And we say with respect to the power of desiring that the beloved is in the lover because the beloved is in the lover's affection by reason of some satisfaction. That is to say, that the lover, when in the company of the beloved, takes pleasure in the beloved or the good things in the beloved. Or that the lover, when not in the company of the beloved, strives with desire for the very person beloved with a love of friendship. Or that the lover strives with a love of friendship for the good things that the lover wills for the beloved, not indeed for any extrinsic reason (as, for example, when one desires something for the sake of something else, or when one wills another's good for the sake of something else), but because of a deeply rooted satisfaction in the beloved. And so also we call love intimate and speak of the depths of love.

And conversely, the lover is indeed in one way in the beloved by a love of desire, and in another way by a love of friendship. For a love of desire is not satisfied with gaining or enjoying the beloved in any external or superficial way, but seeks to possess the beloved completely, reaching the inner things of the beloved, as it were. But in a love of friendship, lovers are in the beloved insofar as they reckon the good or bad things of their friend as their own, and reckon the will of their friend as their own, so that they themselves, as it were, seem to experience and to be affected by things good or bad in their friend. And consequently, it is characteristic of friends "to will the same things and to grieve and rejoice in the same things," as the Philosopher says in the *Ethics*[15] and the *Rhetoric*.[16] And so lovers, since they reckon things pertaining to their friend as their own, would seem to be in the beloved, as if they have become identical with their friend. And so, conversely, the beloved, since they will and act for their friend as they do for themselves, as if reckoning their friend identical with themselves, are in the lover.

And we can also understand the mutual indwelling in a love of friendship in a third way, in a reciprocal way, since friends mutually love one another, and will and do good things for one another.

Reply to Obj. 1. The beloved is contained in the lover in that a satisfaction imprints the beloved in the lover's affection. And conversely, the lover is contained in the beloved in that the lover in some way seeks the innermost things of the beloved. For nothing prevents something from containing, and being contained by, something else in different ways, as, for example, genera are contained in species, and vice versa.

Reply to Obj. 2. Reason's understanding precedes love's affection. And so, as reason searches out the beloved, so love's affection penetrates the beloved, as is evident from what I have said.[17]

Reply to Obj. 3. The argument of this objection holds with respect to the third way of mutual indwelling, but we do not find that way of mutual indwelling in every kind of love.

Notes

1. Peter Lombard, *Glossa*. PL 192:145.
2. Gal. 4:18.
3. Q. 27, A. 3.
4. *De divinis nominibus* 4. PG 3:709.
5. Aristotle, *Ethics* IX, 4. 1166a31–32.
6. *Confessions* IV, 6. PL 32:698.
7. *De Trinitate* VIII, 10. PL 42:960.
8. Q. 27, A. 3.

9. *Politics* II, 1. 1262b11–16.
10. In the body of the article and *ad* 2.
11. Q. 28, A. 1.
12. 1 Jn. 4:16.
13. Phil. 1:7.
14. 1 Cor. 2:10.
15. *Ethics* IX, 3. 1165b27–31.
16. *Rhetoric* II, 4. 1381a3–6.
17. In the body of the article.

Question 49

On Habits in General, Regarding Their Essence

[This question is divided into four articles, two of which are included here.]

Third Article

Do Habits Imply a Relation to Acts?

I proceed in this way to the third article: it seems that habits do not imply a relation to acts.

Obj. 1. Everything acts insofar as it is actual. But the Philosopher says in the *De anima* that "persons who come to have habitual knowledge, are still persons who have potential knowledge, although in a different way than before they acquired learning."[1] Therefore, habits do not imply the relationship that sources have to acts.

Obj. 2. Things that we posit in the definition of something belong intrinsically to that thing. But we posit a source of action in the definition of a power, as the *Metaphysics* makes clear.[2] Therefore, being sources of acts belongs intrinsically to powers. But something intrinsically such is first in every genus. Therefore, habits, if they as well as powers are sources of acts, are consequently secondary to powers. And so the first type of quality will not consist of habits or dispositions.[3]

Obj. 3. Health is sometimes a habit, and leanness and beauty are likewise sometimes habits. But we do not predicate these things in relation to acts. Therefore, it is not essential that habits be sources of acts.

On the contrary, Augustine says in his *De bono conjugali* that "habits are the means whereby we do things when we need to."[4] And the Commentator says in his commentary on the *De anima* that "habits are the means whereby persons act when they should wish to do so."[5]

I answer that having a relation to acts can belong to habits both by reason of the nature of habit and by reason of the subject in which habits inhere. It indeed belongs to every habit by its nature to have a relation to acts, since it belongs to the nature of habit to imply a relationship to a thing's nature, as habits are suitable or unsuitable. But a thing's nature, which is the end of its process of coming to be, is further ordained to another end, which is either an action or the effect that one attains through action. And so a habit implies not only a relation to the very nature of something but also, consequently, to an action, as the action is the nature's end or conduces to the nature's end. And so also the *Metaphysics* defines habit as "a disposition whereby something is well or ill disposed, either intrinsically," that is, by the thing's nature, "or in relation to something else," that is, in relation to the thing's end.[6]

But there are some habits that also first and foremost imply a relation to acts regarding the subjects in which they inhere. This is so, as I have just said, because habits primarily and intrinsically imply a relationship to a thing's nature. Therefore, if the nature of the things in which habits inhere consists in the very relation to acts, then the habits chiefly imply a relation to the acts. And it is evidently the nature and essence of powers to be sources of acts. And so every habit that belongs to a power as the habit's subject chiefly implies a relation to acts.

Reply to Obj. 1. Habits as qualities are actualities and can accordingly be sources of action. But habits are potential with respect to action. And so we call habits "first actualities," and actions "second actualities," as the *De anima* makes clear.[7]

Reply to Obj. 2. Habits essentially regard natures and not powers. And because natures precede action, and powers regard action, we consequently posit habits as a kind of quality before we posit powers as another kind of quality.

Reply to Obj. 3. We call health a habit or habitual disposition in relation to a thing's nature, as I have said.[8] But natures as sources of action consequently imply a relation to acts. And so the Philosopher says in the *De historia animalium* that we call human beings or their bodily members healthy "when they can perform the actions of healthy human beings.'"[9] And we do the same in the case of other human habits.

Fourth Article

Are Habits Necessary?

I proceed in this way to the fourth article: it seems that habits are not necessary.

Obj. 1. Habits are the means whereby things are well or ill disposed toward something, as I have said.[10] But things' forms dispose things well or ill, since forms cause things to be good, just as forms cause things to be beings. Therefore, there is no need for habits.

Obj. 2. Habits imply a relation to acts. But powers sufficiently imply sources of action, since even the powers of nature, which have no habits, are sources of action. Therefore, habits were not necessary.

Obj. 3. Habits are disposed toward good and evil in the same way that powers are. But powers are not always acting. Therefore, neither are habits. Therefore, given the existence of powers, habits were superfluous.

On the contrary, habits are perfections, as the *Physics* says.[11] But things most of all need perfection, since perfection has the character of end. Therefore, habits were necessary.

I answer that, as I have said before,[12] habits imply a disposition in relation to a thing's nature and to a thing's activity or end, and such a disposition well or ill disposes the thing to such activity and such an end. And there are three prerequisites for a thing to need to be disposed toward something else. First, indeed, that the disposed subject is other than the object toward which it is disposed, and is disposed toward the object as potentiality to actuality. And so there is no need for habits or dispositions if there is something whose nature is not a composite of potentiality and actuality, and whose substance is its activity, and that exists for itself, as is evidently true in the case of God.

The second prerequisite is that things with potentiality for something else might be determined in several ways and to different things. And so there is no need for dispositions or habits in things with potentiality for something else but only for that very thing, since such subjects by their nature have a necessary relationship to such an actuality. And so, heavenly bodies, supposing that they are composed of matter and form, have no need for any disposition or habit for their form, since their matter has no potentiality for another form, as I have said in the First Part.[13] Nor need there be any disposition or habit toward their action, since the nature of heavenly bodies has potentiality for only one fixed movement.

The third prerequisite is that several things act together to dispose a subject toward one of the objects for which the subject has potentiality, and that these things can be apportioned in different ways so as to dispose the subject well or ill toward its form or action. And so we call the simple qualities of material elements, which qualities befit the elements' nature in a fixed way, simple qualities and not dispositions or habits. And we call health, beauty, and the like, which imply an apportionment of several things that can be apportioned in different ways, dispositions or habits. And the Philosopher consequently says in the *Metaphysics* that "habits are dispositions,"[14] and that dispositions are "arrangements of things with spatial or potential or specific parts,"[15] as I have said before.[16]

Therefore, there need to be habits, since there are many beings whose natures and actions need several things to act in unison, and these things can be apportioned in different ways.

Reply to Obj. 1. A thing's form perfects its nature, and the subject needs to be inclined by a disposition in relation to the very form.

But the form itself is further ordained to action, which is either an end or the means to an end. And if the form in fact should have only one fixed way of acting, no other disposition besides the form itself is necessary for the action. If, on the other hand, the form is such that it could act in various ways, as the soul can, habits need to incline the form toward its actions.

Reply to Obj. 2. Powers are sometimes inclined toward many things, and so something else needs to determine the powers. But powers do not need habits to determine them if they are not disposed toward many things, as I have said.[17] And so the powers of nature do not perform their actions by means of any habits, since powers of nature of their very selves are limited to one thing.

Reply to Obj. 3. The same habit is not disposed toward good and evil, as I shall make clear later.[18] But the same power is disposed toward good and evil. And so habits are needed to determine powers to good.

Notes

1. *De anima* III, 4. 429b6–10.
2. Aristotle, *Metaphysics* IV, 12. 1019a15–20.
3. On the types and order of qualities, see Q. 49, A. 2.
4. *De bono conjugali* 21. PL 40:390.
5. Averroes, *In De anima*, comm. 18.
6. Aristotle, *Metaphysics* IV, 20. 1022b10–12.
7. Aristotle, *De anima* II, 1. 412a22–28.
8. Q. 49, A. 2, *ad* 1.
9. *Historia animalium* X, 1. 633b23–25.
10. Q. 49, A. 2.
11. Aristotle, *Physics* VII, 3. 246a11–13.
12. Q. 49, AA. 2, 3.
13. Q. 66, A. 2.
14. *Metaphysics* IV, 20. 1022b10.
15. *Metaphysics* IV, 19. 1022b1–2.
16. Q. 49, A. 1, *ad* 3.
17. In the body of the article.
18. Q. 54, A. 3.

Question 50

On the Subjects in Which Habits Inhere

[This question is divided into six articles, five of which are included here.]

First Article

Does the Body Have Any Habits?

I proceed in this way to the first article: it seems that the body has no habits.

Obj. 1. As the Commentator says in his commentary on the *De anima*, "habits are the means whereby persons act when they should will to act."[1] But bodily actions are not subject to the will, since such actions are from nature. Therefore, the body has no habits.

Obj. 2. Bodily dispositions can be easily altered. But habits are characteristics that are difficult to alter. Therefore, bodily dispositions cannot be habits.

Obj. 3. Every bodily disposition is subject to alteration. But alteration belongs only to the third type of quality, and we contradistinguish that type of quality from habits.[2] Therefore, the body has no habits.

On the contrary, the Philosopher says in the *Categories* that we call bodily health or incurable disease a habit.[3]

I answer that habits are dispositions in things with potentiality either for forms or actions, as I have said before.[4] Therefore, no habit exists chiefly in the body as its subject, since habits imply dispositions toward actions. For every bodily action springs either from a natural characteristic of the body or from the soul that moves the body. Therefore, regarding actions that spring from nature, no habit disposes the body, since the powers of nature are limited to one thing, and I have said that habitual dispositions are needed only if subjects have potentiality for many things.[5] And actions that spring from the soul by means of the body indeed belong chiefly to the soul itself and secondarily to the body itself. And habits are proportioned to actions, and so "like actions produce like habits," as the *Ethics* says.[6] And so dispositions for such actions exist chiefly in the soul. But dispositions can exist in the body secondarily, inasmuch as the body is disposed and made apt to be readily at the service of the soul's actions.

If, however, we are speaking about the disposition of a subject toward its form, then a habitual disposition can exist in the body, which we relate to the soul as a subject to its form. And it is in this way that we call health and beauty and the like habitual dispositions. Nonetheless, these dispositions do not completely possess the character of habit, since their causes by their nature can be easily transformed.

And as Simplicius relates in his commentary on the Categories,[7] Alexander held that the body in no way has a habit or disposition of the first type of quality, and said that that type of quality belongs only to the soul.[8] And Aristotle (according to Alexander) did not introduce what he said about health and sickness in the *Categories*[9] as if these belong to the first type of quality, but by way of example. According to this interpretation, Aristotle would mean that, like sickness and health, so also qualities of the first type (which we call habits or dispositions) can be easy or difficult to alter.

But this interpretation is clearly contrary to Aristotle's aim. This is evident both because he employs the same way of speaking when he cites the examples of health and sickness as when he cites the examples or virtue and knowledge,[10] and because he expressly holds in the *Physics* that beauty and health are habits.[11]

Reply to Obj. 1. This objection holds with respect to habits as dispositions toward action, and with respect to bodily actions that spring from nature, but not with respect to actions that spring from the soul, whose source is the will.

Reply to Obj. 2. Because of the variability of material causes, bodily dispositions are not, absolutely speaking, difficult to alter. But bodily dispositions can be difficult to alter in relation to a particular kind of subject, namely, in that they cannot be removed as long as the particular kind of subject remains. Or they can be difficult to alter in relation to other dispositions. But the soul's characteristics are, absolutely speaking, difficult to alter, since their subject is unalterable. And so Aristotle does not say that a state of health difficult to alter is a habit in an absolute sense, but that such a state is "like a habit," as the Greek expresses it.[12] And we call the soul's characteristics habits in an absolute sense.

Reply to Obj. 3. According to some thinkers,[13] bodily dispositions of the first type of quality differ from qualities of the third type[14] in that the latter qualities consist of coming to be and change, as it were, and so we call them conditions or characteristics of being acted upon. And these qualities, when they have attained perfection, their species, as it were, then belong to the first type of quality. But Simplicius in his commentary on the *Categories* rejects this theory.[15] He does so because, according to the theory, heating would belong to the third type of quality, and heat to the first type, whereas Aristotle posits heat in the third type.

And so, as the same Simplicius relates,[16] Porphyry says that conditions or characteristics of being acted upon, and dispositions and habits, differ in material substances by reason of expansion and contraction. For example, if something is the recipient of only enough heat to become hot, and not enough heat to be able to heat anything else, then there is a condition of being acted upon if the heat quickly dissipates, or a characteristic of being acted upon if the heat perdures. And if the thing reaches the point where it can also heat something else, then there is a disposition. And if the disposition is further strengthened to the point where the disposition is difficult to alter, then there will be a habit, with the consequence that the disposition is an expansion or perfection of the condition or characteristic of being acted upon, and the habit an expansion or perfection of the disposition. But Simplicius rejects this theory,[17] since such expansion and contraction does not imply any difference regarding the form itself but implies a difference by reason of the subject sharing in the form in different ways. And so this theory would not differentiate types of quality.

And so we need to say otherwise, that the apportionment of those very characteristics of being acted upon according to the suitability of nature have the character of disposition, as I have said.[18] And so, when there is an alteration regarding the very characteristics of being acted upon, that is, hot and cold, wet and dry, the alteration results in sickness or health. But there is primarily and intrinsically no alteration in such habits and dispositions.

Second Article

Is the Soul the Subject of Habits by Reason of Its Essence,
or Is the Soul Such by Reason of Its Powers?

I proceed in this way to the second article: it seems that habits inhere in the soul by reason of the soul's essence rather than by reason of its powers.

Obj. 1. We speak of dispositions and habits in relation to a nature, as I have said.[19] But we note the soul's nature by its essence rather than by its powers, since the soul by its essence is the nature and form of a special kind of body. Therefore, habits inhere in the soul by the soul's essence and not by its powers.

Obj. 2. Accidents do not belong to other accidents, and habits are accidents. But the soul's powers belong to the genus of accidents, as I have said in the First Part.[20] Therefore, habits do not inhere in the soul by reason of the soul's powers.

Obj. 3. Subjects are prior to the things that inhere in them. But habits, since they belong to the first type of quality, are prior to powers, which belong to the second type of quality. Therefore, habits do not inhere in the soul's powers as the habits' subjects.

On the contrary, the Philosopher in the *Ethics* posits various habits in different parts of the soul.[21]

I answer that habits imply dispositions in relation to a nature or action, as I have said before.[22] Therefore, if we understand habits as having a relation to a nature, and if we are speaking about human nature, then habits cannot inhere in the soul, since the soul itself is the form that completes human nature. And so a habit or disposition can in this respect be in the body by reason of the body's relation to the soul rather than in the soul by reason of the soul's relation to the body. But if we are speaking about a higher nature in which human beings may share (as the Second Letter of Peter says, "that we may share in God's nature,"[23]) then nothing prevents a habit, namely, grace, from being in the soul by the soul's essence, as I shall explain later.[24]

On the other hand, if we understand habits in relation to action, then we find that habits inhere especially in the soul, since the soul is not limited to one action but is disposed toward many actions, and such a disposition is necessary for habits, as I have said before.[25] And since the soul causes actions by means of its powers, habits accordingly inhere in the soul by reason of those powers.

Reply to Obj. 1. The soul's essence does not belong to human nature as a subject to be disposed toward something else but as a form and nature toward which a human being is disposed.

Reply to Obj. 2. An accident as such cannot be the subject in which another accident inheres. But because accidents themselves are interrelated, we understand the subject as underlying one accident to be the subject underlying another. And we in this way say that one accident is the subject of another; for example, we say that surfaces are subjects in which colors inhere. And powers can be subjects of habits in this way.

Reply to Obj. 3. Powers presuppose habits insofar as habits imply dispositions toward a nature, while powers imply relations to actions, and actions are subsequent to natures, since natures cause actions. But habits that have powers for their subject imply relations to action and not to the subject's nature. And so such habits are subsequent to such powers.

Or we may say that powers presuppose habits as the imperfect presupposes the perfect, and as potentiality presupposes actuality. For actuality by nature precedes potentiality, although potentiality precedes actuality in the order of coming to be and of time, as the *Metaphysics* says.[26]

Third Article

Can Powers of the Soul's Sensory Part Have Habits?

I proceed in this way to the third article: it seems that powers of the soul's sensory part cannot have any habit.

Obj. 1. Sense powers are like nutritive powers in being irrational parts of the soul. But we do not hold that the soul's nutritive powers have habits. Therefore, we ought not hold that powers of the soul's sensory part have any habit.

Obj. 2. Sensory parts are common to ourselves and irrational animals. But irrational animals have no habits, since they have no will, and we posit the will is the definition of habit, as I have said before.[27] Therefore, sense powers have no habits.

Obj. 3. The soul's habits consist of scientific knowledge and virtues. And virtue is related to the power of willing in the same way that scientific knowledge is related to the power of understanding. But sense powers have no scientific knowledge, since universals are the object of scientific knowledge, and sense powers cannot understand universals. Therefore, neither can the soul's sensory parts have virtuous habits.

On the contrary, the Philosopher says in the *Ethics* that "some virtues," namely, moderation and courage, "belong to the soul's irrational powers."[28]

I answer that we can consider sense powers in two ways: in one way, as they act at the instigation of nature; in the second way, as they act at the command of reason. Therefore, as they act at the instigation of nature, they are ordained to one thing, just as a nature is. And so, like the powers of nature, sense powers also lack habits, insofar as those powers act at the instigation of nature.

But sense powers, as they act at the command of reason, can then be ordained to various things. And so sense powers can have habits whereby the powers are well or ill disposed toward certain things.

Reply to Obj. 1. Nature does not constitute the soul's nutritive powers to obey the command of reason, and so they have no habits. But nature constitutes sense powers to obey the command of reason, and so they can have habits, for we call sense powers somehow rational insofar as they obey reason, as the *Ethics* says.[29]

Reply to Obj. 2. The sense powers of irrational animals do not act at the command of reason, but if irrational animals are left to themselves, their sense powers act at the instigation of nature. And so irrational animals have no habits ordained for actions. Nonetheless, irrational animals have dispositions like health and beauty, in relation to their nature.

But because human beings' reason disposes irrational animals by conditioning them to do things in this or that way, we can consequently in some way attribute habits to irrational animals. And so Augustine says in his *Octoginta trium quaestionum* that "we see the most savage beasts deterred by fear of pain from the greatest pleasures, and we call such animals tame and gentle when they have become so accustomed."[30] Nonetheless, this behavior lacks the character of habit with respect to using the will, since irrational animals do not possess such a power to use or not to use, and the power to will seems to belong to the nature of habit. And so, properly speaking, irrational animals cannot have any habits.

Reply to Obj. 3. Nature establishes that the will move sense appetites, as the *De anima* says.[31] But nature establishes that rational cognitive powers receive images from sense powers. And so it is more appropriate that habits inhere in appetitive sense powers than in powers of sense perception, since habits inhere in appetitive sense powers only insofar as those powers act at the command of reason.

And yet we may assume that habits also inhere in internal cognitive sense powers themselves, insofar as human beings become enabled to remember well or cogitate well or imagine well. And so also the Philosopher says in the *De memoria* that "practice does much for a good memory,"[32] since the command of reason moves even those powers to act.

And external powers of sense perception, such as seeing, hearing, and the like, are not the subjects of habits; rather, the disposition of the powers' nature ordains the powers for their appointed acts. Similarly, neither are bodily members the subjects of habits, and the powers that command the movements of bodily members, rather than the bodily members, have habits.

Fourth Article

Does the Intellect Itself Have Any Habits?

I proceed in this way to the fourth article: it seems that the intellect itself has no habits.

Obj. 1. Habits are conformed to actions, as I have said.[33] But the actions of human beings are common to the soul and to the body, as the *De anima* says.[34] Therefore, habits are also. But the intellect is not the actuality of the body, as the *De anima* says.[35] Therefore, the intellect is not the subject of any habit.

Obj. 2. Everything in something else is in it in the way in which the other exists. But something that is a form apart from matter is only actuality, while something composed of form and matter has potentiality along with actuality. Therefore, something that is at the same time potential and actual can exist only in something composed of matter and form, and not in something only a form. But the intellect is a form apart from matter. Therefore, only the composite of body and soul, and not the intellect, can have habits, which have potentiality along with actuality, in between both, as it were.

Obj. 3. Habits are "dispositions whereby persons are well or ill disposed toward something," as the *Metaphysics* says.[36] But bodily dispositions cause persons to be well or ill disposed toward intellectual acts, and so also the *De anima* says that "we perceive that human beings with soft flesh are mentally fit."[37] Therefore, cognitive habits inhere in powers that are the actuality of some part of the body, and not in the intellect, which is distinct from the body.

On the contrary, the Philosopher in the *Ethics* posits scientific knowledge and theoretical wisdom and understanding (i.e., the habit of principles) in the soul's very intellectual part.[38]

I answer that thinkers have held various opinions about cognitive habits. For example, those thinkers who held that human beings collectively have one and the same potential intellect were forced to hold that cognitive habits inhere in internal sense powers and not in the intellect itself. For human beings evidently have different cognitive habits, and so those different habits cannot be directly posited in something numerically one that is common to all human beings. And so, if there is numerically one potential intellect that belongs to human beings collectively, the habits of scientific knowledge, which differentiate human beings, could not inhere in that intellect as the habits' subject, but the habits of scientific knowledge will inhere in internal sense powers, which are distinct in each human being.

But this position, indeed first of all, is contrary to Aristotle's intent. For sense powers are evidently rational only because they share in reason and not because of their essence, as the *Ethics* says.[39] And the Philosopher posits intellectual virtues (i.e., theoretical wisdom, scientific knowledge, and understanding) in something essentially rational.[40] And so intellectual virtues inhere in the intellect itself and not in sense powers.

Aristotle also says expressly in the *De anima*[41] that the potential intellect "when it becomes each thing," that is, when it is brought to the actuality of each thing by the thing's intelligible form, "becomes actual in the same way in which we say that knowing is actual, and this indeed happens when the intellect can act on its own," namely, by contemplating. "Thus the intellect indeed has potentiality in some way even then, although not in the same way that it had potentiality before learning or discovering." Therefore, the potential intellect itself is the subject in which inhere the habits of scientific knowledge whereby the intellect is capable of contemplating even when it is not actually doing so.

Second, this position is also contrary to objective truth. For just as powers belong to the things to which their actions belong, so also habits belong to the things to which their actions belong. But acts of understanding and contemplating are the intellect's own acts. Therefore, the habits whereby the intellect contemplates likewise inhere in the proper sense in the intellect itself.

Reply to Obj. 1. As Simplicius relates in his commentary on the *Categories*,[42] some thinkers said that every habit belongs to the human composite, and none to the soul alone, since every action by human beings somehow belongs to the composite, as the Philosopher says in the *De anima*.[43] And this leads to the conclusion that the intellect has no habits, since the intellect is separate from the body.

But this argument has no force. For habits are not the dispositions of objects toward powers but rather the dispositions of powers toward objects. And so a habit needs to inhere in the very power that is the source of acts, and not in something that is related to such a power as its object.

And we say that understanding itself is common to the soul and the body only by reason of sense images, as the *De anima* says.[44] But sense images are evidently related to the potential intellect as objects, as the *De anima* says.[45] And so we conclude that intellectual habits chiefly regard the intellect itself and not sense images, which are common to the soul and the body. And so we need to say that the potential intellect is the subject in which intellectual habits inhere. For it belongs to something that has potentiality for many things to be the subject of habits, and such a potentiality belongs especially to the potential intellect. And so the potential intellect is the subject in which intellectual habits inhere.

Reply to Obj. 2. As potentiality for sensory existing befits bodily matter, so potentiality for intelligible existing befits the potential intellect. And so nothing prevents the potential intellect from having habits, which are in between pure potentiality and complete actuality.

Reply to Obj. 3. Because powers of sense perception internally provide the potential intellect with its proper object, so human beings are rendered fit to understand by the right disposition of those powers, and the right disposition of the body contributes to such a disposition. And so intellectual habits can be in those powers in a secondary way. But intellectual habits inhere chiefly in the potential intellect.

Fifth Article

Does the Will Have Any Habits?

I proceed in this way to the fifth article: it seems that the will has no habits.

Obj. 1. The habits in the intellect are intelligible forms, by means of which the intellect actually understands. But the will does not act by means of any forms. Therefore, the will is not the subject in which any habit inheres.

Obj. 2. Because the active intellect is an active power, we do not attribute any habit to that intellect, as we do to the potential intellect. But the will is especially an active power, since the will moves every other power to its own act, as I have said before.[46] Therefore, the will has no habits.

Obj. 3. Powers of nature have no habits, since those powers are by their nature determined to one thing. But the will is by its nature ordained to incline toward the good ordained by reason. Therefore, the will has no habits.

On the contrary, justice is a habit. But justice inheres in the will, for justice is "the habit whereby persons will and do what is just," as the *Ethics* says.[47] Therefore, the will is the subject in which habits inhere.

I answer that every power that can be ordained to act in different ways needs habits whereby it would be rightly disposed toward its acts. But the will, as a power of reason, can be ordained to act in different ways. And so we need to posit habits in the will, habits whereby the will would be rightly disposed toward its acts.

Also, the very nature of habits makes evident that they are chiefly related to the will, since they are "the means that persons use when they should will to act," as I have said before.[48]

Reply to Obj. 1. As the intellect has forms that are the likenesses of objects, so the will and every appetitive power need to have the means whereby the appetitive power tends toward its object, since the acts of appetitive powers are simply inclinations, as I have said before.[49] Therefore, powers need no characteristic to incline them toward the things to which the nature of the very powers adequately inclines them. But to achieve the end of human life, appetitive powers need to be inclined toward some fixed thing, since the powers' nature does not incline the powers to fixed things, and the powers are disposed toward many and various things. Therefore, the will and other appetitive powers need to have some characteristics to incline them, and we call these characteristics habits.

Reply to Obj. 2. The active intellect is purely active and in no way potential. But the will and every appetitive power cause movement when the powers themselves are moved, as the *De anima* says.[50] And so the active intellect and the will have different natures, since it belongs to something somehow potential to be the subject in which habits inhere.

Reply to Obj. 3. The will by its nature tends toward the good understood by reason. But because that good varies in many respects, habits are needed to incline the will to the good determined by reason, in order that actions more readily ensue.

Notes

1. Averroes, *In De anima* III, comm. 18.
2. On the types and order of qualities, see Q. 49, A. 2.
3. *Categories* 6. 9a1.
4. Q. 49, AA. 2–4.
5. Q. 49, A. 4.
6. Aristotle, *Ethics* II, 1. 1103b21–22.
7. *Super librum Praedictamentorum.* See *Commentaire sur les Categories d' Aristote,* ed. A. Pattin (Leiden: Brill, 1975), p. 319.
8. Alexander of Aphrodisias.
9. *Categories* 6. 8b36–37.
10. Ibid.
11. *Physics* VII, 3. 246b4–5.
12. *Categories* 6. 9a3.
13. Simplicius, *Super librum Praedictamentorum.* See ed. cit., pp. 319–21.
14. Cf. Q. 49, A. 2.
15. See ed. cit., pp. 319–20.
16. Ibid., p. 321.
17. Ibid.
18. Q. 49, A. 2, *ad* 1.
19. Q. 49, A. 2.
20. Q. 77, A. 1, *ad* 5.
21. *Ethics* I, 13. 1103a3–10.
22. Q. 49, AA. 2, 3.
23. 2 Pet. 1:4.
24. Q. 110, A. 4.
25. Q. 49, A. 4.
26. Aristotle, *Metaphysics* VI, 3. 1029a5–6. VIII, 8. 1049b4–12.
27. Q. 50, A. 1, *Obj. 1.* Q. 49, A. 3, "On the contrary."
28. *Ethics* III, 10 1117b23–24.
29. Aristotle, *Ethics* I, 13. 1102b13–14.
30. *Octoginta trium quaestionum* 36. PL 40:25.
31. Aristotle, *De anima* III, 11. 434a12–15.
32. *De memoria et reminiscentia* 2. 452a28–30.
33. Q. 50, A. 1.
34. Aristotle, *De anima* I, 1. 403a8–10.
35. Aristotle, *De anima* III, 4. 429a24–27.

36. Aristotle, *Metaphysics* IV, 20. 1022b10–12.
37. Aristotle, *De anima* II, 9. 421a26.
38. *Ethics* VI, 3. 1139b16.
39. Aristotle, *Ethics* I, 13. 1102b13–14.
40. See n. 37, supra.
41. *De anima* III, 4. 429b6–10.
42. See ed. cit., p. 330.
43. *De anima* I, 1. 403a8–10.
44. Aristotle, *De anima* I, 1. 403a5–10.
45. Aristotle, *De anima* III, 7. 431a14–17.
46. Q. 9, A. 1.
47. Aristotle, *Ethics* V, 1. 1129a7–11.
48. Q. 50, A. 1, *Obj. 1*. Q. 49, A. 3, "On the contrary."
49. Q. 6, A. 4.
50. Aristotle, *De anima* III, 10. 433b16.

Question 51

On the Causes of Habits, Regarding the Formation of Habits Themselves

[This question is divided into four articles, three of which are included here.]

First Article

Do Any Habits Spring from Nature?

I proceed in this way to the first article: it seems that no habits spring from nature.

Obj. 1. The utility of things that spring from nature is not subject to the will. But "habits are the means that persons use when they should will to act," as the Commentator says in his commentary on the *De anima*.[1] Therefore, habits do not spring from nature.

Obj. 2. Nature does not bring about by two causes what it can bring about by one cause. But the soul's powers spring from nature. Therefore, if the habits of the soul's powers were to spring from nature, the soul's habits and the soul's powers would be the same.

Obj. 3. Nature is not wanting in necessary things. But habits are necessary in order to act well, as I have said before.[2] Therefore, if any habits were to spring from nature, it seems that nature would not fail to produce every necessary habit. But this conclusion is evidently not the case. Therefore, habits do not spring from nature.

On the contrary, the *Ethics* posits understanding of principles with other habits,[3] and such understanding springs from nature. And so also we say that we understand first principles by nature.

I answer that things can be natural to something in two ways. In one way, by reason of the thing's specific nature; for example, human beings by reason of their nature are capable of laughter, and fire by reason of its nature moves upward. In the second way, by reason of the individual thing's nature; for example, Socrates and Plato by reason of their individual nature, by their own constitution, are sickly or healthy.

And we call things natural in two ways with respect to both their specific and their individual nature: in one way, in that entire things spring from nature; in the second way, in that things spring from nature in one respect and from an external source in another respect. For example, persons' entire health springs from nature if they restore themselves to health, but their health springs partially from nature and partially from an external source if medicine helps to restore them to health.

Therefore, if we are talking about habits as dispositions of subjects in relation to their forms or natures, habits may be natural in each of the aforementioned ways. For example, some dispositions from nature are requisite for the human species, and we do not find human beings to be without those dispositions. And such dispositions are natural by reason of the nature of our species. But because such dispositions enjoy a certain latitude, different human beings may possess different degrees of such dispositions, according to the nature of individual human beings. And such dispositions can spring either entirely from nature, or partially from nature and partially from an external source, as I have just said about those whom medical skills restore to health.

But habits that are dispositions toward action, habits whose subjects are the soul's powers, as I have said,[4] can indeed be natural both by reason of our specific nature and by reason of an individual human being's nature. Indeed natural by reason of our specific nature, insofar as habits belong to the soul itself, which, as the form of the body, is the source of our being human. And natural by reason of the nature of individuals, regarding their bodies, which are the source of their being material. And yet in neither way is it the case that human beings possess natural habits entirely from nature. Such indeed happens in the case of angels, since they have intelligible forms implanted in them by nature, and human souls do not, as I have said in the First Part.[5]

Therefore, human beings have some habits from nature, as habits that spring partially from nature and partially from an external source. Indeed, cognitive powers have such habits in one way, and appetitive powers in another. For cognitive powers can have natural habits inchoatively, both by reason of our specific nature and by reason of the nature of individual human beings. Indeed, by reason of our specific nature, regarding the soul itself, as, for example, we say that understanding principles is a natural habit. For it befits human beings by the very nature of their intellectual soul that they, when they know what a whole is, and what a part is, immediately know every whole to be greater than one of its parts. And the same is true in the case of other things. But human beings can know what a whole is, and what a part is, only by means of intelligible forms derived from sense images. And it is by this that the Philosopher at the end of the *Posterior Analytics* demonstrates that our knowledge of principles derives from the senses.[6] And there are some inchoatively natural cognitive habits by reason of the nature of individuals, insofar as the disposition of bodily organs render some human beings more fit than other human beings to understand well, since we need sense powers for intellectual activity.

And regarding the soul itself, appetitive powers have natural habits inchoatively only as to the source of the habits and not as to the very substance of the habits; for example, we call the principles of universal law "the seedbeds of virtues."[7] And this is so because the inclination of habits toward their own object, which inclination seems to be the beginning of habits, belongs to the very nature of powers and not to habits.

But regarding the body, there are appetitive habits inchoatively from nature by reason of the nature of individual human beings. For the bodily constitution of some human beings disposes them toward chastity or meekness or the like.

Reply to Obj. 1. This objection is valid about nature as contradistinguished from reason and will, but reason and will themselves belong to human nature.

Reply to Obj. 2. Nature can also add to powers things that nonetheless do not belong to the very powers. For example, it cannot belong to the very intellectual power of angels intrinsically to know everything, since such a power would need to be the actuality of everything, and being the actuality of everything belongs to God alone. For the means by which something is known needs to be an actual likeness of what is known. And so, if an angel's intellectual power were of its very self to know everything, then that power would be the likeness and actuality of everything. And so intelligible forms, which are the likenesses of the things understood, need to supplement the angels' intellectual power itself, since it is by sharing in God's wisdom and not by the angels' own essence that their intellects can actually be the things they understand. And so it is clear that some things that belong to natural habits may not belong to powers.

Reply to Obj. 3. Nature is not equally disposed to produce every different kind of habit, since nature can produce some habits and not others, as I have said.[8] And so it does not follow that all habits would be natural if some habits should be.

Second Article

Do Acts Produce Any Habits?

I proceed in this way to the second article: it seems that acts cannot produce any habits.

Obj. 1. Habits are qualities, as I have said before.[9] But every quality is produced in a subject, since subjects are what receive things. Therefore, since efficient causes as such emit something from themselves rather than receive anything, it seems that an efficient cause's own acts cannot produce any habits in the cause.

Obj. 2. The subjects in which qualities are produced, are altered regarding those qualities, as is evident in the case of things that are heated or cooled. But the things that cause the acts that produce qualities cause the changes related to the qualities, as is evident in the case of things that cause heating and cooling. Therefore, if something's own acts were to produce habits in the thing, then one and the same thing would cause change and undergo change, act and be acted upon. And that is impossible, as the *Physics* says.[10]

Obj. 3. Effects cannot be more excellent than their cause. But habits are more excellent than the acts that precede habits, and this is evidenced by the fact that habits render acts more excellent. Therefore, acts that precede habits cannot produce habits.

On the contrary, the Philosopher teaches in the *Ethics* that acts produce virtuous and vicious habits.[11]

I answer that there are sometimes in efficient causes only the active source of their acts; for example, there is in fire only the active source of generating heat. And such efficient causes' acts cannot produce habits in the causes. And this is the reason why things of nature cannot become accustomed or unaccustomed to anything, as the *Ethics* says.[12]

But we find that other efficient causes have active and passive sources of their acts, as is evident in the case of human acts. For example, appetitive powers produce their acts insofar as cognitive powers, by presenting objects, move appetitive powers, and besides, the power of the intellect, as it reasons about conclusions, has self-evident propositions as the active source of its acts. And so efficient causes by such acts can produce habits, not indeed regarding the acts' primary active source, but regarding the acts' source that, being itself moved, causes movement. For efficient causes' acts dispose whatever is acted upon and moved by something else, and so repeated acts produce characteristics in passive and moved powers, and we call such characteristics habits. For example, morally virtuous habits are produced in appetitive powers as reason so moves the powers, and habits of scientific knowledge are produced in the intellect as first principles so move the intellect.

Reply to Obj. 1. Efficient causes as such do not receive anything. But efficient causes, to the extent that other things move them to act, receive something from the things that move them. And habits are produced in this way.

Reply to Obj. 2. One and the same thing cannot in the same respect cause change and undergo change. But nothing prevents the same thing from causing change and undergoing change in different respects, as the *Physics* says.[13]

Reply to Obj. 3. Acts preceding habits, since the acts spring from an active source, spring from a more excellent source than the habits the acts produce. For example, reason itself is a more excellent source of right action than the morally virtuous habits that customary ways of acting produce in appetitive powers, and understanding principles is a more excellent source of knowledge than scientific knowledge of conclusions.

Third Article

Can One Act Produce a Habit?

I proceed in this way to the third article: it seems that one act can produce a habit.

Obj. 1. Demonstrations are acts of reason. But one demonstration produces scientific knowledge, and scientific knowledge is the habit of particular conclusions. Therefore, one act can produce a habit.

Obj. 2. As acts may increase by being repeated, so acts may increase by being expanded. But repeated acts produce habits. Therefore, one act, if greatly expanded, could also produce a habit.

Obj. 3. Health and sickness are habits. But one act may restore human beings to health. Therefore, one act can produce a habit.

On the contrary, the Philosopher says in the *Ethics* that "one swallow and one day do make the season of spring; so indeed one day and a short period of time do not make persons blessed and happy."[14] But "happiness is activity by completely virtuous habits," as the *Ethics* says.[15] Therefore, one act cannot produce virtuous habits or, by like reasoning, other habits.

I answer that acts produce habits as active sources move passive powers to act, as I have said before.[16] But in order that characteristics be produced in passive things, active things need to dominate what is passive. And so we perceive that fire does not immediately enkindle combustible material, since fire cannot immediately dominate the very material. Rather, fire little by little gets rid of the material's contrary dispositions, and so fire imprints its likeness on the material when it completely dominates the material.

And the active source that is reason cannot in one act completely dominate appetitive powers, since appetitive powers are disposed in different ways and toward different things. (But reason in one act judges that things should be sought in fixed ways and circumstances.) And so reason in one act does not so completely dominate appetitive powers that those powers, for the most part, strive for one and the same thing in accord with nature; rather, uniform striving in accord with nature belongs to virtuous habits. And so many acts, not one, produce virtuous habits.

And we need to note that there are two passive sources in cognitive powers: one, indeed, the potential intellect itself, and the other the intellect that Aristotle calls "passive," which is "particular reason," that is, the cognitive power accompanied by the powers of memory and imagination.[17]

With respect to the first passive source, therefore, the active source can by one act completely dominate the power of the passive source; for example, one self-evident proposition convinces the intellect to give firm assent to a conclusion, and a probable proposition indeed cannot do this. And so many acts of reason, also regarding the potential intellect, are needed to produce habits of probable knowledge, while single acts of reason, regarding the potential intellect, can produce habits of scientific knowledge.

But with respect to lower cognitive powers, the same acts need to be repeated over and over, in order that things be firmly impressed on memory. And so the Philosopher says in the *De memoria et reminiscentia* that "practice strengthens memory."[18]

And single acts can produce bodily dispositions if active sources happen to have great power; for example, strong medicine sometimes immediately brings about health.

Replies to the Objs. The foregoing makes clear the replies to the objections.

Notes

1. Averroes, *In De anima* III, comm. 18.
2. Q. 49, A. 4.
3. Aristotle, *Ethics* VI, 6. 1141a5–8.
4. Q. 50, A. 2.
5. Q. 55, A. 2. Q. 84, A. 3.
6. *Posterior Analytics* II, 15. 100a3.
7. Augustine, *De libero arbitrio* II, 10. PL 32:1256.
8. In the body of the article.
9. Q. 49, A. 1.
10. Aristotle, *Physics* VII, 1. 241b24–26.
11. *Ethics* II, 1. 1103a31–b2.

12. Aristotle, *Ethics* II, 1. 1103a19–26.
13. Aristotle, *Physics* VIII, 5. 257a31–33.
14. *Ethics* I, 7. 1098a18–20.
15. Aristotle, *Ethics* I, 7. 1098a16–17.
16. Q. 51, A. 2.
17. *De anima* III, 5. 430a24–25. Cf. ST I, Q. 78, A. 4.
18. *De memoria et reminiscentia* 1. 451a12–14.

Question 55

On Virtue, Regarding Its Essence

[This question is divided into four articles, one of which is included here.]

Fourth Article

Do We Appropriately Define Virtue?

I proceed in this way to the fourth article: it seems that the definition usually attributed to virtue, namely, "Virtue is a good characteristic of the mind, the characteristic by which we live rightly, of which no one makes wrong use, and which God works in us apart from any works of ours,"[1] is inappropriate.

Obj. 1. Virtue consists of the goodness of human beings, since virtue is "what makes its possessors good."[2] But goodness does not seem to be the same as good, just as whiteness is not the same as white. Therefore, it is inappropriate to say that virtue is a "good characteristic."

Obj. 2. No specific difference is more universal than its genus, since specific differences differentiate genera. But "good" is more universal than "characteristic," since "good" is convertible with "being." Therefore, we should not posit "good" in the definition of virtue as specifically differentiating "characteristic."

Obj. 3. Augustine says in his *De Trinitate*: "When we first encounter something that is not common to us and irrational animals, we encounter something that belongs to the mind."[3] But certain virtues belong even to the irrational parts of the soul, as the Philosopher says in the *Ethics*.[4] Therefore, not every virtue is a good characteristic "of the mind."

Obj. 4. Right order seems to belong to justice, and so the same things are right that we call just. But justice is one kind of virtue.

Therefore, when we define virtue as the characteristic "by which we live rightly," we inappropriately posit "rightly" in the definition.

Obj. 5. All who are proud about something make wrong use of it. But many people are proud about their virtue, for Augustine says in his rule that "pride lays ambush even for good works, in order to destroy them."[5] Therefore, it is false to say that "no one makes wrong use of virtue."

Obj. 6. Virtue makes human beings righteous. But Augustine comments on Jn. 14:12 ("He shall do greater things than these"): "He who created you apart from any work of yours, will not make you righteous apart from any work of yours."[6] Therefore, we inappropriately say that "God works" virtue "in us apart from any work of ours."

On the contrary stands the authority of Augustine, from whose words, and especially from those in his *De libero arbitrio*,[7] we compose the aforementioned definition.

I answer that this definition completely embraces the whole nature of virtue. For we compose the complete nature of anything from all of its causes. And the aforementioned definition includes all the causes of virtue. For when we speak of "good characteristic," we understand virtue's formal cause by its genus and specific difference (just as we understand the formal cause of anything), since "characteristic" is virtue's genus, and "good" its specific difference. Nonetheless, the definition would be more appropriate if we were to substitute "habit," which is the proximate genus of virtue, for "characteristic."

And although virtue has no matter out of which it is formed, just as other accidents do not, virtue has the matter with which it deals, and the matter in which it rests, namely, its subject. And the matter with which virtue deals is the object of a virtue. But since objects limit virtue to specific kinds of virtue, and we are here giving the definition of virtue in general, we could not posit such matter in the aforementioned definition. And so, when we say that virtue is a good characteristic "of the mind," we substitute virtue's subject for its material cause.

And action itself is the end of virtue, since virtues are habits related to action. But we should note that some habits related to action (e.g., vicious habits) are always directed to evil, and that some habits are sometimes directed to good and sometimes to evil (just as probable opinions are sometimes disposed toward truth and sometimes toward error), and that virtues are habits that are always disposed toward good. And so we say that virtues are the habits "by which we live rightly," in order to distinguish virtues from the habits that are always disposed toward evil. And we say that virtues are habits "of which no one makes wrong use," in order to distinguish virtues from the habits that are sometimes directed to good and sometimes to evil.

And the efficient cause of infused virtue, which is the virtue defined here, is God. And that is why the definition says: "which God works in us apart from any work of ours." But if we were to omit this clause, the rest of the definition will indeed be common to all virtues, both those acquired and those infused.

Reply to Obj. 1. Being is what first falls within the intellect's grasp, and so we predicate of everything that we comprehend, that it is being, and consequently one and good (which are convertible with being). And so we say that being-ness is being and one and good, and that oneness is being and one and good, and we speak likewise about goodness. But we do not so speak about particular forms, such as whiteness and health, since we do not comprehend under the aspect of white and healthy everything that we comprehend.

And yet we should consider that, as we call accidents and nonsubsistent forms beings because they are the reason why something exists, and not because they themselves possess existing, so also we call accidents and nonsubsistent forms good or one because they themselves are the reason why something is good or one, and indeed not because of any other goodness or unity. And so we call virtue good because virtue is the reason why something is good.

Reply to Obj. 2. The good that we posit in the definition of virtue is not good in general, which is convertible with being and exists in other things besides characteristics. Rather, the good we posit in the definition of virtue is the good of reason, as Denis says in his *De divinis nominibus* that "the good of the soul consists in being in accord with reason."[8]

Reply to Obj. 3. There can only be virtue in the irrational part of the soul inasmuch as that part shares in reason, as the *Ethics* says.[9] And so reason, or mind, is the special subject in which human virtue inheres.

Reply to Obj. 4. Justice has a special right order that concerns the external things involved in human intercourse, and these things constitute the special matter of justice, as I shall make clear later.[10] But the right order that implies a relation to the requisite human end and to God's law (which is the rule of the human will, as I have said before[11]) is common to every virtue.

Reply to Obj. 5. Persons can make wrong use of virtue as an object, as, for example, when they wrongly esteem it—when they despise it or are proud about it—but not as a source of action, namely, in such a way that virtuous acts are evil.

Reply to Obj. 6. God produces infused virtue in us without us being its efficient cause but not without us consenting to it. And it is in this way that we should understand the expression: "which God works in us apart from any work of ours." And God, with us as efficient causes, produces in us the things that we do, since he is at work in every will and nature.

Notes

1. Cf. Peter Lombard, *Sententiae* II, dist. 27, A. 2.
2. Aristotle, *Ethics* II, 6. 1106a15.
3. *De Trinitate* XII, 8. PL 42:1005.
4. *Ethics* III, 10. 1117b23.
5. *Epistola 211.* PL 33:960.
6. *Sermo ad populum 169.* PL 38:923.
7. *De libero arbitrio* II, 19. PL 32:1268.
8. *De divinis nominibus* 4. PG 3:733.
9. Aristotle, *Ethics* I, 13. 1102b13–14.
10. Q. 60, A. 2. II–II, Q. 58, A. 8.
11. Q. 19, A. 4.

Question 57

On Distinguishing Intellectual Virtues

[This question is divided into six articles, four of which are included here.]

Second Article

Are There Only Three Habits of the Theoretical Intellect, Namely, Theoretical Wisdom, Scientific Knowledge, and Understanding?

I proceed in this way to the second article: it seems that we inappropriately distinguish three virtues of the theoretical intellect, namely, theoretical wisdom, scientific knowledge, and understanding.

Obj. 1. We should not distinguish a species from a genus as if both were species of the same genus. But theoretical wisdom is one kind of scientific knowledge, as the *Ethics* says.[1] Therefore, in enumerating species of intellectual virtue, we should not distinguish theoretical wisdom from scientific knowledge.

Obj. 2. In distinguishing powers, habits, and acts, which we do by noting their objects, we regard differences chiefly by the objects' formal nature, as is evident from what I have said before.[2] Therefore, we should distinguish different habits by their formal objects and not by their material objects. But principles of demonstration ground our knowledge of conclusions. Therefore, we should not hold the understanding of principles to be a habit or virtue distinct from knowledge of conclusions.

Obj. 3. We call virtues that by their essence inhere in the rational part of the soul, intellectual virtues. But reason, even theoretical reason, draws conclusions by hypothetical syllogisms in the same way that it draws conclusions by categorical syllogisms. Therefore, just as we hold the scientific knowledge produced by a categorical syllogism to be a virtue of the theoretical intellect, so also should we hold the probable knowledge produced by a hypothetical syllogism to be such a virtue.

On the contrary, the Philosopher in the *Ethics* posits only three virtues of the theoretical intellect, namely, theoretical wisdom, scientific knowledge, and understanding.[3]

I answer that, as I have said before,[4] there are virtues of the intellect whereby it is made completely able to contemplate truth, since contemplating truth is its good act. And we can contemplate truth in two ways: in one way, as self-evident; in the second way, as known through something else. And self-evident truths stand as principles, and the intellect immediately perceives such truths. And so we call the habit that makes the intellect completely able to contemplate such truths, understanding, that is, the habit of principles.

And the intellect by rational inquiry and not immediately perceives the truths it knows through something else, and the truths so known stand as the ultimate conclusions of rational inquiry. And such truths can indeed be the ultimate conclusions of rational inquiry in two ways: in one way, as ultimate in one kind of knowledge; in the second way, as ultimate in regard to all human knowledge. But "truths subsequent in our knowledge are prior and more knowable in the order of nature," as the *Physics* says.[5] Therefore, what is last with respect to the whole of human knowledge is by nature first and most knowable. And such things constitute the object of theoretical wisdom, which contemplates the highest cause, as the *Metaphysics* says.[6] And so theoretical wisdom appropriately judges and integrates everything, since we can completely and comprehensively judge only by tracing things to their first cause.

And scientific knowledge makes the intellect completely able to contemplate truths that are ultimate in this or that kind of knowable thing. And so, as there are different kinds of knowable things, there are different habits of scientific knowledge, although there is only one theoretical wisdom.

Reply to Obj. 1. Theoretical wisdom is a scientific knowledge inasmuch as it possesses what is common to every scientific knowledge, namely, to demonstrate conclusions by principles. But in addition to what other kinds of scientific knowledge possess, theoretical wisdom has something special, namely, to judge everything, and to do so both regarding conclusions and regarding first principles. Therefore, theoretical wisdom is essentially a more perfect virtue than scientific knowledge.

Reply to Obj. 2. If one and the same act relates formal objects to powers or habits, we do not distinguish the habits or powers by their formal and material objects. For example, it belongs to the same power of sight to see color and to see light, which is the ground of seeing color and is seen at the same time as color itself. But we can contemplate principles of demonstration in themselves without contemplating conclusions. We can also at the same time contemplate principles and conclusions, as we draw the latter from the former. Therefore, contemplating principles in the latter way belongs to scientific knowledge, which contemplates conclusions as well as principles, but contemplating principles as such belongs to understanding.

And so, if one should consider the matter rightly, one does not distinguish these three virtues as co-equal with one another but in a certain order. (The same is true in the case of wholes with potentiality, one part of which is more perfect than another; for example, the rational soul is more perfect than the sensory soul, and the sensory soul is more perfect than the vegetative soul.) For scientific knowledge in such a way depends on understanding as more important than itself. And both scientific knowledge and understanding depend on theoretical wisdom as the most important, since theoretical wisdom includes both understanding and scientific knowledge, as theoretical wisdom evaluates the conclusions and principles of scientific knowledge.

Reply to Obj. 3. Virtuous habits are steadfastly disposed toward good and in no way disposed toward evil, as I have said before.[7] But the intellect's good is truth, and its evil is error. And so we call only habits whereby we always affirm truth and never error, intellectual virtues. On the contrary, probable opinion and hypothetical knowledge can partake of truth or error. And so probable opinion and hypothetical knowledge are not intellectual virtues, as the *Ethics* says.[8]

Third Article

Are Intellectual Habits That Are Skills Virtues?

I proceed in this way to the third article: it seems that skills are not intellectual virtues.

Obj. 1. Augustine says in his *De libero arbitrio* that "no one makes wrong use of virtue."[9] But some persons make wrong use of their skills; for example, craftsmen by means of knowledge of their craft do evil. Therefore, skills are not virtues.

Obj. 2. Virtues do not belong to virtues. But "virtues belong to skills," as the *Ethics* says.[10] Therefore, skills are not virtues.

Obj. 3. The skills proper to free persons excel the skills proper to manual workers. But as the skills proper to manual workers are practical, so the skills proper to free persons are theoretical. Therefore, skills, if they were to be intellectual virtues, would have to be reckoned among theoretical intellectual virtues.

On the contrary, the Philosopher maintains in the *Ethics* that skills are virtues, and yet he does not reckon them among the theoretical virtues, which he holds reside in the part of the soul that produces knowledge.[11]

I answer that skills are simply right reasoning about works to be produced. And yet the goodness of the works does not consist in any disposition of the human will but in the intrinsic goodness of the very works produced. For craftsmen as such deserve praise for the quality of the works they produce, and not for the disposition of the will with which they produce the works.

Thus skills, strictly speaking, are habits related to action. And yet skills have something in common with theoretical habits, since it also belongs to theoretical habits themselves how the things contemplated are disposed, and not how the human will is disposed toward the things contemplated. For example, it does not matter how the appetitive part of the soul disposes geometricians, whether they are happy or angry, provided they demonstrate truths, just as it does not matter how the will of craftsmen is disposed, as I have just said. And so skills are essentially virtues in the same way that theoretical habits are, namely, inasmuch as both produce works that are good only regarding the ability to produce works well, and not regarding the works' use, which is the special good that complementary virtues seek.

Reply to Obj. 1. If craftsmen produce works of poor quality, the works are not products of craftsmanship but, rather, contrary to craftsmanship. Just so, if persons knowingly lie, their words are not in accord with, but contrary to, their knowledge. And so, just as knowledge is always disposed toward good, as I have said,[12] so also are skills, and we accordingly call skills virtues. Skills nonetheless fall short of the complete character of virtue in this respect, since they do not cause their use to be good, and something else is necessary to make their use itself good, although there can be no good use of skills apart from the skills.

Reply to Obj. 2. In order that human beings use in a morally right way the skills that they possess, their will needs to be good, and moral virtue brings this about. Therefore, the Philosopher says that virtue, namely, moral virtue, belongs to skills, since particular moral virtues are necessary for the morally right use of skills. For example, justice, which makes the will rightly ordered, evidently inclines craftsmen to do conscientious work.

Reply to Obj. 3. Even in theoretical activities, certain kinds of works (e.g., the composition of syllogisms and proper statements, or the work of counting or measuring) are produced. And so we by analogy call any theoretical habits ordained for such works of reason skills. And we call these habits skills proper to free persons in order to distinguish such skills from those ordained for works produced by the body. (And works produced by the body are in a way works proper to slaves, since the body is like a slave in being subject to the soul, and human beings are free by reason of their soul.) And we without qualification call ways of knowing not ordained for any such work scientific ways of knowing and not skills. Nor need the character of skill be more appropriate for the skills proper to free persons than for the skills proper to manual workers if the former skills are more excellent than the latter.

Fourth Article

Is Practical Wisdom a Virtue That Differs from Skills?

I proceed in this way to the fourth article: it seems that practical wisdom is not a virtue that differs from skills.

Obj. 1. Skills are right reasoning about works. But different kinds of works do not cause things to lose their nature as skills, for very different works are the objects of different skills. Therefore, since practical wisdom is right reasoning about works, it seems that we should also call practical wisdom itself a skill.

Obj. 2. Practical wisdom has more in common with skills than theoretical habits do, for the objects of both practical wisdom and skills are "things that may be disposed otherwise than they are," as the *Ethics* says.[13] But we indeed call theoretical habits skills. Therefore, much more should we call practical wisdom a skill.

Obj. 3. "To deliberate well belongs to practical wisdom," as the *Ethics* says.[14] But some skills may involve deliberation, as the *Ethics* says[15]; for example, military skill and navigational skill and medical skill involve deliberation. Therefore, practical wisdom is indistinguishable from skill.

On the contrary, the Philosopher in the *Ethics* distinguishes practical wisdom from skill.[16]

I answer that we need to distinguish virtues where we find essentially different virtues. And I have said before that some habits have the character of virtue only because they cause the ability to produce good works, while other habits have the character of virtue both because they cause the ability to produce good works, and because they cause good use of the works.[17] And skills cause only the ability to produce good works, since skills are not concerned about what craftsmen desire. But practical wisdom not only causes the ability to produce good works but also causes good use of the works. For practical wisdom, as presupposing rightly ordered desire, is concerned about what persons desire.

And the reason for this difference is because skill is "right reasoning about things that we can make," while practical wisdom is "right reasoning about things that we can do." And making and doing are different, since as the *Metaphysics* says,[18] making (e.g., building, sawing, and the like) is an action that passes into external matter, while doing (e.g., seeing, willing, and the like) abides in the very cause that acts. Thus practical wisdom is ordained for such human acts, which consist in the exercise of powers and habits, in the same way that skills are ordained for external productions, since both practical wisdom and skills consist of right reasoning about the things to which each is related.

And the perfection and correctness of reasoning in theoretical things depends on the principles wherewith reason syllogizes, just as I have said before that scientific knowledge depends on, and presupposes, understanding, that is, the habit of principles.[19] But ends in regard to human acts are disposed like principles in regard to theoretical things, as the *Ethics* says.[20] And so, for practical wisdom (i.e., right reasoning about things that we can do), human beings need to be rightly disposed regarding ends, and right desire indeed results in such a disposition. And so, for practical wisdom, human beings need moral virtues, which produce right desire.

And the good of artifacts is the good proper to the works themselves, and not the good proper to the human will, and so skills do not presuppose right desire. And so we praise craftsmen who deliberately err, more than craftsmen who indeliberately do so. But it is more contrary to practical wisdom that persons should deliberately err than that they should indeliberately do so, since a rightly ordered will is essential to practical wisdom but not to skills.

Therefore, practical wisdom is evidently a virtue that differs from skills.

Reply to Obj. 1. All of the different kinds of artifacts exist outside human beings, and so the nature of virtue in the skills producing those objects does not differ. But practical wisdom is right reasoning about human acts themselves, and so the nature of its virtue differs from the virtue in skills, as I have said.[21]

Reply to Obj. 2. As to the subject in which practical wisdom inheres, and the matter with which it deals, practical wisdom has more in common with skills than theoretical habits do, for both practical wisdom and skills inhere in the part of the soul that has probable knowledge, and concerns things that may be disposed in different ways. But skills as virtues have more in common with theoretical habits than with practical wisdom, as is evident from what I have previously said.[22]

Reply to Obj. 3. Practical wisdom deliberates rightly about things belonging to the entire life of human beings and the final goal of human life. But in the case of some skills, there is deliberation about things that belong to the skills' own ends. And so we call some persons wise commanders or wise ship captains since they deliberate rightly about warfare or seafaring, but we do not call them absolutely wise. Rather, we call absolutely wise only those who deliberate rightly about things of benefit to the entire life of human beings.

Fifth Article

Is Practical Wisdom a Necessary Virtue for Human Beings?

I proceed in this way to the fifth article: it seems that practical wisdom is not a necessary virtue for human beings.

Obj. 1. As skills are ordained for things that we can make, and skills consist of right reasoning about such things, so practical wisdom is ordained for things that we can do, and we judge the lives of human beings accordingly. For practical wisdom consists of right reasoning about things that we can do, as the *Ethics* says.[23] But in the case of things that we can make, skills are necessary only in order that the things be made, and such skills are not necessary after the things have been made. Therefore, perhaps human beings also only need practical wisdom in order to become virtuous, and not to live rightly after they have become virtuous.

Obj. 2. "We deliberate rightly by practical wisdom," as the *Ethics* says.[24] But human beings can act both by their own good counsel and by another's. Therefore, in order to live rightly, human beings do not themselves need to possess practical wisdom, but it suffices for them to follow the counsels of wise persons.

Obj. 3. Intellectual virtues are the virtues by which we are enabled always to affirm truth and never error. But this does not seem to be so in the case of practical wisdom. For in deliberating about things to be done, it is human to err sometimes, since human things that we can do are things that may be disposed in different ways. And so the Book of Wisdom says: "The designs of mortals are fearful, and our plans for the future uncertain."[25] Therefore, it seems that we should not hold that practical wisdom is an intellectual virtue.

On the contrary, the Book of Wisdom, when speaking about God's wisdom, reckons practical wisdom with the other virtues necessary for human life: "She teaches moderation and practical wisdom, justice and fortitude, and nothing is more useful for human beings than these."[26]

I answer that practical wisdom is a virtue especially necessary for human living. For living rightly consists of acting rightly. And in order for persons to act rightly, they need not only to do certain things but also to do them in certain ways, namely, to act by right choice, not simply out of impulse or emotion. And since means are the object of choice, rectitude in choosing has two requirements, namely, the requisite end, and means suitably ordained for that end. And the virtues that perfect the soul's appetitive part, whose object is the human good and end, suitably dispose human beings to their requisite end. But for there to be things suitably ordained for the requisite end, a habit of reason needs directly to dispose human beings, since deliberating and choosing, which are concerned about means, are acts of reason. And so reason needs to have an intellectual virtue that perfects reason to be suitably disposed toward means. And this virtue is practical wisdom. And so practical wisdom is a necessary virtue for living rightly.

Reply to Obj. 1. We do not regard the good of a skill to be in craftsmen themselves but in the very products of their skill, since skills consist of right reasoning about things that we can make. For making, which passes into external matter, perfects the things made, not their maker, just as movements are the actuality of moveable things. And the objects of skills are the things that we can make. But we observe that the good of practical wisdom is in the human beings who act, whose perfection consists in the very acting, for practical wisdom is right reasoning about things that we can do, as I have said.[27] And so skills require that craftsmen make good products, and not that craftsmen act in a morally good way. And it would be more necessary that artifacts themselves work well (e.g., that knives cut well, or that saws saw well) if those things were to have active rather than passive properties, since artifacts have no mastery over their acts.

And so craftsmen themselves need their skills only in order to produce good artifacts and to preserve them, and not in order to live rightly. But human beings need practical wisdom both in order to become good and in order to live rightly.

Reply to Obj. 2. When human beings do good things because moved by another's counsel and not because of their own reason, their actions are not yet altogether perfect as regards their reason directing them, and their will moving them to act. And so, although they do good things, they nonetheless do not do them rightly in an absolute sense, and acting rightly in an absolute sense is living rightly.

Reply to Obj. 3. We understand truths of the practical intellect otherwise than we understand truths of the theoretical intellect, as the *Ethics* says.[28] For we understand truths of the theoretical intellect by the intellect's conformity to things. And because the intellect can be unerringly conformed to things only in the case of necessary things and not in the case of contingent things, so theoretical habits are intellectual virtues only in the case of necessary things and not in the case of contingent things.

But we understand truths of the practical intellect by the intellect's conformity to right desire. And such conformity indeed has no place in necessary things, which the human will does not cause, but only in the contingent things that we can bring about, whether these are interior things that we can do, or external things that we can make. And so we posit virtues of the practical intellect only about contingent things: skills, indeed, about things that we can make, and practical wisdom about things that we can do.

Notes

1. Aristotle, *Ethics* VI, 7. 1141a19, b2–3.
2. Q. 54, A. 2, *ad* 1. I, Q. 77, A. 3.
3. *Ethics* VI, 7. 1141a19.
4. Q. 57, A. 1.
5. Aristotle, *Physics* I, 1. 184a18–23.
6. Aristotle, *Metaphysics* I, 1. 981b28–29. I, 2. 982b9–10.
7. Q. 55, AA. 3,4.

8. Aristotle, *Ethics* VI, 3. 1139b17–18.

9. *De libero arbitrio* II, 18 and 19. PL 32:1267–68.

10. Aristotle, *Ethics* VI, 5. 1140b22–23.

11. *Ethics* VI, 3. 1139b16–18. VI, 7. 1141a19.

12. Q. 57, A. 2, *ad* 3.

13. Aristotle, *Ethics* VI, 6. 1140b35–1141a8.

14. Aristotle, *Ethics* VI, 5. 1140a25–28.

15. Aristotle, *Ethics* III, 3. 1112b3–6.

16. *Ethics* VI, 3. 1139b16–18. VI, 5. 1140b2–4, 21–22.

17. Q. 57, A. 1. Q. 56, A. 3.

18. Aristotle, *Metaphysics* VIII, 8. 1050a30–b2.

19. Q. 57, A. 2, *ad* 2.

20. Aristotle, *Ethics* VII, 8. 1151a16–20.

21. In the body of the article.

22. In the body of the article, and the preceding article.

23. Aristotle, *Ethics* VI, 5. 1140b3–4.

24. Aristotle, *Ethics* VI, 5. 1140a25–28. VI, 7. 1141b9–14. VI, 9. 1142b31–33.

25. Wis. 9:14.

26. Wis. 8:17.

27. In *Obj. 1* and the preceding article.

28. Aristotle, *Ethics* VI, 1. 1139a16–17.

Question 58

On Distinguishing Moral Virtues from Intellectual Virtues

[This question is divided into five articles, two of which are included here.]

Fourth Article

Can There Be Moral Virtue Without Intellectual Virtue?

I proceed in this way to the fourth article: it seems that there can be moral virtue without intellectual virtue.

Obj. 1. Moral virtues are "habits by way of nature, habits in accord with reason," as Cicero says.[1] But even though natures act in accord with a higher power of reason that moves them, that power of reason nevertheless does not need to be joined to natures in the same subjects, as is evidently the case in the things of nature, which are not endowed with knowledge. Therefore, human beings can possess moral virtues by way of nature, virtues inclining them to act in accord with reason, even when intellectual virtues do not perfect the nature of those human beings.

Obj. 2. Human beings attain perfect use of their reason through intellectual virtues. But human beings who do not exercise their reason very vigorously may sometimes be virtuous and acceptable to God. Therefore, it seems that there can be moral virtue without intellectual virtue.

Obj. 3. Moral virtues cause human beings to incline to act rightly. But some human beings have such inclinations from nature even without judgments of reason. Therefore, there can be moral virtues without intellectual virtue.

On the contrary, Gregory says in his *Moralia* that "other virtues, unless they should do according to practical wisdom the things they seek to do, cannot be virtues at all."[2] But practical wisdom is an intellectual virtue, as I have said before.[3] Therefore, there cannot be moral virtues without intellectual virtues.

I answer that there can indeed be moral virtues without certain intellectual virtues (e.g., theoretical wisdom, scientific knowledge, and skills) but not without understanding and practical wisdom. Indeed, there can be no moral virtue without practical wisdom, since moral virtues are habits related to choice, that is, habits that cause right choice. And two things are necessary in order that choice is right. First, that there is the requisite intention of the human end, and moral virtues, which incline the will toward the good befitting reason (which good is the requisite end) accomplishes this. Second, that human beings rightly understand the means to the requisite end, and human beings can only do so if their reason rightly deliberates, judges, and commands. And such activities of reason belong to practical wisdom and the virtues associated with it, as I have said.[4] And so there can be no moral virtue without practical wisdom.

And consequently, neither can there be moral virtues without understanding. For it is by understanding that we know the principles that we know by nature, both in regard to theoretical and practical things. And so, just as right reasoning in regard to theoretical things, since it springs from principles known by nature, presupposes understanding of the principles, so also does practical wisdom, which consists of right reasoning about things that we can do.

Reply to Obj. 1. Things devoid of reason have inclinations from nature apart from choice, and so such inclinations do not need reason. But the inclinations proper to moral virtues involve choice, and so, for moral virtues to be perfect, intellectual virtues need to perfect reason.

Reply to Obj. 2. Virtuous persons do not need to exercise reason vigorously regarding everything but only regarding the things to be done virtuously. And so every virtuous person exercises reason vigorously. And so even those who seem simple-minded, because they lack worldly cleverness, can be practically wise, and the Gospel of Matthew accordingly says: "Be wise as serpents and simple as doves."[5]

Reply to Obj. 3. An inclination from nature toward a virtuous good is a virtuous beginning but not completely virtuous. For the stronger such inclinations are, the more dangerous they may be, unless they are united to right reason, which makes right choices of means suitable for the requisite end. Similarly, the faster a blind horse runs, the more forcibly it collides with something, and the worse its injury. And so, although moral virtues do not consist of right reason (as Socrates said[6]), they are not only "in accord with right reason," since they incline toward what is in accord with right reason (as Platonists held[7]), but they need to be done "with right reason," as Aristotle says in the *Ethics*.[8]

Fifth Article

Can There Be Intellectual Virtue Without Moral Virtue?

I proceed in this way to the fifth article: it seems that there can be intellectual virtue without moral virtue.

Obj. 1. The perfection of something prior does not depend on the perfection of something subsequent. But acts of reason precede and move sense appetites. Therefore, intellectual virtues, which perfect the power of reason, do not depend on moral virtues, which perfect the will. Therefore, there can be intellectual virtue without moral virtue.

Obj. 2. Moral acts are the matter of practical wisdom, just as things that we can make are the matter of skills. But there can be skills apart from their proper matter; for example, there are smiths apart from iron. Therefore, there can likewise be practical wisdom apart from moral virtues, even though practical wisdom, of all intellectual virtues, seems to be the one most associated with moral virtues.

Obj. 3. "Practical wisdom is the virtue that deliberates rightly," as the *Ethics* says.[9] But many persons deliberate rightly who nonetheless lack moral virtues. Therefore, there can be practical wisdom apart from moral virtue.

On the contrary, willing to do evil is directly contrary to moral virtue, and not contrary to anything that can be apart from moral virtue. But "to do evil willingly" is contrary to practical wisdom, as the *Ethics* says.[10] Therefore, there cannot be practical wisdom apart from moral virtue.

I answer that there cannot be practical wisdom apart from moral virtue, but there can be other intellectual virtues apart from moral virtue. This is because practical wisdom consists of right reasoning about things that we can do, both in general and in particular, and actions involve particular things. And right reasoning requires the principles from which valid arguments spring. And valid arguments about particular things require both universal principles and particular principles. Regarding universal principles about things that we can do, the natural understanding of principles (whereby human beings know that they should not do anything evil), or even some practical scientific knowledge, indeed rightly disposes human beings. But this does not suffice to reason rightly about particular things. For emotions may in particular cases sometimes overwhelm those universal principles known by understanding or scientific knowledge. For example, when desire overwhelms individuals, the object of their desire seems good to them, although it is contrary to the universal judgment of reason.

And thus, as natural understanding or habits of scientific knowledge render human beings rightly disposed regarding universal principles, so, in order that human beings be rightly disposed regarding particular principles about things that they can do, that is, regarding ends, human beings need to be perfected by habits that cause right judgment about ends to be somehow inborn in them. And moral virtues accomplish this. For virtuous persons judge rightly about virtuous ends, since "persons perceive ends in the way in which persons are disposed," as the *Ethics* says.[11] And so human beings need to possess moral virtues in order to reason rightly about things that they can do, and such right reasoning is practical wisdom.

Reply to Obj. 1. Acts of reason understanding ends precede acts of the will willing the ends. But acts of the will willing ends precede acts of reasoning to choose means, and such reasoning belongs to practical wisdom. So also in the case of theoretical things, understanding principles is the foundation of syllogistic reasoning.

Reply to Obj. 2. We do not rightly or wrongly determine the principles of artifacts by the disposition of our will, as we do ends, which are the principles of moral acts. Rather, we determine the principles of artifacts only by the contemplation of our reason. And so skills do not need virtues that perfect the will, as practical wisdom does.

Reply to Obj. 3. Practical wisdom not only deliberates rightly but also judges rightly and commands rightly. And we can rightly judge and command only if we remove the impediment of emotions overwhelming the judgments and commands of practical wisdom. And moral virtues accomplish this.

Notes

1. *De oratore* II, 53.
2. *Moralia* XXII, 1. PL 76:212.
3. Q. 58, A. 3, *ad* 1. Q. 57, A. 5.
4. Q. 57, AA. 5, 6.
5. Mt. 10:16.
6. Cf. Aristotle, *Ethics* VI, 13. 1144b19–20.
7. Cf. St. Thomas, *Commentary on the Ethics*, lect. 11, n. 1283.
8. *Ethics* VI, 13. 1144b21.
9. Aristotle, *Ethics* VI, 5. 1140a25–28. VI, 7. 1141b10. VI, 9. 1142b31–32.
10. Aristotle, *Ethics* VI, 5. 1140b22–25.
11. Aristotle, *Ethics* III, 5. 1114a32–b1.

Question 59

On the Relation of Moral Virtues to Emotions

[This question is divided into five articles, three of which are included here.]

Second Article

Can Emotions Accompany Moral Virtues?

I proceed in this way to the second article: it seems that emotions cannot accompany moral virtues.

Obj. 1. The Philosopher says in the *Topics* that "a meek person is one who does not experience emotion, and a patient person is one who experiences emotion and remains steadfast."[1] And every moral virtue has the same character. Therefore, emotion does not accompany any moral virtue.

Obj. 2. Virtues are right dispositions of the soul, just as health is the right disposition of the body, as the *Physics* says.[2] And so "virtue seems to be the healthy state of the soul," as Cicero says in his *Tusculanae disputationes*.[3] But we call the soul's emotions "diseases of the soul," as Cicero says in the same work,[4] and health is incompatible with disease. Therefore, neither are virtues compatible with emotions of the soul.

Obj. 3. Moral virtues need the perfect exercise of reason even in regard to particulars. But emotions prevent such exercise, for the Philosopher says in the *Ethics* that "pleasures overwhelm the judgments of practical wisdom,"[5] and Sallust says in his *Bellum Catilinae* that "the mind does not easily perceive truth when they," namely, the soul's emotions, "interfere."[6] Therefore, emotions do not accompany moral virtues.

On the contrary, Augustine says in *The City of God*: "If the will is wicked, it will have those wicked movements," namely, wicked emotions, "and if the will is rightly ordered, emotions will be both blameless and praiseworthy."[7] But moral virtues exclude nothing praiseworthy. Therefore, moral virtues do not exclude emotions and can coexist with the very emotions.

I answer that the Stoics and Aristotelians disagreed about this matter, as Augustine relates in *The City of God.*[8] For the Stoics held that the soul's emotions cannot exist in a wise or virtuous person. On the other hand, the Aristotelians, whose school Aristotle founded, held that emotions can coexist along with moral virtues, but only if kept to a mean, as Augustine says in *The City of God.*[9]

And as Augustine says in the same place, the Stoics and the Aristotelians differ more in words than in their opinions. For the Stoics did not distinguish between the intellectual appetite (which is the will) and the sense appetites (which are divided into irascible and concupiscible appetites). Consequently, the Stoics, unlike the Aristotelians, did not distinguish the soul's emotions from other human affections, in that the soul's emotions are movements of sense appetites, and other affections (which are not emotions of the soul) are movements of the intellectual appetite that we call the will. Rather, the Stoics distinguished emotions from other affections only in that they called emotions any affections contrary to reason. And wise or virtuous persons cannot have any such affections if the affections are deliberately caused. But virtuous persons may happen to have such affections if the affections should arise suddenly. The latter is the case because, as Augustine relates the words of Aulus Gellius: "It is not in our power whether the mental images we call fancies, at times befall our soul. And such images, when terrifying things cause them, necessarily move wise persons' souls, so that their souls for a short while either quake with fear or are constrained by melancholy, since these emotions block the judgments of reason. And yet wise persons neither approve of such emotions nor consent to them."[10]

Therefore, if we, like the Stoics, should call emotions inordinate affections, emotions cannot exist in virtuous persons in such a way that they consent to the emotions after deliberating. But if we should call emotions any movements of sense appetites, then emotions as ordained by reason can exist in virtuous persons. And so Aristotle says in the *Ethics* that "some inaccurately define virtues as emotionless and restful states, since they do not qualify their statement."[11] Rather, they should say that virtues are states of repose from emotions "as and when emotions are inappropriate."

Reply to Obj. 1. The Philosopher introduces this example, as he introduces many other examples in his works on logic, as the opinion of others and not as his own opinion. And it was the opinion of the Stoics that emotions would not accompany virtues. And the Philosopher in the *Ethics* rejects this opinion, saying that virtues are not emotionless states.[12]

We can nonetheless say that we should understand as an inordinate emotion the emotion that the statement says a meek person does not experience.

Reply to Obj. 2. This argument and all like arguments that Cicero introduces in his *Tusculanae disputationes* to this effect are valid about emotions insofar as emotions signify inordinate affections.

Reply to Obj. 3. If emotions blocking judgments of reason prevail on the soul to consent to the emotions, the emotions prevent deliberation and judgment by reason. But if emotions should result from judgments of reason, as when commanded by reason, the emotions help to execute the commands of reason.

Fourth Article

Are Emotions the Object of Every Moral Virtue?

I proceed in this way to the fourth article: it seems that emotions are the object of every moral virtue.

Obj. 1. The Philosopher says in the *Ethics* that "moral virtues concern joys and sorrows."[13] But joy and sorrow are emotions, as I have said before.[14] Therefore, emotions are the object of every moral virtue.

Obj. 2. The subject in which moral virtues inhere, shares in reason, as the *Ethics* says.[15] But the part of the soul that shares in reason, is the subject in which emotions inhere, as I have said before.[16] Therefore, emotions are the object of every moral virtue.

Obj. 3. We find some emotion in every moral virtue. Therefore, either emotions are the object of every moral virtue or of none. But emotions are the object of some moral virtues, such as courage and moderation, as the *Ethics* says.[17] Therefore, emotions are the object of every moral virtue.

On the contrary, as the *Ethics* says, emotions are not the object of justice, and justice is a moral virtue.[18]

I answer that moral virtues perfect the will by ordering the will itself to the good of reason. But the good of reason consists of what reason controls and orders. And so everything that reason can order and control can be the object of moral virtues. But reason orders both the emotions of sense appetites and the actions of the intellectual appetite, that is, the will, and emotions do not inhere in the will, as I have said before.[19] And so emotions are not the object of every moral virtue. Rather, emotions are the object of some moral virtues, and actions of the will the object of other moral virtues.

Reply to Obj. 1. Some moral virtues concern joys and sorrows as the consequences of the virtues' own acts and not as the virtues' own matter. For every virtuous person is delighted in virtuous acts and is saddened at the contrary. And so the Philosopher adds after the cited words: "If acts and emotions are the object of virtues, and joy or sorrow results from every emotion and every act, then virtues will concern joys and sorrow," namely, as consequences.[20]

Reply to Obj. 2. Not only do sense appetites, in which emotions inhere, share in reason, but the will, in which emotions do not inhere, also does, as I have said.[21]

Reply to Obj. 3. Some virtues have emotions as their own matter, but other virtues do not. And so not every virtue has the same character, as I shall show later.[22]

Fifth Article

Can There Be Any Moral Virtue Apart from Emotion?

I proceed in this way to the fifth article: it seems that there can be moral virtue apart from emotion.

Obj. 1. The more moral virtues overcome emotions, the more perfect moral virtues are. Therefore, moral virtues in their most perfect existence are completely emotionless.

Obj. 2. Everything is perfect when it is removed from its contrary and from anything that tends toward its contrary. But emotions tend toward sin, and sin is contrary to virtue. And so the Letter to the Romans speaks about "sinners' emotions."[23] Therefore, perfect virtue is completely emotionless.

Obj. 3. Virtue conforms us to God, as Augustine makes evident in his *De moribus Ecclesiae*.[24] But God does everything without emotion. Therefore, virtues are most perfect when they are emotionless.

On the contrary, "every just person rejoices in just deeds," as the *Ethics* says.[25] But joy is an emotion. Therefore, there can be no justice without emotion. And still less can there be any other virtue without emotion.

I answer that if we should call emotions inordinate affections, as the Stoics did, then virtue is obviously perfect when emotion is absent.

But if we should call emotions all the movements of sense appetites, then moral virtues with emotions as their object, as their special matter, evidently cannot exist without emotions. This is so because such moral virtues, if they were to exist without emotions, would consequently cause sense appetites to be completely inactive, and it is not part of virtues that things subject to reason be devoid of their own acts. Rather, it is part of virtues that things subject to reason, by performing their own acts, execute the commands of reason. And so, as virtues ordain bodily members for the members' requisite external acts, so virtues ordain sense appetites for the appetites' own ordained movements.

And moral virtues with actions of the will rather than emotions as their object can exist without emotions (and justice is such a virtue), because these virtues direct the will to its own acts, and its own acts do not consist of emotions. But joy, at least the joy inhering in the will, nonetheless results from just acts, and the joy inhering in the will is not an emotion. And when perfect justice multiplies this joy, the joy will redound to sense appetites, since lower powers accompany the movements of higher powers, as I have said before.[26] And so, by reason of such an overflow, the more virtues shall be perfect, the more emotion they cause.

Reply to Obj. 1. Virtues overcome inordinate emotions but cause controlled emotions.

Reply to Obj. 2. Emotions lead to sin if they are inordinate, but they do not if they are controlled.

Reply to Obj. 3. We consider the good in anything by the state of the thing's nature. But God and angels have no sense appetites, as human beings do. And so God and angels have good actions completely apart from any emotion, just as they act apart from any body, while emotions accompany the good actions of human beings, just as their bodies assist their actions.

Notes

1. *Topics* IV, 5. 125b22–24.
2. Aristotle, *Physics* VII, 3. 246b2–5.
3. *Tusculanae disputationes* IV, 13.
4. *Tusculanae disputationes* IV, 10.
5. *Ethics* VI, 5. 1140b12–21.
6. *Bellum Catilinae* 51.
7. *The City of God* XIV, 6 PL 41:409.
8. *The City of God* IX, 4. PL 41:258.
9. Ibid.
10. *The City of God* IX, 4. PL 41:259.
11. *Ethics* II, 3. 1104b24–28.
12. Ibid.
13. *Ethics* II, 3. 1104b8–9.
14. Q. 23, A. 4. Q. 31, A. 1. Q. 35, AA. 1, 2.
15. Aristotle, *Ethics* I, 13. 1103a1–3.
16. Q. 22, A. 3.
17. Aristotle, *Ethics* III, 6. 1115a6–7. III, 10. 1117b25–27.
18. Aristotle, *Ethics* V, 1-3. 1129a4–1131a29.
19. Q. 22, A. 3.
20. *Ethics* II, 3. 1104b13–16.
21. In the body of the article.
22. Q. 60, A. 2.
23. Rom. 7:5.
24. *De moribus Ecclesiae Catholicae et Manichaeorum* 6. PL 32:1315, 1319.
25. Aristotle, *Ethics* I, 8. 1099a17–18.
26. Q. 17, A. 7. Q. 24, A. 3.

Question 61

On the Cardinal Virtues

[This question is divided into five articles, one of which is included here.]

Second Article

Are There Four Cardinal Virtues?

I proceed in this way to the second article: it seems that there are not four cardinal virtues.

Obj. 1. Practical wisdom directs other moral virtues, as is evident from what I have said before.[1] But what directs other things is more important. Therefore, practical wisdom alone is the chief virtue.

Obj. 2. The chief virtues are in some respect moral virtues. But practical reason and right desire dispose us for moral actions, as the *Ethics* says.[2] Therefore, there are only two cardinal virtues.

Obj. 3. Even among other than cardinal virtues, one is more important than another. But in order to call a virtue chief, it need be chief only with respect to some virtues and not with respect to every virtue. Therefore, it seems that there are many more chief virtues.

On the contrary, Gregory says in his *Moralia*: "The whole structure of good action is founded on four virtues."[3]

I answer that we can understand the number of things either by their formal principles or by the subjects in which they inhere, and we by both ways of understanding find that there are four cardinal virtues. For the formal source of the virtues about which we are currently speaking is the good of reason. And we can indeed consider the good of reason in two ways. In one way, insofar as the good of reason consists in the very contemplation of reason, and then there will be one chief virtue, the virtue that we call practical wisdom.

In the second way, we can consider the good of reason as we

impose the ordinations of reason on things. And the latter way concerns either actions, and then there is the virtue of justice, or emotions, and then there need to be two virtues. For we need to impose ordinations of reason on emotions because emotions resist reason. And emotions can indeed resist reason in two ways. In one way, as emotions incite us to act contrary to reason, and so we need to control our emotions, and we call such control of emotions the virtue of moderation. In the second way, as emotions keep us from doing what reason dictates (as, e.g., fear of danger or of work does), and so human beings need to be strengthened regarding what is proper to reason, so as not to yield to their emotions, and we call this strength of character the virtue of courage.

We likewise find the same number of cardinal virtues by considering the subjects in which they inhere. For we find that the virtues about which we are currently speaking inhere in four subjects, namely, one that essentially belongs to reason (the one that practical wisdom perfects) and three that share in reason. One of the latter is the will, which is the subject in which the virtue of justice inheres, the second is the concupiscible appetite, which is the subject in which the virtue of moderation inheres, and the third is the irascible appetite, which is the subject in which the virtue of courage inheres.

Reply to Obj. 1. Practical wisdom is without qualification the most important of all moral virtues. But we hold each of the other cardinal virtues to be chief in its own genus.

Reply to Obj. 2. Virtues inhere in three subjects that share in reason, as I have said.[4]

Reply to Obj. 3. We trace every other moral virtue, some of which are more important than others, to the aforementioned cardinal virtues, both with respect to the subjects in which the other virtues inhere and with respect to their formal character.

Notes

1. Q. 58, A. 4.
2. Aristotle, *Ethics* VI, 2. 1139a24–27.
3. *Moralia* II, 49. PL 75:592.
4. In the body of the article.

Question 63

On the Causes of Virtues

[This question is divided into four articles, two of which are included here.]

First Article

Are Virtues in Us by Nature?

I proceed in this way to the first article: it seems that virtues are in us by nature.

Obj. 1. Damascene says in his work: "Virtues are from nature, and they are equally in every person."[1] And Anthony says in a sermon to monks: "It is wickedness if the will should transform nature; it is virtue if the will should observe the condition of nature."[2] And a gloss on the Gospel of Matthew 4:23 ("Jesus went about," etc.) says: "He teaches natural virtues, namely, chastity, justice, humility, which human beings possess by nature."[3]

Obj. 2. Virtuous good consists in being in accord with reason, as is evident from what I have said.[4] But everything in accord with reason is natural for human beings, since the nature of human beings consists of reason. Therefore, virtues are in human beings by nature.

Obj. 3. We say that things innate in us are natural to us. But virtues are innate in some persons, for the Book of Job says: "Mercy increased in me from infancy and is in me from the day I sprang from the womb."[5] Therefore, virtues are in human beings by nature.

On the contrary, things in human beings by nature are common to them and not taken away by sin, since even devils retain things that are good by nature, as Denis says in his *De divinis nominibus*.[6] But virtues are not in every human being, and sin casts virtues out. Therefore, virtues are not in human beings by nature.

I answer that some thinkers (e.g., those who held the theory of latent forms[7]) said that material forms are entirely produced from within. And others (e.g., those who held that external causes produce material forms[8]) said that material forms are entirely produced from without. Still others said that material forms derive partially from within, namely, inasmuch as the forms preexist potentially in matter, and partially from without, namely, inasmuch as we trace the forms to acts by efficient causes.

So also, indeed, did some hold that scientific knowledge and virtues are entirely produced from within, namely, in such a way that all virtues and scientific knowledge preexist in the soul by nature. And they held that training and exercise take away the hindrances to scientific knowledge and virtues that the burden of the body brings to the soul, just as polishing iron brightens it. And this was the view of the Platonists.[9] And others, like Avicenna,[10] said that scientific knowledge and virtues are entirely produced from without, that is, by the causal action of intelligent substances. Still others said that scientific knowledge and virtues are in us by nature as capacities and not by way of perfections, as the Philosopher says in the *Ethics*.[11] And the latter view is more correct.

And to show this, we need to consider that we call something natural to human beings in two ways: in one way, by human beings' specific nature; in the second way, by human beings' individual nature. And each thing belongs to a species by reason of its form, and each thing is individuated by its matter. And the form of human beings is the rational soul, and the matter of human beings is the body. Therefore, what befits human beings by reason of their rational soul is natural to them by reason of their species, and what is natural to them by the particular composition of their body is natural to them by reason of their individual nature. For what is specifically natural to human beings regarding their body is in some way related to the soul, namely, inasmuch as such a body is proportioned to such a soul.

And virtues are in both ways somehow inchoatively natural to human beings. Virtues are indeed natural to human beings by their specific nature inasmuch as their reason by nature has knowledge of some principles, both about things that we can know and about things to be done, and these principles are the seeds of intellectual and moral virtues. Virtues are also natural to human beings by their specific nature inasmuch as the will has a natural desire for the good that is in accord with reason. And virtue is natural to human beings by their individual nature inasmuch as the body's disposition better or worse disposes individuals toward certain virtues. This happens inasmuch as sense powers are actualities of certain parts of the body, and the parts' disposition helps or hinders those powers in their acts. And so the parts' disposition helps or hinders the powers of reason, which those sense powers serve. And so one human being has a natural aptitude for scientific knowledge, another a natural aptitude for courage, another a natural aptitude for moderation. And we possess both intellectual and moral virtues in these ways by reason of certain inchoative aptitudes.

But we do not completely possess these virtues from nature. For natures are determined to one and the same course of action, and one and the same course of action does not bring these virtues to perfection. Rather, virtues are perfected in different ways, according to the different things with which the virtues deal, and according to different circumstances.

Thus we have virtues from nature potentially and inchoatively and incompletely. (The theological virtues, which are entirely produced from without, are an exception.)

Reply to the Objs. The foregoing makes clear the response to the objections. For the arguments of the first two objections are valid insofar as we, as rational, have seeds of virtue from nature. And the argument of the third objection is valid insofar as, by the natural disposition of the body that persons have innately, one person has the aptitude to be compassionate, another person the aptitude to live moderately, another person the aptitude for some other virtue.

Second Article

Does Repetition of Acts Produce Virtues in Us?

I proceed in this way to the second article: it seems that repetition of acts cannot produce any virtue in us.

Obj. 1. A gloss of Augustine on the statement of Rom. 14:23,

"Everything not of faith is sin," says: "The whole life of unbelievers is sin, and nothing is good without the supreme good. Where knowledge of the truth is lacking, virtue is counterfeit even in the best moral conduct."[12] But we cannot acquire faith by works; rather, it is God who produces faith in us, as the Letter to the Ephesians says: "By his favor, you are saved through faith."[13] Therefore, we cannot acquire any virtue by repetition of acts.

Obj. 2. Sin, since it is contrary to virtue, is incompatible with virtue. But human beings can avoid sin only through God's grace, as the Book of Wisdom says: "I learned that I could in no other way be moderate than if God should bestow the gift."[14] Therefore, only God's gift and not our repetition of acts can produce virtues in us.

Obj. 3. Acts that lead to virtue lack the perfection of virtue. But effects cannot be more perfect than their cause. Therefore, antecedent acts cannot produce any virtue.

On the contrary, Denis says in his *De divinis nominibus* that good is more powerful than evil.[15] But evil acts produce vicious habits. Therefore, much more can good acts produce virtuous habits.

I answer that I have spoken before in a general way about acts producing habits.[16] And we now need to note specifically regarding virtues that the virtues of human beings perfect the very human beings in goodness, as I have said before.[17] And the nature of good consists in "manner, kind, and rank," as Augustine says in his *De natura boni,*[18] or of "number, weight, and measure," as the Book of Wisdom says.[19] Therefore, we need to assess the good of human beings by some norm. And that norm is indeed twofold, namely, human reason and God's law, as I have said before.[20] And since God's law is a higher norm, so his law governs more things than human reason does. Consequently, God's law also governs whatever human reason governs, but the converse is not true.

Therefore, human acts, insofar as they spring from reason, under whose power and rule the good measured by the norm of human reason consists, can produce virtues ordained for that good. But human acts, whose source is reason, cannot produce virtues that dispose human beings for the good measured by God's law and not by human reason; rather, only God's action can produce such virtues in us. And so Augustine, when defining the latter kind of virtues, includes the following clause: "which God works in us apart from our action."[21]

Reply to Obj. 1. And also regarding the latter virtues, the argument of the first objection is valid.

Reply to Obj. 2. Divinely infused virtues, especially if considered in their perfection, are incompatible with any mortal sin. But humanly acquired virtues may be compatible with sinful, even mortally sinful, acts. For the exercise of habits that we possess is subject to our will, as I have said before,[22] and one sinful act does not destroy the habits of acquired virtues, since habits, not acts, are directly contrary to habits. And so, although human beings cannot without grace avoid mortal sin, so as never to sin mortally, they are nonetheless not prevented from acquiring virtuous habits, whereby they may abstain for the most part from evil deeds and especially from deeds very contrary to reason.

There are also some mortal sins that human beings can in no way avoid without grace, namely, sins directly contrary to the theological virtues, which we possess by the gift of grace. I shall, however, clarify this matter more fully later.[23]

Reply to Obj. 3. Some seeds or sources of acquired virtues preexist in us by nature, as I have said before.[24] And these sources are indeed more excellent than the virtues acquired by the sources' power. For example, understanding of theoretical principles is more excellent than scientific knowledge of conclusions, and the correctness of reason from nature is more excellent than the correction of appetites caused by appetites sharing in reason. And such correction indeed belongs to moral virtues. Therefore, human acts, since they spring from higher sources, can produce acquired human virtues.

Notes

1. *De fide orthodoxa* III, 14. PG 94:1045.
2. St. Anthony (A.D. c. 250–356) is considered the father of monasticism. The quotation is from St. Athanasius, *Vita sancti Antonii* 20. PG 26:873.
3. *Glossa ordinaria.* PL 114:88.
4. Q. 55, A. 4, *ad* 2.
5. Job 31:18.
6. *De divinis nominibus* 4. PG 3:725.
7. Anaxagoras.

8. Plato, *Phaedo* 49. 100B–101E. *Timaeus* 18. 50E. Avicenna, *Metaphysics*, tract. 9, chap. 5.
9. Cf. Plato, *Meno* 15. 81C.
10. *De anima*, part 5, chap. 5.
11. *Ethics* II, 1. 1103a25–26.
12. *Glossa ordinaria*. PL 114:516.
13. Eph. 2:8.
14. Wis. 8:21.
15. *De divinis nominibus* 4. PG 3:717.
16. Q. 51, AA. 2, 3.
17. Q. 55, AA. 3, 4.
18. *De natura boni* 3. PL 42:553.
19. Wis. 11:21.
20. Q. 19, AA. 3, 4.
21. *De libero arbitrio* II, 19. PL 32:1268.
22. Q. 49, A. 3, in the section "On the contrary."
23. Q. 109, A. 4.
24. Q. 63, A. 1. Q. 51, A. 1.

Question 64

On the Mean of Virtues

[This question is divided into four articles, one of which is included here.]

Second Article

Is the Mean of Moral Virtues a Mean of Things or of Reason?

I proceed in this way to the second article: it seems that the mean of moral virtues is a mean of things and not of reason.

Obj. 1. The good of moral virtues consists in the mean. But good exists in things themselves, as the *Metaphysics* says.[1] Therefore, the mean of moral virtues is a mean of things.

Obj. 2. Reason is the power of understanding. But moral virtues consist in the mean of actions and emotions rather than the mean of understandings. Therefore, the mean of moral virtues is a mean of things and not of reason.

Obj. 3. The means that we understand by arithmetic and geometrical proportions are the means of things. But such is the mean of justice, as the *Ethics* says.[2] Therefore, the mean of moral virtues is a mean of things and not of reason.

On the contrary, the Philosopher says in the *Ethics* that "moral virtues, which are determined by reason, consist of the mean in relation to us."[3]

I answer that we can understand the mean of reason in two ways. In one way, as the mean exists in acts of reason themselves, as if the very acts of reason were brought to a mean. And in this sense, the mean of moral virtues is not a mean of reason, since moral virtues perfect acts of the will and not acts of reason. In the second way, we can say that the mean of reason is the mean that reason imposes on some matter. And then every mean of moral virtues is a mean of reason, since we say that moral virtues consist in the mean by conforming to right reason, as I have said.[4]

But the mean of reason may also sometimes be a mean in things, and then, as in the case of justice, the mean of moral virtue needs to be a mean in things. And the mean of reason is sometimes not a mean in things, and then we understand the mean in relation to ourselves, and such is the mean in the case of every moral virtue other than justice. And justice is different because justice concerns actions, which consist in external things, and we need absolutely and as such to establish what is right about external things, as I have said before.[5] And so the mean of reason in the case of justice is the same as the mean of things, namely, in that justice renders to each person what is due to that person, neither more nor less. But other moral virtues concern internal emotions, about which we cannot in one and the same way establish what is right, since human beings are disposed toward emotions in various ways. And so we need to establish the right order of reason in emotions in relation to ourselves, whom emotions affect.

Reply to the Objs. And the foregoing makes clear the answer to the objections. The arguments of the first two objections are valid about the mean of reason, namely, the mean found in the acts of reason themselves. And the argument of the third objection is valid about the mean of justice.

Notes

1. Aristotle, *Metaphysics* V, 3. 1027b26–29.
2. Aristotle, *Ethics* V, 4. 1132a2–7.
3. *Ethics* II, 6. 1106b36–1107a2.
4. Q. 64, A. 1.
5. Q. 60, A. 2.

Question 65

On the Connection between Virtues

[This question is divided into five articles, two of which are included here.]

First Article

Are Moral Virtues Interconnected?

I proceed in this way to the first article: it seems that moral virtues are not necessarily connected.

Obj. 1. The practice of acts sometimes produces moral virtues, as the *Ethics* proves.[1] But human beings become practiced in the acts of one virtue without becoming practiced in the acts of another virtue. Therefore, we can possess one moral virtue without possessing another.

Obj. 2. Magnificence[2] and high-mindedness are particular moral virtues. But persons can possess other moral virtues without possessing magnificence and high-mindedness. For the Philosopher says in the *Ethics* that "the poor cannot be magnificent,"[3] although they possess other virtues, and that "one who deserves little honor and so esteems his worth, is moderate but not high-minded."[4] Therefore, moral virtues are not connected.

Obj. 3. As moral virtues perfect the soul's will, so intellectual virtues perfect the soul's intellect. But intellectual virtues are not connected, since persons can possess one kind of scientific knowledge without possessing another kind. Therefore, moral virtues are also not connected.

Obj. 4. If moral virtues are connected, this is only because they are linked to practical wisdom. But being linked to practical wisdom does not suffice to link moral virtues to one another. For it seems that persons can be wise about things that they can do that belong to one virtue, without being wise about things that they can do that belong to another virtue. (Just so, persons can possess skill with respect to some things that they can make, without possessing skill with respect to other things that they can make.) And practical wisdom is right reasoning about things that human beings can do. Therefore, moral virtues do not need to be connected.

On the contrary, Ambrose says in his commentary on the Gospel of Luke (6:20): "Virtues are interconnected and linked in such a way that persons who possess one virtue, show themselves to possess many."[5] Augustine likewise says in his *De Trinitate* that "virtues in the human soul are in no way separate from one another."[6] And Gregory says in his *Moralia* that "one virtue without others is either no virtue at all or incomplete virtue."[7] And Cicero says in his *Tusculanae disputationes*: "If you admit that you do not possess one virtue, you will necessarily possess none."[8]

I answer that we can understand moral virtues as either complete or incomplete. Incomplete virtues (e.g., moderation and courage) are indeed only tendencies in us toward acts of particular kinds of good things to be done, whether we have such inclinations by nature or habituation. And if we understand moral virtues in this way, they are not connected. For example, we see that some individuals who are not ready to act chastely are nonetheless by their natural constitution or habitual behavior ready to act generously.

And complete moral virtues are habits that incline us to do good deeds rightly. And if we so understand moral virtues, we need to affirm that they are connected, as almost everyone holds. And two arguments, corresponding to the different ways in which thinkers distinguish the cardinal virtues, are assigned for this connection. For, as I have said, some distinguish those virtues by certain general characteristics proper to each (e.g., that judgment belongs to practical wisdom, right order to justice, restraint to moderation, strength of soul to courage) in whatever matter we consider those things.[9] And so it is clearly evident why the virtues are connected, for strength of soul is not to be praised as a virtue if it is without moderation or right order or judgment. And the argument is the same about the other virtues. And Gregory in his *Moralia* assigns this reason for the connection of the virtues, saying that "virtues, if disconnected, cannot be" essentially "perfect" as virtue, "since there is no true practical wisdom that is not just, moderate, and courageous."[10] And he holds the same about the other virtues. And Augustine assigns a like reason in his *De Trinitate*.[11]

But others distinguish the aforementioned cardinal virtues by their matter. And Aristotle in the *Ethics* accordingly assigns the reason why the virtues are connected to the fact that persons can possess no moral virtues apart from practical wisdom,[12] as I have said before.[13] This is because it belongs to moral virtues, as habits of choosing, to make right choices. And right choice requires not only an inclination toward a requisite end, which morally virtuous habits directly bring about, but also that persons directly choose means to such an end, which practical reason does by deliberating about, judging, and commanding the means. Likewise, neither can persons possess practical wisdom without possessing moral virtues. This is because practical wisdom is right reasoning about things that we can do, and such reasoning proceeds from the ends of the things that we can do, as principles, and moral virtues rightly dispose persons to those ends. And so, as we cannot possess theoretical knowledge without understanding principles, we cannot possess practical wisdom without moral virtues. And it evidently follows from this that moral virtues are connected.

Reply to Obj. 1. Some moral virtues perfect human beings regarding their common condition, namely, regarding things to be done that arise without exception in every human life. And so human beings need at the same time to become practiced in acts regarding the matter of all these virtues. And they will indeed acquire every such morally virtuous habit if they become practiced in acting rightly regarding every such matter. But they may become practiced in acting rightly about one matter and not in acting rightly about another matter (e.g., in being rightly disposed about emotions of anger but not rightly disposed about emotions of desire). If so, they will indeed acquire a habit to control emotions of anger, and yet that habit will not possess the character of virtue because of a defect of practical wisdom, which is overwhelmed regarding emotions of desire. Similarly, inclinations from nature do not possess the full character of virtue if they should lack practical wisdom.

And some moral virtues (e.g., magnificence and high-mindedness) perfect human beings regarding a superior condition. And because there is no occasion for some human beings to become practiced in acts regarding the matter of such virtues, persons can possess other virtues (if we are speaking about acquired virtues) without actually possessing those virtuous habits. And yet such persons, by acquiring other moral virtues, have a ready potentiality to possess those virtues. For example, persons who have by practice acquired the virtue of generosity regarding modest gifts and consumption will with a modicum of practice acquire the habit of magnificence if they should come into a great deal of money. Similarly, geometricians with a modicum of application acquire scientific knowledge of conclusions that they have never considered before. And people say that they possess what is at hand for them to possess, as the Philosopher says in the *Physics*: "Things slightly deficient seem almost not to be deficient at all."[14]

Reply to Obj. 2. The foregoing makes clear the answer to the second objection.

Reply to Obj. 3. Intellectual virtues concern different matters unrelated to one another, as is evident in the case of different kinds of scientific knowledge and different skills. And so we do not find in intellectual virtues the connection that we find in moral virtues, which concern emotions and actions. And emotions and actions are evidently interrelated. For all emotions spring from emotions that are primary, namely, love and hate, and terminate in other emotions, namely, joy and sorrow. And similarly, all the actions that constitute the matter of moral virtues are related to one another and also to the emotions. And so the whole matter of moral virtues falls within one and the same character of practical wisdom.

Nonetheless, everything intelligible is related to first principles. And all intellectual virtues accordingly depend on moral virtues, as I have said.[15] And universal principles, which are the object of understanding, do not depend on conclusions, which are the object of other intellectual virtues. Similarly, moral virtues depend on practical wisdom, since the will in one respect moves reason, and reason in another respect moves the will, as I have said before.[16]

Reply to Obj. 4. The things toward which moral virtues incline us are related to practical wisdom as principles, while things that we can make are related to skills only as matter and not as principles. And although there can be right reasoning in one matter and not in another, we can nonetheless in no way call reasoning right if there be a defect in any principle of reasoning. For example, if one were to err regarding this principle, "Every whole is greater than one of its parts," one could not attain knowledge of geometry, since one would necessarily err greatly in conclusions derived from the principle.

And besides, things that we can do, are interrelated, while things that we can make, are not, as I have said.[17] And so a defect in practical wisdom regarding some things that we can do, would also bring about a defect regarding other things that we can do. And such does not happen in the case of things that we can make.

Second Article

Can There Be Moral Virtues Without the Theological
Virtue of Charity?

I proceed in this way to the second article: it seems that there can be moral virtues without the theological virtue of charity.

Obj. 1. The *Librum sententiarum* of Prosper says that "every virtue except charity can be common to the upright and the wicked."[18] But "charity can exist only in the upright," as the same text says. Therefore, human beings can possess other virtues without possessing charity.

Obj. 2. "Human beings can by their acts acquire moral virtues," as the *Ethics* says.[19] But human beings can possess charity only by infusion, as the Letter to the Romans says: "God's love is poured into our hearts by the Holy Spirit, who has been given to us."[20] Therefore, human beings can possess other virtues without possessing charity.

Obj. 3. Moral virtues, since they depend on practical wisdom, are interconnected. But charity does not depend on practical wisdom; indeed, charity surpasses practical wisdom, as the Letter to the Ephesians says: "The love of Christ that surpasses knowledge."[21] Therefore, moral virtues are not connected to charity and can exist without it.

On the contrary, the First Letter of John says: "Those who do not love, abide in death."[22] But virtues perfect the spiritual life, since they themselves are the means "whereby we live rightly," as Augustine says in his *De libero arbitrio*.[23] Therefore, there can be no virtues without the love that is charity.

I answer that human beings can by their acts acquire moral virtues insofar as those virtues result in something good related to ends that do not surpass the natural capacity of human beings, as I have said before.[24] And the moral virtues so acquired can exist without charity, as they did in the case of many pagans.

But moral virtues, insofar as they result in the good related to our final supernatural end, perfectly and truly possess the character of virtue and cannot be acquired by human acts; rather, God infuses such virtues. And such moral virtues cannot exist without charity. For I have said before that other moral virtues cannot exist without practical wisdom, and that practical wisdom cannot exist without moral virtues, since moral virtues cause us to be rightly disposed toward certain ends, and practical wisdom reasons from those ends.[25] And for practical wisdom to reason rightly, it is far more necessary that human beings are rightly disposed regarding their supernatural end, which is accomplished by charity, than they are rightly disposed regarding other ends, which is accomplished by moral virtues. Similarly, in theoretical things, right reasoning most of all requires the first, indemonstrable principle, that is, that contradictory propositions cannot be simultaneously true. And so it is evidently the case that infused practical wisdom cannot exist without charity, and, consequently, that other infused moral virtues, which cannot exist without practical wisdom, likewise cannot exist without charity.

Thus it is evident from what I have said that only infused virtues are perfect and to be called virtues in an absolute sense, since they rightly dispose human beings for their final end absolutely. But other virtues, namely, acquired virtues, are virtues in some respect but not absolutely, for they rightly dispose human beings regarding their final end in particular kinds of things to be done but not regarding their final end absolutely. And so a gloss of Augustine on Rom. 14:23 ("Everything not of sin," etc.) says: "Where recognition of the truth is wanting, the virtue even in good conduct is counterfeit."[26]

Reply to Obj. 1. The cited text understands virtues according to the incomplete nature of virtue. On the other hand, if we understand moral virtues according to the complete nature of virtue, moral virtues "make their possessor good"[27] and so cannot exist in the wicked.

Reply to Obj. 2. The argument of this objection is valid regarding acquired moral virtues.

Reply to Obj. 3. Although charity surpasses knowledge and practical wisdom, infused practical wisdom nonetheless depends on charity, as I have said.[28] And consequently, all infused moral virtues depend on charity.

Notes

1. Aristotle, *Ethics* II, 1. 1103a31–b2.
2. Magnificence is the virtue of public spiritedness in underwriting communal celebrations and projects. The virtue obviously presupposes the possession of wealth.
3. *Ethics* IV, 2. 1122b26–29.
4. *Ethics* IV, 3. 1123b5–8.
5. *Super Lucam* 5. PL 15:1653.
6. *De Trinitate* VI, 4. PL 42:927.
7. *Moralia* XXII, 1. PL 76:212.
8. *Tusculane disputationes* II, 14.
9. Q. 61, AA. 3, 4.
10. *Moralia* XXII, 1. PL 76:212.
11. *De Trinitate* VI, 4. PL 42:927.
12. *Ethics* VI, 13. 1144b36.
13. Q. 58, A. 4.
14. *Physics* II, 5. 197a29.
15. In the body of the article.
16. Q. 9, A. 1. Q. 58, A. 5, *ad* 1.
17. In the Reply to *Obj. 3.*
18. Prosper of Aquitaine, *Librum sententiarum* 7. PL 51:428.
19. Aristotle, *Ethics* II, 1. 1103a31–b2.
20. Rom. 5:5.
21. Eph. 3:19.
22. 1 Jn. 3:14.
23. *De libero arbitrio* II, 19. PL 32:1268.
24. Q. 63, A. 2.
25. Q. 65, A. 1. Q. 58, AA. 4, 5.
26. *Glossa ordinaria.* PL 114:516.
27. Aristotle, *Ethics* II, 6. 1106a15.
28. In the body of the article.

Question 66

On the Equality of Virtues

[This question is divided into six articles, three of which are included here.]

Third Article

Are Moral Virtues More Excellent Than Intellectual Virtues?

I proceed in this way to the third article: it seems that moral virtues are more excellent than intellectual virtues.

Obj. 1. Things more necessary and perduring are better than things less necessary and less perduring. But moral virtues are "more perduring than scientific disciplines,"[1] which are intellectual virtues, and moral virtues are also more necessary for human life. Therefore, moral virtues are more important than intellectual virtues.

Obj. 2. It belongs to the nature of virtues that "they make their possessors good."[2] But we call human beings good by reason of their moral virtues and not by reason of their intellectual virtues, except, per chance, by reason of their practical wisdom. Therefore, moral virtues are better than intellectual virtues.

Obj. 3. Ends are more excellent than means. But "moral virtues cause us to intend ends rightly, while practical wisdom causes us to chose means rightly," as the *Ethics* says.[3] Therefore, moral virtues are more excellent than practical wisdom, which is the intellectual virtue concerned about moral things.

On the contrary, moral virtues reside in the part of the soul that shares in reason, while intellectual virtues reside in the part of the soul that is essentially reason, as the *Ethics* says.[4] But the part of the soul that is essentially reason, is more excellent than the part of the soul that shares in reason. Therefore, intellectual virtues are more excellent than moral virtues.

I answer that we can in two ways call things greater or lesser: in one way, absolutely; in the second way, in some respect. But nothing prevents something from being absolutely better, as, for example, "It is better to philosophize than to be rich," and yet not better in some respect, namely, "in the case of one who experiences need."[5] And when we consider anything according to its specific nature, we consider it absolutely. And virtues are specified by their object, as is evident from what I have said.[6] And so, absolutely speaking, virtues with more excellent objects are more excellent. And the object of reason is evidently more excellent than the object of the will, for reason understands things as universals, while the will inclines toward real things, which exist as individual things. And so, absolutely speaking, intellectual virtues, which perfect reason, are more excellent than moral virtues, which perfect the will.

But if we should consider virtues in relation to acts, then moral virtues, which perfect the will, and whose function it is to move other powers to act, as I have said,[7] are more excellent.

And virtues are called virtues because they are the sources of acts, since virtues perfect powers. Therefore, it also follows that the character of virtue belongs more to moral virtues than to intellectual virtues, although intellectual virtues are, absolutely speaking, more excellent habits.

Reply to Obj. 1. Moral virtues are more perduring than intellectual virtues because we practice them in things that belong to ordinary life. But the objects of scientific disciplines, which objects are necessary and invariable, are evidently more perduring than the objects of moral virtues, which objects consist of particular things to be done.

And the fact that moral virtues are more necessary for ordinary human life, shows that they are more excellent in this respect, and not that they are more excellent absolutely. Indeed, theoretical intellectual virtues are more excellent because they are not ordained for anything else, as the useful is ordained as means for something else. And such is the case because, by means of theoretical intellectual virtues, we begin to possess happiness, which consists in true knowledge, as I have said before.[8]

Reply to Obj. 2. Absolutely speaking, we call human beings good in regard to moral virtues rather than intellectual virtues because the will moves other powers to their acts, as I have said before.[9] And so this likewise proves only that virtues are better in one respect.

Reply to Obj. 3. Practical wisdom directs moral virtues not only by choosing means but also by prescribing ends. And each virtue aims to achieve the mean in its own matter, and the right reasoning of practical wisdom indeed determines that mean, as the *Ethics* says.[10]

Fourth Article

Is Justice Superior to Other Moral Virtues?

I proceed in this way to the fourth article: it seems that justice is not superior to other moral virtues.

Obj. 1. It is a greater deed to give one's possessions to others than to repay one's debts to others. But giving one's possessions to others belongs to the virtue of generosity, and repaying one's debts to others belongs to the virtue of justice. Therefore, it seems that generosity is a greater virtue than justice.

Obj. 2. What is most perfect in anything seems to be what is greatest in that thing. But "patience has a perfect effect," as the Letter of James says.[11] Therefore, it seems that patience is greater than justice.

Obj. 3. "High-mindedness produces greatness in every virtue," as the *Ethics* says.[12] Therefore, high-mindedness makes even justice itself greater. Therefore, high-mindedness is greater than justice.

On the contrary, the Philosopher says in the *Ethics* that "justice is the most excellent of the virtues."[13]

I answer that we can call virtues specifically greater or lesser either absolutely or in some respect. We indeed call a virtue greater insofar as it reflects a greater good of reason, as I have said before.[14] And justice, as more closely connected to reason, accordingly surpasses all the other moral virtues. And both the subject in which justice resides and the object of justice make this evident. The subject in which justice resides indeed manifests this, since justice resides in the will, and the will is the rational appetite, as is evident from what I have said.[15] And the object or matter of justice manifests this, since justice concerns actions, and actions dispose human beings not only in regard to themselves but also in relation to others. And so "justice is the most excellent of the virtues," as the *Ethics* says.[16]

And of the other moral virtues, which concern emotions, the greater the things concerning which movements of desire are subject to reason, the more each virtue reflects the good of reason. And the greatest thing belonging to human beings is life, on which all other things depend. And so courage, which subjects movements of desire to reason in things proper to life and death, is the chief moral virtue that deals with emotions, although courage is subordinate to justice. And so the Philosopher says in the *Rhetoric* that "the virtues most esteemed by others are necessarily the greatest, since virtue is the power to do good. Therefore, others most of all esteem the courageous and the just, since the virtue of the former," namely, courage, "is indeed useful in war, and the virtue of the latter," namely, justice, "is useful both in war and in peace."[17]

And after courage ranks moderation, which subjects desire to reason regarding things that are directly ordained for life, both in the case of the life of the individual and in the case of the life of the species, namely, food and sex, respectively.

And so also we call these three virtues, together with practical wisdom, the most worthy virtues.

But we say that particular virtues are greater in some respect as they assist or adorn one of the chief virtues. Similarly, substances are, absolutely speaking, more worthy than accidents, but accidents are more worthy than substances in one respect, in that accidents perfect substances in accidental ways of existing.

Reply to Obj. 1. Acts of generosity need to be grounded in acts of justice, since "giving would not be generous if givers were not to give things that belong to them," as the *Politics* says.[18] And so generosity would be impossible without justice, which distinguishes what belongs to one person from what belongs to another. But justice can exist without generosity. And so the virtue of justice, absolutely speaking, is greater than the virtue of generosity, since justice is more universal and the foundation of generosity. On the other hand, generosity is greater in one respect, in that it adorns and supplements justice.

Reply to Obj. 2. We say that patience has a "perfect effect" in the bearing of evils. And patience in bearing evils excludes not only unjust punishment (which justice also excludes), or only anger (which meekness excludes), but also inordinate sorrow, which is the root of all of the above. And so patience is more perfect and greater in this respect, that it destroys the root of evil in this matter.

But patience is not, absolutely speaking, more perfect than all the other virtues. This is because courage not only endures annoyances without disquiet, which endurance belongs to patience, but also fights against those things when there should be need to do so. And so every courageous person is patient, but the converse is not true, since patience is only one part of courage.

Reply to Obj. 3. High-mindedness is only possible when other virtues preexist, as the *Ethics* says.[19] And so high-mindedness is related to other virtues as their embellishment. And so it is greater than all the others in one respect but not absolutely.

Fifth Article

Is Theoretical Wisdom the Greatest Intellectual Virtue?

I proceed in this way to the fifth article: it seems that theoretical wisdom is not the greatest intellectual virtue.

Obj. 1. One who commands is greater than one who is commanded. But practical wisdom seems to give commands to theoretical wisdom. For the *Ethics* says that a science, namely, the science of politics, "preordains what kind of scientific disciplines ought to flourish in political communities, and what kind each citizen should learn, and to what extent,"[20] and the science of politics belongs to practical wisdom, as the *Ethics* also says.[21] Therefore, since theoretical wisdom is also included among scientific disciplines, it seems that practical wisdom is greater than theoretical wisdom.

Obj. 2. It belongs to the nature of virtue to dispose human beings to be happy, for virtue is "the disposition of perfect things for what is best for them," as the *Physics* says.[22] But practical wisdom is right reasoning about things to be done, which deeds bring human beings to the state of happiness, and theoretical wisdom does not contemplate human acts, the acts by which human beings attain happiness. Therefore, practical wisdom is a greater virtue than theoretical wisdom.

Obj. 3. The more perfect knowledge is, the greater it seems to be. But we can possess more perfect knowledge about human things, about which we have scientific knowledge, than we can about divine things, about which we have theoretical wisdom, according to the distinction of Augustine in his *De Trinitate.*[23] This is because we cannot understand divine things, as the Book of Job says: "Behold how great God is, he who surpasses our knowledge."[24] Therefore, scientific knowledge is more important than theoretical wisdom.

Obj. 4. Knowledge of principles is worthier than knowledge of conclusions. But theoretical wisdom draws conclusions from indemonstrable principles, which are the object of understanding, just as other kinds of scientific knowledge do. Therefore, understanding is a greater virtue than theoretical wisdom.

On the contrary, the Philosopher says in the *Ethics* that among intellectual virtues, theoretical wisdom is "like the head."[25]

I answer that we consider a virtue's specific greatness by the virtue's object, as I have said.[26] But the object of theoretical wisdom surpasses the objects of all the other intellectual virtues, since theoretical wisdom contemplates the highest cause, that is, God, as the *Metaphysics* says.[27] And it is because we judge about effects by their causes, and about lower causes by their higher cause, that theoretical wisdom is able to judge, and has the function of disposing, and is architechtonic (so to speak) in relation to every other intellectual virtue.

Reply to Obj. 1. Since human things are the object of practical wisdom, and the highest cause is the object of theoretical wisdom, practical wisdom can be greater than theoretical wisdom "only if human beings were to be the greatest things in the world," as the *Ethics* says.[28] And so we need to say, as the same work says, that practical wisdom does not command theoretical wisdom itself, but rather vice versa,[29] since "the spiritual person judges everything, and no one judges such a person," as the First Letter to the Corinthians says.[30] For practical wisdom is not disposed to assert itself about the highest things, which theoretical wisdom contemplates, but gives commands about things ordained for theoretical wisdom, namely, how human beings ought to attain theoretical wisdom. And so practical wisdom, or the science of politics, is the servant of theoretical wisdom in this respect, since practical wisdom leads theoretical wisdom in procession and opens the way for it, just as the porter leads a king in procession and opens the way for him.

Reply to Obj. 2. Practical wisdom contemplates things that are the means whereby human beings attain happiness, and theoretical wisdom contemplates the very object of happiness, that is, the highest intelligible thing. And there would indeed be perfect happiness in acts of theoretical wisdom if theoretical wisdom were to have perfect contemplation regarding its object. But the acts of theoretical wisdom in this life, since they are imperfect regarding their chief object, that is, God, are consequently the beginning of, or the sharing in, future happiness. And so theoretical wisdom is more closely disposed toward happiness than practical wisdom is.

Reply to Obj. 3. "One kind of knowledge is more important than another either because the object of the one is more excellent than the object of the other, or because the knowledge attains certitude," as the Philosopher says in the *De anima*.[31] Therefore, if several subjects are equally good and excellent, the intellectual virtue that attains more certain knowledge will be the greater virtue. But a virtue that attains less certainty about higher and greater matters will be more important than a virtue that attains more certainty about lesser matters. And so the Philosopher says in the *De coelo* that it is important to be able to know things about celestial matters, even by weak and probable reasoning.[32] And he says in the *De partibus animalium* that "it is more desirable to know a little about more excellent things than to know a great deal about rather lowly things."[33]

Therefore, human beings, especially in the condition of their present life, cannot perfectly attain theoretical wisdom, to which knowledge about God belongs, so as to have it in their possession, as it were. Rather, "such wisdom belongs to God alone," as the *Metaphysics* says.[34] And yet the modicum of knowledge about God that human beings can possess through theoretical wisdom is more important than any other knowledge.

Reply to Obj. 4.   The truth and knowledge of indemonstrable principles depend on the nature of the principles' terms; for example, when a person knows what a whole is, and what a part is, the person knows immediately that every whole is greater than one of its parts. But all being is the peculiar effect of the highest cause, namely, God. Therefore, to know the nature of being and nonbeing, of whole and part, and of other things that result from being, belongs to theoretical wisdom. And we form the indemonstrable principles from such things, as the principles' terms. And so theoretical wisdom employs indemonstrable principles, which are the object of understanding, not only by drawing conclusions from them, as other sciences do, but also by judging about them, and by arguing against adversaries. And so theoretical wisdom is a greater virtue than understanding.

Notes

1. Aristotle, *Ethics* I, 10. 1100b14.
2. Aristotle, *Ethics* II, 6. 1106b15.
3. Aristotle, *Ethics* VI, 12. 1144a8.
4. Aristotle, *Ethics* I, 13. 1103a1–3.
5. Aristotle, *Topics* III, 2. 118a10–11.
6. Q. 54, A. 2. Q. 60, A. 1.
7. Q. 9, A. 1.
8. Q. 3, A. 6.
9. Q. 56, A. 3.
10. Aristotle, *Ethics* II, 6. 1107a1–2. VI, 13. 1144b21–24.
11. Jas. 1:4.
12. Aristotle, *Ethics* IV, 3. 1123b30.
13. *Ethics* V, 1. 1129b27–29.
14. Q. 66, A. 1.
15. Q. 8, A. 1. Q. 26, A. 1.
16. See n. 13, supra.
17. *Rhetoric* I, 9. 1366b3–7.
18. Aristotle, *Politics* II, 5. 1263b13–14.
19. Aristotle, *Ethics* IV, 3. 1124a2–4.
20. Aristotle, *Ethics* I, 2. 1094a28–b2.
21. Aristotle, *Ethics* VI, 7. 1141a21–22.
22. Aristotle, *Physics* VII, 3. 246b23–24.

23. *De Trinitate* XII, 14. PL 42:1009.
24. Job 36:26.
25. *Ethics* VI, 7. 1141a19–20.
26. Q. 66, A. 3.
27. Aristotle, *Metaphysics* I, 1. 981b28–29.
28. Aristotle, *Ethics* VI, 7. 1141a21–22.
29. Aristotle, *Ethics* VI, 12. 1143b33–36. VI, 13. 1145a6–11.
30. 1 Cor. 2:15.
31. *De anima* I, 1. 402a2–4.
32. *De coelo* II, 12. 291b27–29.
33. *De partibus animalium* I, 5. 644b31–35.
34. Aristotle, *Metaphysics* I, 2. 982b28–30.

GLOSSARY

Accident: *an attribute that inheres in another and cannot subsist in itself.* What subsists in itself and does not inhere in another is a substance. John, for example, is a substance, while his height is an accident; his height does not exist apart from him. *See* Actuality, Property, Substance.

Action: *activity.* There are two basic kinds of action. Immanent action, the activity of living things, perfects the being that acts. Plants have the immanent activities of nutrition, growth, and reproduction. Animals have the additional immanent activities of sense perception and sense appetites. Human beings have the additional immanent activities of intellection and willing. God alone has perfectly immanent activity, that is, immanent activity without any accompanying transient effect. Transient action produces an effect in something other than the cause that acts. In other words, transient action is efficient causality. Action in the strict sense is transient action. *See* Cause.

Actuality: *the perfection of a being.* Existing is the primary actuality of every being. A specific (substantial) form actualizes finite beings and distinguishes one kind of being from another. Particular (accidental) characteristics further actualize finite beings. Joan, for example, is perfected and actualized by her act of existing, her human form, and her particular attributes (her knowledge, her virtue, her physical attributes). *See* Accident, Form, Matter, Potentiality, Substance.

Appetite: *the active tendency of finite beings to actualize their capacities.* Inanimate material beings have natural appetites. Plants have additional vegetative appetites (for nourishment, growth, and reproduction). Animals have additional sense appetites (concupiscible, irascible). Human beings hae an additional intellectual appetite (the will). *See* Concupiscible, Irascible, Will.

245

Cause: *a being that influences the being or coming-to-be of something else.* In common parlance, the term refers primarily to an efficient cause, that is, a cause that by its activity produces an effect; a builder and those who work under him, for example, are the efficient causes of the house they construct. Efficient causes can be univocal or nonunivocal. An efficient cause is univocal when it and its effect belong to the same species; human beings, for example, are univocal efficient causes of the bodies of the human beings they beget. An efficient cause is nonunivocal when it and its effect do not belong to the same species; God, for example, is the nonunivocal efficient cause of the things he creates, since he belongs to no species and so shares no species or genus with any creature.

But there are other causes than efficient causes. A final cause is the end for the sake of which an efficient cause acts; a builder, for example, builds a house to provide shelter (objective purpose) and to make money (subjective purpose). An exemplary cause is the idea or model of a desired effect in the mind of an intellectual efficient cause that preconceives the effect; a builder, for example, conceives the form of the house that he intends to build.

Efficient, final, and exemplary causes are extrinsic to the effects they cause. In addition, form, which makes an effect to be what it is, and matter, which receives a form, are correlative intrinsic causes; a house, for example, is composed of bricks and wood (the matter), which are given a structure or shape (the form). *See* Form, Matter, Source.

Concupiscible: *type of sense appetite whose object is the pleasant.* Love and hate, desire and aversion, joy and sorrow are examples of movements of the concupiscible appetite. *See* Appetite, Irascible.

Efficient Cause: *see* Cause.

Emotions: *movements of sense appetites.* Emotions may be ordinate (in accord with right reason) or inordinate (contrary to, and disruptive of, right reason). Emotions involve either desire for the pleasant or fear of difficult things that are useful. *See* Concupiscible, Irascible, Moral Virtues.

Essence: *what makes something to be what it substantially is*. The human essence, for example, makes human beings to be what they are as substances, namely, rational animals. When the essence of a being is considered as the ultimate source of the being's activities and development, it is called the being's nature; human nature, for example, is the ultimate source of the human activities (activities of reason and activities according to reason) whereby human beings develop themselves. *See* Accident, Form, Property, Substance.

Exemplary Cause: *see* Cause.

Final Cause: *see* Cause.

Form: *the cause that intrinsically makes a being to be substantially or accidentally what it is*. The human form, for example, makes John to be what he is as a substance, and other forms make him to be what he is accidentally (tall, thin, red-headed). *See* Accident, Substance.

Formal Cause: *see* Cause.

Habit: *the characteristic disposition or inclination to be or act in a certain way*. Habits may belong to the body, the intellect, or the will, be innate or acquired, be natural or supernatural, be good or bad. For example, logical argumentation is a habit of the intellect; moderation is a habit of the will; timidity may be an innate habit; cleanliness is an acquired habit; courage is a natural habit; faith is a supernatural habit; generosity is a good habit; stinginess is a bad habit. *See* Virtue.

Happiness: *the perfect or complete attainment of the good or end that nature constitutes human beings to desire and strive for*. As such, happiness is an objective state of perfection and not a subjective state of euphoria, although possession of the ultimate objective perfection of human beings will entail joy and satisfaction. For Aristotle, human beings become happy, that is, reach a state of perfection, when they engage in activities of reason and live in accord with right reason. For St. Thomas, human beings can only become happy when they behold God as he is in himself, although activities of reason and activities in accord with right reason in this life will bring human beings to a state of incomplete and imperfect happiness. St. Thomas typically uses different words to denote this-world and next-world happiness:*"felicitas"* to denote this-world happiness, *"beatitudo"* to denote next-world happiness.

Intellect: *the faculty of understanding, judgment, and reasoning.* St. Thomas, following Aristotle, holds that there is an active power of the intellect that moves the passive or potential power of the intellect to understand the essences of material things, form judgments, and reason discursively.

Intellectual Virtues: *the virtues consisting of the right disposition of the intellect toward truth.* Theoretical intellectual virtues concern understanding principles, scientific knowledge, and theoretical wisdom. Practical intellectual virtues concern practical wisdom and skills. *See* Practical Wisdom, Science, Skills, Theoretical Wisdom.

Irascible: *type of sense appetite whose object is the useful that is difficult to achieve.* The object does not appear as something pleasant and can be achieved only by overcoming opposition. Hope and despair, fear and anger are examples of the irascible appetite. *See* Appetite, Concupiscible.

Justice: *the moral virtue that consists of the right disposition of the will to render to others what is due to them.* This is general justice, sometimes called legal justice because the political community's laws prescribe the general obligations of citizens to one another and the community. For St. Thomas, there are two kinds of particular justice. Commutative justice concerns the obligation of individuals and groups to respect the rights of others and to be fair in commercial transactions. Distributive justice concerns the obligations of the community to ensure that individuals and groups receive a share of the community's goods proportional to the individual's and the group's contribution to the community. *See* Moral Virtues.

Material Cause: *see* Cause.

Matter: *the cause of "stuff" out of which and with which something material is produced.* The material causes of a house, for example, are its bricks, mortar, wood. Prime matter individualizes and so limits a specific substantial form, and it provides the subject and capacity for material things to change from one substance to another. Although prime matter is no-thing, it is a source or cause in everything material. It can receive any communicable substantial form and so has limitless capacity for any such form. *See* Cause, Form, Potentiality.

Moral Virtues: *virtues consisting of the right disposition of the will toward requisite ends* (e.g., just, courageous, moderate deeds). Practical wisdom directs moral virtues by prescribing their ends and by choosing means to attain the ends. Justice concerns external actions, and other moral virtues concern emotions. *See* Emotions, Justice, Practical Wisdom.

Motion: *movement.* Motion literally and primarily refers to loco-motion, that is, change of position. But the term can refer more broadly to any change or transition from one state or condition to another. According to St. Thomas, it is a self-evident first principle of understanding that whatever undergoes motion does so as a result of causal action by something else.

Nature: *see* Essence.

Potentiality: *the capacity to be or become something.* The potentiality of a being limits its actuality; frogs, for example, can swim, but they cannot fly. Finite beings can change accidentally; John, for example, can go bald. Finite material things can also change from one substance into another; grass, for example, when consumed by a cow, becomes part of the cow. Potentiality in the active sense is the same as power. *See* Accident, Actuality, Matter, Power.

Power: *the active capacity to perform a certain type of activity.* For example, the power of sight. *See* Potentiality.

Practical Wisdom (Prudence): *the practical intellectual virtue that consists of characteristically right reasoning about the things that human beings should do.* Practical wisdom concerns human action and so differs from theoretical wisdom, which concerns the ultimate causes of things irrespective of human action relating to the things. Practical wisdom prescribes the ends of moral virtues and chooses the means to attain those ends. As the most important natural virtue connected with human action, practical wisdom is sometimes considered as if it were one of the moral virtues. *See* Habit, Intellectual Virtues, Moral Virtues, Theoretical Wisdom.

Property: *a quality or characteristic that necessarily belongs to a substance; a proper accident.* Joan's ability to use language, for example, unlike the color of her hair, is a characteristic proper to her as a human being. *See* Accident, Substance.

Prudence: *see* Practical Wisdom.

Science (Aristotelian): *knowledge about things through knowledge of their causes.* Science studies the efficient, final, material, and formal causes of things. Physical, psychological, and social sciences study the secondary causes of material and human things, while philosophy (metaphysics) studies the first causes of being as such. For Aristotle, philosophy is the highest science; for St. Thomas, theology, the study of God in the light of Christian revelation, is the highest science. *See* Cause.

Skills: *practical intellectual virtues that consist of right reasoning about how to make things.* *See* Intellectual Virtues.

Soul: *the substantial form of a living material thing.* The soul is the ultimate intrinsic source whereby living material things differ from nonliving material things. There are three kinds of souls: the vegetative soul capable of nutrition, growth, and reproduction; the sensory soul capable of sense perception; the rational soul capable of intellection. According to Aristotle and St. Thomas, the only soul in human beings is the rational soul, which also has the powers of the vegetative and sensory souls. The rational soul is intrinsically independent of matter for its existence and activity. *See* Form, Substance.

Source: *that from which something else proceeds.* The essence of a frog, and specifically its form, for example, is an ontological source or cause, that is, the source or cause from which the frog's activity proceeds. The premises of arguments are logical sources or principles from which conclusions logically proceed. *See* Cause.

Species: *the substantial identity of material things insofar as that identity is common to many things.* The species concept (e.g., human being) is composed of a genus concept (e.g., animal), which indicates the essence of certain material things in an incompletely determined way, and a specific difference distinguishing things of the same genus (e.g., rational). The species concept, or definition, thus expresses the whole substance or essence of a particular kind of material thing.

Specific Difference: *see* Species.

Subject: *that in which something else inheres.* In the strict sense, subjects are substances underlying accidents. In a broader sense, prime matter can be called the subject of substantial form, the soul the subject of powers, and powers the subject of virtues. *See* Accident, Form, Matter, Substance.

Substance: *what exists in itself and not in another.* Finite individual substances "stand under" (Latin: *substare*) accidents and persist through accidental changes. Human beings, for example, are composed of substance (the body-soul composite) and accidents (size, shape, color, etc.). *See* Accident, Property, Subject.

Synderesis: *the habit of first moral principles.* Human beings have an innate disposition to understand the first principles of human action. Human beings are disposed by nature to recognize that they should seek the good proper to their nature, and that the human good includes preserving one's life in reasonable ways, mating and educating offspring in reasonable ways, and living cooperatively with others in an organized community. *See* Habit.

Theoretical Wisdom: *the intellectual virtue consisting of characteristically right reasoning about the ultimate causes of things. See* Intellectual Virtues.

Virtue: *human excellence.* Like its Greek equivalent *(arete)*, the Latin-derived term indicates a perduring quality of a human being and so a characteristic disposition. St. Thomas distinguishes three kinds of virtue: intellectual, moral, and theological. Intellectual virtues have for their objects intellectual activities. Concerning theoretical truth, intellectual virtues comprise understanding principles, scientific knowledge, and theoretical wisdom. Concerning practical truth, intellectual virtues comprise practical wisdom and skills. Moral virtues consist of characteristic readiness to act in particular matters as practical wisdom dictates. Practical wisdom and moral virtues may be acquired or infused. There are three infused theological virtues: faith, hope, and charity. *See* Habit, Intellectual Virtues, Moral Virtues, Practical Wisdom, Science, Theoretical Wisdom.

Will: *the intellectual appetite, the intellectual faculty of desire.* The will necessarily wills the ultimate human perfection, happiness, but freely wills particular goods, since the latter are only partially good.

Wisdom: *see* Practical Wisdom, Theoretical Wisdom.

BIBLIOGRAPHY

On Aristotle's philosophical system, see:

Grene, Marjorie. *A Portrait of Aristotle*. Chicago: University of Chicago Press, 1967.

Veatch, Henry B. *Aristotle: A Contemporary Appreciation*. Bloomington: Indiana University Press, 1974.

For an up-to-date, scholarly chronology of the life and works of St. Thomas, see:

Torrell, Jean-Pierre. *Saint Thomas Aquinas*. Vol. 1: *The Person and His Work*. Translated by Robert Royal. Washington: The Catholic University of America Press, 1996.

Tugwell, Simon. *Albert and Thomas: Selected Writings*. Introduction to St. Thomas, pp. 201–351. New York: Paulist Press, 1988.

For an accurate and well-integrated condensed translation of the whole *Summa*, see:

Aquinas, St. Thomas. *Summa Theologiae: A Concise Translation*. Edited and translated by Timothy McDermott. Westminster, Md.: Christian Classics, 1989.

For a guide to the context of St. Thomas's thought, see:

Pieper, Joseph. *Guide to St. Thomas*. Translated by Richard and Clara Winston. New York: Pantheon, 1962.

For expositions of St. Thomas's general philosophy, see:

Copleston, Frederick. *A History of Philosophy*. Vol. 2, pp. 302–424. Westminster, Md.: Newman, 1950. Also available in Image Books, Doubleday. Vol. 2, part 2.

Davies, Brian. *The Thought of Thomas Aquinas*. Oxford: Oxford University Press, 1992.

Gilson, Etienne. *The Christian Philosophy of St. Thomas Aquinas*. New York: Random House, 1956.

McInerny, Ralph. *A First Glance at St. Thomas Aquinas: A*

Handbook for Peeping Thomists. Notre Dame, Ind.: University of Notre Dame Press, 1990.

On the ethics of St. Thomas in general, see:

Elders, Leon J., and Hedwig, K., eds. *The Ethics of St. Thomas Aquinas*. Studi tomistici 25. Vatican City: Libreria Editrice Vaticana, 1984.
—. *Lex et Libertas: Freedom and Law According to St. Thomas Aquinas*. Studi tomistici 30. Vatican City: Libreria Editrice Vaticana, 1987.
Mullady, Brian T. *The Meaning of the Term "Moral" in St. Thomas Aquinas*. Studi tomistici 27. Vatican City: Libreria Editrice Vaticana, 1986.

On the vision of God as the ultimate human goal, see:

Lonergan, Bernard. "The Natural Desire to See God." In *Collection*. New York: Herder and Herder, 1967.

On choice and human action, see:

Donagan, Alan. *Choice: The Essential Element in Human Action*. New York: Routledge, 1987.
—. *Human Ends and Human Action: An Exploration in St. Thomas's Treatment*. Milwaukee: Marquette University Press, 1985.
Powell, Ralph. *Freely Chosen Reality*. Washington: University Press of America, 1983.
Sokolowski, Robert. *Moral Action: A Phenomenological Study*. Bloomington: Indiana University Press, 1985.

On virtue, see:

Geach, Peter. *The Virtues*. Cambridge, Eng.: Cambridge University Press, 1977.

On practical wisdom, see:

Westberg, Daniel. *Right Practical Reason: Aristotle, Action, and Prudence in Aquinas*. Oxford: Oxford University Press, 1994.

On Thomist natural law, see:

Aquinas, St. Thomas. *A Treatise on Law*. ST I–II, QQ. 90–97. Translated, with commentary, by Robert J. Henle. Notre Dame, Ind.: University of Notre Dame Press, 1993.

Armstrong, Ross A. *Primary and Secondary Precepts in Thomistic Natural-Law Teaching*. The Hague: Nijhoff, 1966.

Lee, Patrick. "Permanence of the Ten Commandments: St. Thomas and His Modern Commentators." *Theological Studies* 42 (1981):422–43.

May, William. *Becoming Human: An Introduction to Christian Ethics*. Dayton: Plaum, 1975.

Regan, Richard J. *The Moral Dimensions of Politics*. Chap. 1. New York: Oxford University Press, 1986.

Reilly, James P. *St. Thomas on Law*. Etienne Gilson Series 12. Toronto: Pontifical Institute of Medieval Studies, 1990.

On contemporary interpretations of natural law, see:

Finnis, John M. *Fundamentals of Ethics*. Washington: Georgetown University Press, 1983.

—. *Natural Law and Natural Rights*. Oxford: Clarendon Press, 1980.

George, Robert P. *Natural-Law Theory: Contemporary Essays*. Oxford: Oxford University Press, 1992.

Hittinger, Russell. *Critique of the New Natural-Law Theory*. Notre Dame, Ind.: University of Notre Dame Press, 1987.

McCormick, Richard A. *Ambiguity and Moral Choice*. Milwaukee: Marquette University Press, 1973.

Porter, Mildred J. *The Recovery of Virtue: The Relevance of Aquinas for Christian Ethics*. Louisville, Ky.: John Knox Press, 1990.

On papal teaching, see:

John Paul II, Pope. "Centesimus annus." *Acta Apostolicae Sedis* 83 (1991):793–867. [English title: "The Hundredth Year of *Rerum Novarum*."]

—. "Evangelium vitae." *Acta Apostolicae Sedis* 87 (1995):401–522. [English title: "The Gospel of Life."]

—. "Veritatis splendor." *Acta Apostolicae Sedis* 85 (1993):1133–1228. [English title: "The Splendor of Truth."]

On recent bibliography, see:

Ingardia, Richard. *Thomas Aquinas: International Bibliography, 1977–1990.* Bowling Green, Ohio: Philosophical Documentation Center, Bowling Green State University, 1993.

Index

Ambrose, St., 145, 228
Anthony of Egypt, St., 219
Aristophanes, 157
Aristotelians, 212
Aristotle:
    on actuality and potentiality, 57, 85, 171;
    on animals' movements 44;
    on beauty, 168;
    on causes, 55, 59, 61;
    on change, 185;
    on choice, 79, 82, 85, 90;
    on the cognitive sense, 187;
    on courage, 238;
    on deeds done out of fear 45;
    on deliberation, 93, 94, 198;
    on emotions, 145, 146, 211, 213, 215;
    on ends, 2, 3, 56, 65, 208;
    on ends and means, 54, 81, 82;
    on evil, 119;
    on excellence absolutely and relatively, 236;
    on form and movement 113;
    on friendship, 26, 34, 147, 148, 156;
    on genera and specific differences, 143;
    on generosity, 238;
    on good as actuality, 115, 225;
    on good and human acts, 129, 132, 199;
    on happiness, 13, 18, 23, 25, 33, 186;
    on habit of first principles, 174, 181;
    on habits, 162–64, 174;
    on health, 162–63, 167, 168;
    on high-mindedness, 227, 237, 239;
    on human acts, 174, 175;
    on human beings, 5;
    on intellect's object, 9, 29, 74, 175, 176;
    on interconnection of moral virtues, 227, 229;
    on involuntary things, 42, 43;
    on justice, 129, 177, 225, 237, 238;
    on kinds of theoretical knowledge, 193, 194;
    on knowledge, 161, 175, 194, 196;
    on knowledge of causes from effects, 10;
    on knowledge's influence on the will, 53, 55;
    on likes quarreling, 157;
    on love, 147, 148, 151, 157, 159;
    on magnificence, 227;
    on making and doing, 198–99;
    on measure and things measured, 134;
    on mental agility, 174;
    on moral action, 217, 231;
    on moral virtue, 208, 211–14, 225, 227, 235;
    on motion's continuity, 77;
    on nature, 61;
    on pleasure and wisdom, 13, 14, 47;
    on politics as practical wisdom, 239;
    on power of reason to command will, 103;
    on power of will to command other powers and bodily members, 56–57, 106, 109, 113, 146, 172, 173;
    on powers, 161, 170;
    on practical and theoretical knowledge, 202, 239;
    on practical wisdom, 200, 207, 207–8, 211, 235;
    on practice and memory, 173, 187;
    on privation, 122;
    on reason, 64, 137;
    on relative excellence of different kinds of knowledge, 241;

257